COMM **210**

Fundamentals of Public Communication

by Richard Nitcavic

COMM 210

2013–2014

Ball State University

Printed in the United States of America

10 9 8 7 6 5 4 3 2 1

ISBN 978-0-7380-6184-9

Hayden-McNeil Publishing
14903 Pilot Drive
Plymouth, MI 48170
www.hmpublishing.com

Nitcavic 6184-9 F13-S

COMM 210

Table of Contents

COMM **210**

Acknowledgement

The faculty of Communication Studies and the Instructors of COMM 210 wish to dedicate this academic year to Dr. Richard Nitcavic, former Director of COMM 210. Dr. Nitcavic died suddenly in the spring of 2005. He and his expertise and enthusiasm will be missed.

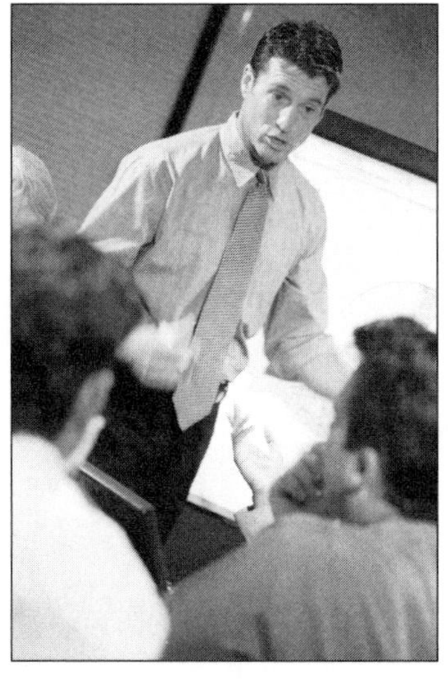

CHAPTER 1

The Process of Public Communication and You

Objectives

After reading this chapter, you should be able to

1. identify the differences between a course in public speaking and other college courses;
2. explain the importance of public communication in your everyday life;
3. identify your responsibilities as an ethical public speaker;
4. explain the key principles and elements of the communication process; and
5. identify the characteristics of effective public speakers.

Topical Outline

THE UNIQUE NATURE OF THE PUBLIC SPEAKING COURSE
- Stress and stage fright
- Pursuit of personal interests
- Personal relevance
- Memorable relationships

THE IMPORTANCE OF PUBLIC SPEAKING
- Accomplishment of personal goals
- Pursuit of personal responsibility

THE COMMUNICATION PROCESS
- Models
- Components
- Fundamental principles

THE EFFECTIVE PUBLIC SPEAKER

THE ROLE OF CULTURE

Key Concepts

- Attention
- Channel
- Circularity of communication
- Co-culture
- Communication and culture
- Communication models
- Communication process
- Content
- Decode
- Delivery
- Dominant U.S. culture
- Encode
- Ethical behavior
- Ethics
- Expertise
- Feedback
- Freedom of speech
- Group communication
- Helical model
- Internal noise
- Interpersonal communication
- Intrapersonal communication
- Irreversibility of communication
- Levels of communication
- Mass-mediated communication
- Meaning
- Memory
- Message
- Multicultural audience
- Noise
  - External noise
  - Internal noise
- Non-U.S. culture
- Perception
- Physical context
- Public communication
- Receiver
- Selectivity of perception
- SMCR model
- Social context
- Source
- Stage fright
- Stress
- Uniqueness of a public speaking course
- Values of public speaking

The Process of Public Communication

PERSPECTIVE

I. Occasionally, some students will dismiss the importance of studying principles of public communication by saying, "This course is just common sense." Frequently, these students imply that because they talk and listen every day, they know all there is to know about effective communication. Often, few objective observers would agree. In fact, many interviewers and employers cite a lack of communication skills (interpersonal, group, and public) as a weakness of potential and actual employees. We hope that you will take this opportunity to develop skills and attitudes that will benefit you throughout your career and daily life.
   A. We hope that you will find the concepts and principles of public speaking sensible. If you do, you are likely to add them to the "common sense" that directs your life.
   B. We hope that during this course you will take advantage of the opportunity to apply communication principles and develop your personal communication effectiveness.

II. In Western culture, the study of public speaking originated as the study of ways one human being could influence other human beings through oral communication. Since the time of the ancient Greeks, Western scholars have been recording their thoughts on the ways an individual can best persuade, inform, and entertain other humans through effective speech. In modern times, scholars have applied the methods of scientific investigation to test many of the traditional theories and principles of the field and to develop new theories and principles.
   A. If you have had relatively little instruction in oral communication, you may have developed a variety of habits and attitudes that reduce the effectiveness and efficiency of your communication. You may have developed misconceptions about communication that are preventing you from reaching your full potential as a human being.
   B. This course is designed to give you an introduction to the study and performance of public speaking competency. You will receive a body of information that will serve as a guideline for the preparation of your speeches and a framework for classroom activities designed to improve your communication skills. The skills you develop will help you in a variety of communication situations.
   C. This course will require you to apply the principles you study. Along with reading this book, you will use interactive media. Additionally, instead of listening to nothing but an instructor's lectures, you and your peers will deliver presentations. By responding to these presentations, you will have a chance to contribute to the growth of one another.

III. ***Purpose statement.*** The purpose of this chapter is to acquaint you with the nature, values, and elements of the public communication process.

IV. ***Preview.*** First, we will examine ways that the study of public speaking is a unique activity. Next, we will consider the importance of public communication. Third, we will compare public communication to other forms of communication. And, finally, we will identify characteristics of the successful public speaker.

Chapter Body

I. **The study of public speaking is a unique activity.** Years from now, when you look back on your college years, there will be some courses you can hardly remember. Maybe you will forget the book, the professor, your learning experiences, or even a whole course. But most students remember their public speaking course. This course makes a strong impression for several reasons.
   A. First, many students feel stress when giving and/or listening to a speech.
      1. Nearly everyone experiences "stage fright" about giving speeches. That fear or uncertainty may contribute to the impact this course will have in your memory.
      2. Some students feel stress when they are audience members. For instance, listening to a speaker's controversial stand on abortion, hearing a classmate take a racially biased position, or watching a demonstration on condom use for safer sex, may challenge you as an audience member. Freedom of speech can be stressful.
      3. This book contains suggestions for dealing with stress and reducing your nervousness so that your public speaking experiences are more effective.
   B. A second factor that makes this course unique is that you will be able to study topics of personal interest as you gather material for your presentations. In addition to studying the principles of speech communication, you will be able to explore issues you want to study.
   C. A third reason this course has staying power is that your study of communication will be relevant to your everyday life. In many other college courses, students may perceive that they study subjects with little practical application. Some students find it hard to understand why they need to learn about microbiology or ancient European history, for example, or they may complain about the variety of subjects they may be required to study in college. The value of a liberal education may take years to appreciate; the value of communication competence is readily apparent in the here and now.
      1. In study after study, researchers have found that employers identify strong oral communication skills as among the most sought after abilities in prospective employees. Hence, this course is among the four core requirements of your University Core Curriculum.

2. You can immediately apply and benefit from communication skills in other classes, your current jobs, and everyday relations with people.

D. Fourth, you may develop memorable relationships with your instructor and peers. You will find few courses in which you will share information and discuss as many topics as you will in this course. You will have an opportunity to know your communication instructor and classmates better than you might in most courses.
   1. Perhaps the relationships will come from the nature of the interaction. You and your classmates will participate in activities and give speeches on a variety of topics. You will have the chance to exchange, support, and test ideas in discussions that will challenge your thinking.
   2. Teachers of public speaking know the importance of individual coaching and instruction. They are usually more than eager to provide one-on-one assistance, when they can work it into their schedules.

II. **The Importance of Public Speaking.** Probably every college professor acts as though her or his subject should be the students' first priority. Many public speaking instructors believe that developing your communication skills warrants all the time and energy you can give. By studying and improving communication skills, you can significantly improve your performance in other subjects and the way you interact with other people. Those changes can benefit you for a lifetime. Hence, teachers of public speaking expect you to devote the time and energy required to research, plan, and practice your presentations. The study of communication can help you accomplish your goals and meet your responsibilities. Hence, not allowing yourself to grow by failing to expend the time and energy required to apply the principles in this course will be frustrating to your instructor.

A. First, we need skills for effective communication with people we talk to every day. Because we spend more time communicating than in any other waking activity, a high level of communication competence is desirable.
   1. Improved communication can help you to achieve your personal goals and satisfy your personal needs.
      a. In your close relationships, for example, if you can clearly express your needs you are more apt to have them satisfied.
      b. In a work situation, the person who can give clear directions, persuade others, and speak well is more apt to be promoted.
      c. When meeting a business person of another culture, your increased sensitivity can increase your chances for a successful interaction.
   2. This course provides instruction in speaking and listening.

a. We spend the majority of our waking hours engaged in some form of communication. Of that time, we spend more time listening than we do talking, reading, or writing.
b. How much time have you spent studying listening? Beyond having a teacher, parent, friend, or spouse tell us to "LISTEN!" most of us have received few suggestions about how to listen effectively or have tried seriously to improve our critical listening skills.
c. For most of us, our formal education in speaking has been little better. Perhaps in high school, you already have had a course in public speaking or even studied debate. But when you consider the influence communication has on your everyday life, you probably have had relatively little formal education in speaking or listening.

3. For some students, this may be the only communication course you take. That makes your responsibility for learning improved speaking and listening in this course an important one. By investing substantial time and energy in your learning, you may reap significant benefits from this class. Only you can change your behaviors.
   a. All the theoretical learning in the world won't make a bit of difference unless you take the responsibility for improving your communication skills.
   b. Here is a chance to do something for yourself, to better your opportunities, to enhance your interaction with other people.
4. Sometimes students complain that a public speaking class is an unrealistic situation. Actually, the communication situations in a speech class parallel real life.
   a. In this class you probably will begin giving speeches to people you hardly know, but by the end of the course you may know those people well.
   b. Although you sometimes may need to give presentations to total strangers, most of your presentational speaking will be to people you know.
      (1) You are more apt to give a talk to people in your community than to total strangers.
      (2) You are more apt to give a report to coworkers than to people in another company.
      (3) You are more apt to give a message to a religious group to which you belong than to people of a different religious group.

B. Second, we need to learn ways to uphold our freedom of speech with responsible action.
   1. You are fortunate to be studying communication in a society that considers free speech a key element in making our society a success.
   2. Freedom of speech, guaranteed by the First Amendment of the *Constitution of the United States*, is a right that some international students consider a privilege.

3. We not only have a right to express our ideas, but also the responsibility to support them ethically.
   a. You may find more opportunity for discussion in this public speaking course than in your other college courses.
   b. You should remember that with your freedom comes an expectation of ethical behavior.
      (1) You will be expected to give opinions based on facts.
      (2) You will be expected to express ideas that respect your classmates.
      (3) You will be expected to listen as well as speak responsibly.
      (4) You will be expected to take responsibility for your own behaviors.
      (5) You will be expected to uphold your freedom of speech with ethical conduct.

III. **The Communication Process.** Communication is not something that one person does to another person. Communication is a continuous, ever-changing, circular, process of interaction.
   A. Many theorists have developed models of communication. Communication models give us a way to visualize, or make more concrete, an abstract process.
      1. They simplify the complexities of communication.
      2. They help us to understand the important components of the communication process and the relationships among them.
      3. Consider two classic models. Look at Frank Dance's (1967) helical model and David Berlo's (1960) SMCR model.

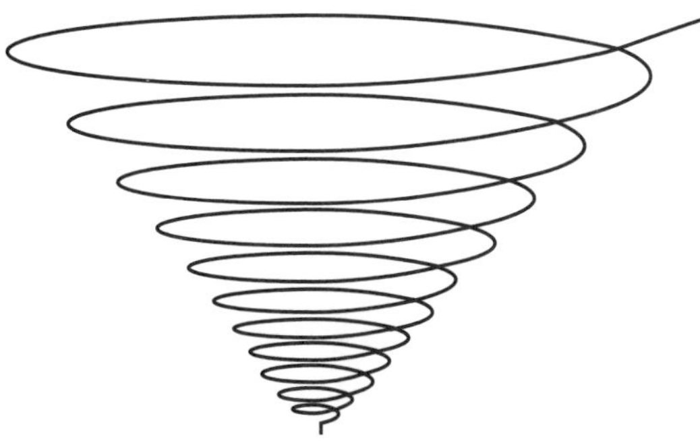

Figure 1.1 Dance's Helical Model

         a. Dance related communication to a helix.
            (1) The bottom of the helix is small. As the helix moves upward it becomes larger. But movement up the helix is slow—a process of circular, back-and-forth motion. In the beginning, communicators share but a small portion of themselves in their relationships. Through a slow process of give and take, their relationships develop as, little by little, they commit more of themselves.

(2) Dance's *helical model* helps us to remember that the communication process is ever-changing, circular, expanding, and building upon the past.

b. The *Source-Message-Channel-Receiver* model (SMCR model) advanced by David Berlo, has served as another useful way to view the communication process. The model helps us to focus on the elements that must be operating effectively for communication to occur. The model helps us identify the location of potential barriers to effective communication. More comprehensive models also include as elements: feedback, noise, and communication context.

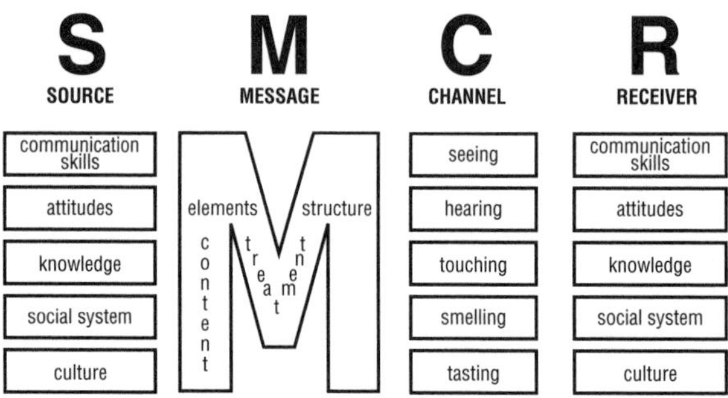

Figure 1.2 SMCR Model

c. Using the two models in combination, we can look at the elements and the characteristics of the communication process.

B. The significant elements of the communication process include the source, message, channel, receiver, feedback, noise, and context or environment. The process of communication cannot function effectively and efficiently if problems or barriers exist in any one of these elements of the model.

1. A *source* transmits a message through a channel to a receiver.
   a. Sources bring to the communication event their communication skills, their attitudes, their knowledge, the social systems to which they belong, and their cultures.
   b. The source *encodes*, or creates, the message by putting ideas into words and actions. An effective source encodes messages in a way that's appropriate for the intended receiver(s).
2. The *message* includes verbal elements (content) and nonverbal elements (delivery)—what speakers say and the way they say it.
   a. The message must have qualities that will lead the receiver to perceive the meaning that the source intended.
   b. Hence, words, phrasing, and the way they are organized become significant aspects of the verbal message. Additionally, the ways that sources use their voice and body become important aspects of the nonverbal message.

3. *Channel* refers to the means by which the message gets from the sender to the receiver.
   a. Some theorists conceptualize the channels as one's senses. Although each person may use them differently, each of us who is not sensorially impaired communicates through all five senses: sound, sight, touch, smell, and taste.
      (1) When you hear someone speak, you use the aural or sound channel.
      (2) When you look at the speaker's facial expressions, you use your sight.
      (3) When you shake the speaker's hand afterward, you use touch to convey meaning.
      (4) When you smell the speaker's cologne, you use another channel.
      (5) When you eat the refreshments provided at a speaking event, you use your sense of taste.
   b. Other theorists consider channels as the technology used to deliver the message, for example, the air waves (for face-to-face oral communication), the telephone line, the World Wide Web, the paper used for handwriting, or a human intermediary. From this perspective, the channel is the medium which carries the message from source to receiver.
   c. Communication is likely to be more effective if multiple senses are involved and the medium has the capability to convey the intended meaning.
4. The *receiver*, like the source, brings to the communication situation all of his or her communication skills, attitudes, knowledge, social system, and culture.
   a. The receiver *decodes*, or translates, the source's message attaching meaning and understanding to the speaker's (verbal and nonverbal) message.
   b. When the source and receiver differ significantly in their frame of reference (for example, in attitudes, knowledge, social system, and culture), the decoding process is likely to result in messages different from the ones intended.
   c. While decoding, or processing the message, the receiver then becomes the source of a new message by providing feedback.
5. *Feedback* is any verbal or nonverbal response to a source, such as a question from the audience, a puzzled look, or nod of agreement. If receivers do not provide feedback (or sources do not allow or pay attention to feedback) the effectiveness of the communication process decreases. The source and the receiver(s) may fail to realize that they are not sharing the same meaning.

6. *Noise* is anything that interferes with the process. Noise may be external or internal to the receiver.
   a. *External noise* is sometimes referred to as physical noise because it presents a physical barrier that prevents the message from getting through to the receiver. For example, if someone coughs and the audience fails to hear part of the message, the noise is external to the listener.
   b. *Internal noise* can be physiological or psychological.
      (1) If a listener is distracted by a thought about lunch or an upcoming exam (psychological noise), a lack of concentration will interfere with reception of the speaker's message.
      (2) If the listener's ears are "stopped up" from a cold, the physiological problem might interfere with the reception of the message.
7. *Context/Environment.* One cannot consider a communication event without taking into account the role of the context. The context, or environment, is the situation in which the communication occurs and includes the physical context, social context, number of people involved, relationship of participants, surrounding events, culture, rituals, and noise.
   a. The *physical context* is the place in which the communication occurs. Think for a moment about listening to a local politician in the football stadium parking lot after a game versus listening in a convention hall. The temperature outdoors, the time of day, the surrounding people, and the accompanying activities all affect your reception of the message.
   b. The *social context* can influence communication.
      (1) If you are asked to "say a few words," the social expectations will be different at a fundraising dinner for the local Humane Society than at a going-away party for a coworker.
      (2) Such factors as the level of formality, use of appropriate language, familiarity with the audience members, use of humor, content of the message, appropriate dress, and other factors may be influenced by social context.

C. Fundamental Principles of the Communication Process.
   1. *Communication is circular.* Because the sender and receiver encode and decode simultaneously through feedback, communication is a circular, ongoing process.
      a. First one person speaks, then the second person responds, then the first, and back and forth in a simultaneous process.

   b. At any given moment, everyone involved in the interaction can be both a sender and receiver of messages, encoding one message while decoding another.
2. *Communication is based on our perception.* Perception is an individual's way of understanding reality. Perception depends on a variety of influences including: attention, selectivity, and memory.
   a. You cannot pay attention to all the stimuli reaching your senses. No one can. If you are listening to a professor give a lecture, the actual message coming from the professor (including vocal aspects, words, gestures, facial expression, and use of the overhead, for example) competes with other stimuli in the room (the person yawning next to you, the thoughts about what you did last night, and more).
   b. An infinite number of internal and external messages are coming at us at any given time. What we decide to pay attention to (selective attention) and how we process those messages (based on our experiences and selective memory) influence the messages we receive (or create from the selected stimuli).
   c. Because each of us perceives, remembers, and understands differently, the outcomes of the communication process are unique to the people and situations involved. Hence, truly effective communication is extremely difficult.
      (1) We can't talk with two people and constantly monitor all of their physical behaviors and words during the conversation. The process is too complex.
      (2) The more people who enter the situation, the more complex the process becomes. With a larger group, we have the perceptions of more people to take into account. On the other hand, we lose much information about individuals because they are farther away and provide less feedback.
      (3) An effective public speaker will recognize the influence of various aspects of the communication process and use every technique possible to enhance effectiveness.
3. *Communication is irreversible.* Communication is not something we can take back.
   a. Think of a time when you had a disagreement with someone you love. Perhaps you said something that hurt the person. Afterward, you might have apologized and said, "Forget it, I didn't really mean it." Even if you "didn't mean it," you cannot erase the memory and effects of your words and actions. In the case of a strong argument, it may haunt the relationship for a long time.
   b. If you stand up and speak in a staff meeting—and you later decide you said something stupid—you cannot wish away the

effects caused by your remarks. Instead, you must build on the past rather than ignore it.

c. Think of what happens when a person tells an ethnic joke to start a speech, then later discovers the audience is offended. The speaker may apologize, but the perceptions of the audience members may not change.

4. Because communication is circular, is based on our perception, and is irreversible, *all communication must build on previous interaction.*

D. *Levels of Communication.* The communication process can occur on multiple levels: intrapersonal, interpersonal, group, public, and mass-mediated.

1. *Intrapersonal communication* refers to the communication you have with yourself. Your thoughts, your self-talk, your recognition of your own feelings and attitudes.
2. *Interpersonal communication*, or dyadic communication, occurs between two people. Brief exchanges between strangers, conversations between friends, ongoing discussions with a significant other all fall into this category.
3. *Group communication* usually concerns three or more people who interact and influence one another in the pursuit of a common interest. A study group, an athletic team, and families are different types of groups.
4. *Public communication* is one person communicating face-to-face with an audience. The size of the audience may vary, but the interaction between speaker and audience is more limited than in the previous levels of communication.
5. *Mass-mediated communication*, or mass communication for short, is the communication which takes place over some form of technology because the audience is so large that its members cannot be grouped together in one place. Newspapers, television, and the Internet are all examples of mass communication. A speaker does not have direct access to the audience and the audience's feedback is usually delayed.
6. All five of these levels share a common process: a source attempting to influence a receiver through the creation of appropriate messages. Although each level has some unique forces affecting the outcome of communication, you will be able to apply the skills and principles of public speaking to other levels of communication as well.

a. Whether talking directly to the boss, working with a team, or speaking to a large group of employees, an individual can benefit from speaking clearly, substantiating ideas, giving a variety of support, using an effective conversational style, and recognizing and adapting to individual differences.

b. Whereas interpersonal communication is usually more intimate, public communication is usually more "everything else."
    (1) When we talk to a group of people we normally should make the communication an extension of our "normal self" but increase our volume, vocal variety, and use of supporting material.
    (2) The extension of a message to several people or a large group of people means that the speaker must do more to adapt to the physical and psychological expectations of the context and people involved.

IV. **Characteristics of the Successful Public Speaker.** While this course specifically addresses your skills as a communicator, your college program, taken as a whole, aims to develop the attributes of a successful public speaker.
  A. Several goals of your University's Core Curriculum program are attributes typical of effective public speakers:
    1. sound ethics;
    2. lifelong learning;
    3. sensitivity to a multicultural audience;
    4. the ability to recognize and solve problems; and
    5. the ability to locate, synthesize, and apply knowledge (in this class we refer to this ability as using sound reasoning and support).
  B. An effective speaker has expertise on the topic. Your major program seeks to develop your expertise on topics that will dominate your professional presentations. In this course, we shall focus on using your life experiences, the library, and other forms of research to bolster your expertise.
  C. In this class, we hope you will seek to strengthen the five attributes of an effective public speaker that are goals of the University Core Curriculum program (see IV. A. 1–5. above), as well as focus on additional attributes of effective speaking, including:
    1. a creative delivery that stimulates interest while communicating well;
    2. a style of language that represents a natural, but appropriate, extension of your personality; and
    3. a conversational tone when delivering a planned message.
  D. A final attribute or characteristic of effective public speakers is primarily your responsibility—a positive self-concept.

V. **Communication and Culture.** Some people claim that the traditions of public speaking in the United States are too "white," too male, and too one-way.
  A. Many aspects of traditional public speaking situations are functions of the dominant U.S. culture.

1. When you hear the phrase "public speaking," what images pop into your mind? Do you see a male speaker standing up in front of a passive group of audience members?
    a. The speaker may try to be interesting with a joke, some examples, maybe a visual aid.
    b. Too often, audience members sit quietly and nod their heads politely while they endure.
    c. This stereotype of public speaking is probably familiar to you.
2. Certainly, public speakers need to fulfill expectations regarding traditions and convention, but such an approach fails to take into account the many possible modes of public presentation.

B. We are part of a diverse culture. The concept of the "American melting-pot" is yielding to the concept of the "American tossed salad." In the United States we have all kinds of people. By mixing us together, we are tastier and more nourishing, but we each retain our own flavor. Because of immigration patterns and the higher growth rate of U.S. minorities, authorities predict that "by 2056, the 'average' U.S. citizen will trace her or his decent to Africa, Asia, the Hispanic countries, the Pacific Islands—almost anywhere but white Europe" (Wittmer, 1992, p. 73).

C. The most successful communicators have a flexibility that allows them to adapt to various U.S. co-cultures and non-U.S. cultures.
1. They can creatively involve a diverse audience.
2. They can demonstrate openness and respect toward others.

D. In this textbook, we will discuss the traditions of the field of public speaking, while we discuss communication concern for people of various cultures.
1. We use the term "dominant U.S. culture" to refer to what has traditionally developed in a one-way, male-oriented, U.S. society of Western-European origins.
2. We call it dominant because it is just that—dominant. One need not be part of the majority to be dominant, as evidenced in South Africa.

E. So, how does dominance affect public speaking?
1. The dominant culture and co-cultures display many different views of their origin, rules for "proper" behavior, and characteristics of their "common" language.
2. In co-cultures, language tends to develop in ways that provide members a sense of commonality and a means of self-protection from the dominant culture.
    a. U.S. co-cultures can include people of common ethnic or racial background, people who are gay or lesbian, the disabled, the homeless, the elderly, even prostitutes (Samovar & Porter, 1991).

b. The cultures of such groups can affect their members' expectations and the way they might perceive and react to a message.

Closing Remarks

All of the characteristics of a successful public speaker are ones that you can acquire, including the characteristic of cultural sensitivity. Although some characteristics are easier to learn and shape than others, you can take positive steps to acquire all. Although everyone comes to this course with predetermined ideas and skills, by recognizing that change is possible, by learning the skills and finding the motivation to change, you can change your feelings about your public speaking ability. As the expression goes, effective public speakers are made, not born.

References and Suggestions for Further Readings

Aristotle. (1960). *The Rhetoric of Aristotle: An expanded translation with supplementary examples for students of composition and public speaking.* by Lane Cooper. NY: Appleton-Century-Crofts.

Avila, A. (1992). A brief history, current problems and recommendations for improving communication with Mexican Americans. In J. Wittmer, (Ed.). *Valuing diversity and similarity: Bridging the gap through interpersonal skills.* Minneapolis, MN: Educational Media Corporation.

Berlo, D. (1960). *The process of communication.* NY: Holt, Rinehart and Winston.

Border, G. A. (1991). *Cultural orientation: An approach to understanding intercultural communication.* Angled Cliffs, NJ: Prentice-Hall.

Brislin, R. (1994). *Intercultural communication training.* Thousand Oaks, CA: Sage.

Brummett, B. (1986). Absolutist and relativist stances toward the problem of difference: A model for student growth in public speaking education. *Communication Education, 35*, 269–274.

Caballero, J. (1992). *Children around the world.* Atlanta: Humanics.

Carter, T. P. (1989). *Mexican Americans in schools: A history of educational neglect.* NY: College Entrance Examination Board.

Clark, R. M. (1984). *Family life and school achievement: Why poor black children succeed or fail.* Chicago: University of Chicago Press.

Comer, J. P., & Poussaint, A. F. (1992). *Raising black children.* NY: Penguin Books.

Condon, J. C. (1984). *With respect to the Japanese: A guide for Americans.* Yarmouth, ME: Intercultural Press.

Condon, J. C. (1985). *Good neighbors: Communicating with the Mexicans.* Yarmouth, ME: Intercultural Press.

Dance, F. E. X. (1967). Toward a theory of human communication. *Human communication theory: Original essays.* Ed. F. E. X. Dance. (pp. 288–309). NY: Holt, Rinehart and Winston.

Delpit, L., & Nelson-Barber, S. (in press). Rethinking issues of context and culture for the new teacher. *Anthropology & Education Quarterly.*

Diggs, A. D. (1993). *Success at work: A guide for African-Americans.* Fort Lee, NJ: Barricade Books.

Dodd, C. H. (1991). *Dynamics of intercultural communication.* Dubuque, IA: Brown & Benchmark.

Duran, R. L., & Zakahi, W. R. (1987). Communication performance and communication satisfaction: What do we teach our students? *Communication Education, 36*, 13–22.

Epstein, E. (1988, March). Square one special module. 3.2.1. *Contact,* p. 22.

Fersh, S. (1989). *Learning about peoples and culture.* NY: McDougal, Littell.

Fieg, J. P., & Mortlock, E. (1989). *A common core: Thais and Americans.* Yarmouth, ME: Intercultural Press.

Finkelstein, B., Imamura, A. E., & Tobin, J. J. (1991). *Transcending stereotypes: Discovering Japanese culture and education.* Yarmouth, ME: Intercultural Press.

Fisher, G. (1988). *Midgets: The role of culture and perception in international relations.* Yarmouth, ME: Intercultural Press.

Frymier, A. B. (1993). The impact of teacher immediacy on students' motivation: Is it the same for all students? *Communication Quarterly, 41*, 454–464.

Gamble, T., & Gamble, M. (1994). *Public Speaking in the age of diversity.* Boston: Allyn and Bacon.

Geber, B. (1990). Managing diversity. *Training, 27*, 23–30.

Gibbs, J. T., & Huang, L. N. (Eds.). (1991). *Children of color: Psychological interventions with minority youth.* San Francisco: Jossey-Bass.

Gochenour, T. (1990). *Considering Filipinos.* Yarmouth, ME: Intercultural Press.

Gochenour, T. (1993). *Beyond experience: The experiential approach to cross-cultural education.* Yarmouth, ME: Intercultural Press.

Gonzalez, A., Houston, M., & Chen, V. (Eds.). (1994). *Our Voices: Essays in culture, ethnicity, and communication.* Los Angeles, CA: Roxbury.

Greatbatch, D., & Heritage, J. (1986). Generating applause: A study of rhetoric and response at party political conferences. *American Journal of Sociology, 92*, 110–57.

Gudykunst, W. B. (1994). *Bridging differences: Effective intergroup communication.* Thousand Oaks, CA: Sage.

Gudykunst, W. B., & Nishida, T. (1994). *Bridging Japanese/North American differences.* Thousand Oaks, CA: Sage.

Hamlet, J. D. (1994). Understanding traditional African American preaching. In A. Gonzalez, M. Houston, V. Chen (Eds.). *Our Voices: Essays in culture, ethnicity, and communication.* Los Angeles, CA: Roxbury.

Hecht, M. L., Collier, M. J., & Ribeau, S. A. (1993). *African American communication: Ethnic identity and cultural interpretation.* Newbury Park, CA: Sage.

Heim, P., & Golant, S. K. (1994). *Hardball for women: Winning at the game of business.* NY: Plume.

Henry, W. A. (1990, April 9). Beyond the melting pot. *The Nation,* 28–35.

Hill, R. (1972). *The strengths of black families.* NY: Amerson-Hall.

Hopson, D. P., & Hopson, D. S. (1993). *Raising the rainbow generation: Teaching your children to be successful in a multicultural society.* NY: Simon & Schuster.

Hudson, W., Hudson, C. W., & Ellis, V.F. (1990). *Black history activity and enrichment handbook: An easy-to-use collection of ideas, activities and games designed to help explore African-American history and culture.* Orange, NJ: Just Us Books.

King, N., & Huff, K. (1985). *Host family survival kit: A guide for American host families.* Yarmouth, ME: Intercultural Press.

Kochman, T. (1981). *Black and white styles in conflict.* Chicago: University of Chicago Press.

Kreps, G. L., & Kunimoto, E. N. (1994). *Effective communication in multicultural health care settings.* Thousand Oaks, CA: Sage.

Kunjufu, J. (1985). *Countering the conspiracy to destroy black boys.* Chicago: Images.

Kunjufu, J. (1988). *To be popular or smart: The black peer group.* Chicago: Images.

MacArthur, B. (1994). *The Penguin book of twentieth-century speeches.* NY: Penguin.

Major, C. (1994). *Juba to jive: The dictionary of African-American slang.* NY: Viking.

Marshall, T. (1989). *The whole world guide to language learning.* Yarmouth, ME: Intercultural Press.

Matiella, A. C. (1991). *Positively different.* Santa Cruz, CA: Network Publications.

Matthews, G. (1992). *Teaching principles of intercultural communication through world music.* A paper presented at the Speech Communication Association Convention, Atlanta, GA.

McClain, P. D. (1993). *Minority group influence: Agenda setting, formulation, and public policy.* Westport, CT: Greenwood.

McDaniel, D. O. (1993). *Broadcasting in the Malay world: Radio, television, and video in Brunei, Indonesia, Malaysia, and Singapore.* Norwood, NJ: Ablex.

Nordenstreng, K., & Schiller, H. I. (1993). *Beyond national sovereignty: International communications in the 1990s.* Norwood, NJ: Ablex.

Nydell, M. K. (1987). *Understanding Arabs: A guide for Westerners.* Yarmouth, ME: Intercultural Press.

Nyquist, J. D., & Wulff, D. H. (1992). *Preparing teaching assistants of instructional roles: Supervising TAs in communication.* Annandale, VA: Speech Communication Association.

Paige, R. M. (1993). *Education for the intercultural experience.* Yarmouth, ME: Intercultural Press.

Parker, W. M. (1988). *Consciousness-raising: A primer for multicultural counseling.* Springfield, IL: Thomas.

Pearson, J. C., Turner, L. H., & Todd-Mancillas, W. (1991). *Gender and communication.* Dubuque, IA: Brown & Benchmark.

Perry, T., & Fraser, J. W. (1993). *Freedom's plow: Teaching in the multicultural classroom.* NY: Routledge.

Radtke, L., & Stam, H. J. (1993). *Power and gender.* Thousand Oaks, CA: Sage.

Rainbow Activities: 50 multi-cultural/human relations experiences. (1977). South El Monte, CA: Creative Teaching.

Rubin, R. B. (1985). The validity of the communication competency assessment instrument. *Communication Monographs, 52*, 173–185.

Samovar, L. A., & Porter, R. E. (1991). *Communication between cultures.* Belmont, CA: Wadsworth.

Schloff, L., & Yudkin, M. (1993). *He and she talk: How to communicate with the opposite sex.* New York: Plume.

Simons, G. F., Vazquez, C., & Harris, P. R. (1993). *Transcultural leadership: Empowering the diverse workforce.* Yarmouth, ME: Intercultural Press.

Stewart, R. A., & Roach, K. D. (1993). A model of instructional communication as a framework for analyzing and interpreting student ratings of instruction. *Communication Quarterly, 41*, 427–442.

Storti, C. (1989). *The art of crossing cultures.* Yarmouth, ME: Intercultural Press.

Stricklin, M. (1987). Q methodology and the measurement of self perception. *Operant Subjectivity, 10*, 114–124.

Sue, D. W., & Sue, D. (1990). *Counseling the culturally different: Theory and practice.* NY: Wiley.

Thompson, B. W., & Tyagi, S. (1993). *Beyond a dream deferred: Multicultural education and the politics of excellence.* Minneapolis: University of Minnesota Press.

Wang, G. (1993). *Treading different paths: Informatization in Asian nations.* Norwood, NJ: Ablex.

Watzlawick, P. H., Beavin, J. H., & Jackson, D.D. (1967). *Pragmatics of human communication: A study of interactional patterns, pathologies and paradoxes.* NY: Norton.

Wenzhong, H., & Grove, C. L. (1991). *Encountering the Chinese: A guide for Americans.* Yarmouth, ME: Intercultural Press. [see also Wen-Chung, H.].

Whitehead, F. (1994). *Culture wars: Opposing viewpoints.* San Diego, CA: Greenhaven.

Wiley, R. *Why black people tend to shout: Cold facts and wry views from a black man's world.* NY: Penguin.

Wiseman, R. L. (1994). *Communication in the multinational organization.* Thousand Oaks, CA: Sage.

Wittmer, J. (1992). *Valuing diversity and similarity: Bridging the gap through interpersonal skills.* Minneapolis, MN: Educational Media Corporation.

Woods, P. L., & Liddell, F. H. *I, too, sing America: The African American books of days.* NY: Workman.

CHAPTER 2

Intrapersonal Processes, Listening, and You

Objectives

After reading this chapter, you should be able to

1. recognize the importance of intrapersonal communication in public speaking and listening;
2. identify different types of listening;
3. apply methods of effective listening to improve your own skills; and
4. identify a format for analyzing the appropriateness of speaking techniques in presentations delivered to a variety of audiences including those made up of individuals from U.S. American co-cultures and foreign cultures.

Topical Outline

INTRAPERSONAL PROCESSES
- Frame of reference
- Creativity
- Imagined communication
- Risk-taking behaviors
- Cognitive patterns

THE PROCESS OF LISTENING
- Learning effective listening skills
- Types of listening

IMPROVING LISTENING SKILLS
- Note-taking
- Preview/review
- Concentration
- Interaction
- Context
- Observation
- Ideas

SPEECH ANALYSIS

Key Concepts

Cognitive mapping
Cognitive patterns
Concentration
Context
Creativity
Evaluative listening
Frame of reference
Hearing
Imagined communication
Interactive process
Internal communication
Intrapersonal processes
Listening
Listening for comprehension
Listening for ideas
Listening for pleasure
Listening rate
Nonverbal cues
Note-taking
Passive listening
Previewing
Reviewing
Risk-taking behavior
Selective listening
Self-talk
Speech analysis
Therapeutic listening
Willingness to take risks

Intrapersonal Processes and Listening

PERSPECTIVE

I. Most individuals seldom think about the process of encoding and decoding messages. For the most part, we naively assume that because we are using a single language to communicate we need not be concerned with the way we come to share meaning. However, the way we communicate with ourselves (our process of intrapersonal communication) profoundly affects the way we approach communication with others. Additionally, the way we approach listening profoundly affects the meaning we derive from a speaker. Furthermore, providing feedback can encourage a speaker. Listening encouragement causes the speaker to do better because he or she can interpret and adjust to the feedback. Even a negative response can be more encouraging than no response, because at least the speaker knows to give more explanation or give another argument to prove the point. Feedback is essential to the interactive process. Feedback from a responsive listener actually can make the speaker perform better in that an enthusiastic listener can stimulate the speaker's enthusiasm. The speaker's nervousness is reduced because of being able to better concentrate on the message and audience. Finally, responsive listening is advantageous to the listener, who can better comprehend the speaker by paying attention and responding appropriately.

II. ***Purpose statement:*** This chapter will examine the processes of intrapersonal communication and listening as they relate to our growth as effective communicators.

III. ***Preview:*** We shall first identify six forces that influence the process of intrapersonal communication; second, discuss the nature of the listening process; third, identify ways to improve the process of listening; and fourth, provide a system for analyzing speeches.

Chapter Body

I. **Intrapersonal Processes.** "Intrapersonal" means within the person. Intrapersonal communication processes happen inside of you, or internally. Some people equate these processes with thinking. Although thinking is part of the process, intrapersonal communication includes more than what we think. More importantly intrapersonal processes include the way we think and the way we communicate with ourselves. Intrapersonal communication affects the way we receive messages from others and affects the way we send messages to others. Intrapersonal communication processes depend upon an individual's frame of reference, creativity, imagination, risk-taking behavior, and cognitive patterns. The use of the computer may also have important influences on intrapersonal processes.

A. *Frame of Reference.* Your frame of reference refers to the way you view your world.
   1. Your frame of reference consists of all that you bring internally to the communication situation: your beliefs, attitudes, and values; your memory of experiences; your cultural background; your stereotypes and expectations; your self-concept; your feelings and level of stress; your thinking patterns; and other psychological factors.
   2. Your frame of reference is your structure for encoding and decoding messages.
   3. As a speaker, understanding the frames of reference of your listeners will allow you to adapt your message for high levels of clarity and/or persuasive impact. As a listener, attempting to understand the way the speaker's frame of reference may differ from your own can help you to understand better the speaker and your reaction to the speaker.

B. *Creativity.* One of the most important skills you can shape is that of creativity. Basically, creative thinking involves visualizing something in an innovative, new, or unique but useful way.
   1. Csikszentmihalyi (1996) claims that creativity is important because "most of the things that are interesting, important and *human* are the results of creativity....And when we are involved in [creativity], we feel that we are living more fully than during the rest of life" (pp. 1–2).
   2. Humans have long valued artists because their creativity provides new ways of imagining or conceptualizing our world. In our personal and work lives, creativity can be important to each of us, particularly when solving problems.
   3. You can increase your creativity by learning to think in less traditional ways.
      a. Being a slave to tradition makes one worry about risk and/or failure to the point that self-criticism inhibits creativity. During the creative process, assume that the words "wrong," "stupid," "useless," and "ugly" have no meaning; let yourself go; and strive for quantity. After you have created, judge your creation(s) by traditional standards of goodness, brilliance, usefulness, and beauty. If your creation doesn't measure up to these standards, play on—improve or reject your creation or come to an understanding that tradition is not as good as your creation. An understanding of the superiority of your creation will allow you to justify it to yourself, if not the world.
      b. Habitual and routine thinking patterns and structures prevent free, open problem-solving. Hence, you are more likely to be creative if you change the conditions in your environment.
   4. The extent to which you have developed your creative thinking affects the way you send and receive messages, the way you interact with others, and your potential for success in new situations.

C. *Imagined Communication.* Another key aspect of intrapersonal communication is sometimes called self-talk or imagined communication. In imagined communication, individuals talk to someone else or to themselves as if they were another person. However, the communication takes place in their minds (internally instead of externally).

1. In one basic communication course of over two hundred students, all except six students said they experience these kinds of conversations. The two hundred students gave a variety of examples of imagined conversations.
    a. Some students imagine communications before they take place. For example, while they plan their classroom presentations, they see themselves in front of the audience, imagine how fantastic they look, see some classmates listening attentively, and picture their instructor making a positive response. This approach, by the way, can help most speakers to succeed in public communication situations by reducing their anxiety.
    b. Other students reported imaginary communication after a speaking event. Many said that after a speech, they replayed the situation mentally, imagining what could have been done better. Many individuals relieve stressful situations by hearing themselves saying what they should have said during the exchange.
    c. Many students reported having imagined communication with people as a way of exploring problems, preparing for things to come, or venting anger over something that had already happened. One reported "talking" to a friend who had moved away, another "talked" to a former professor she admires, and several "talked" to someone emotionally close who had died. (Similarly, in June 1996, the news media reported that Hillary Clinton imagined communicating with her hero, Eleanor Roosevelt, as a method to reduce stress and "think things out.")
    d. Other students reported imagined conversations with famous people, with themselves as if they were another person, or with an imaginary friend.
2. Imaginary communication is a phenomenon that most people avoid discussing. Most of us learned at an early age that people who talk to themselves are crazy. Yet, nearly all students surveyed reported this kind of behavior. Many reported talking aloud to themselves—alone in a car was one of the favorite locations for that.
3. Although you may not be taught to imagine communicating with yourself, you may discover that it helps you to prepare for future communication, deal with your feelings, and learn from past communication. Imagined communication is an important aspect of your intrapersonal communication processes.

D. *Risk-taking Behaviors*. Your willingness to take risks is largely dependent on your interpretation of past experience. If you have found risk-taking to be fun, adventuresome, or thrilling, then you are more inclined to make risky moves. At least a minimum amount of risk is necessary for growth and development.

1. Some people consider as risk-taking behaviors only those actions that are life-threatening, such as driving cars at high speeds, skiing without understanding the course, or engaging in other dangerous stunts. For our purposes, we are focusing on risk-taking in communication. When we communicate, we risk rejection by others. Additionally, behaviors that threaten our self-concept or intrapersonal processes are "risky."
    a. Often, before you speak, you may consider the risk of communicating. As an old saying goes, "If I tell you who I am, and you don't like who I am, that's all that I have." When you talk in class, express your ideas in a business meeting, give a presentation, or decide to communicate (or not to communicate), your behaviors will be interpreted by others. Others may agree or disagree, be interested or bored, understand or misunderstand, be persuaded or argue. Because the frame of reference is at least slightly different for every individual, you never really know completely the ways other people will react to you. But effort on your part to understand and adapt to your listeners will reduce the risk of rejection.
    b. The way we communicate is closely linked to our self-image. Most individuals find risky and threatening any efforts to change their self-image. Hence, many students in a public speaking class must face the risk of personal change. On one extreme is the student who sees himself or herself as a person who "just can't speak well in public." On the other extreme is the student who sees herself or himself as "a perfect communicator" who needs no improvement and will accept no criticism. We encourage you to "face your demons" and take risks to grow in your ability to speak before groups. William Haney, a professor with decades of experience as a consultant to business, academic, governmental, and military organizations, wrote, "Optimally, one's energies are directed toward realizing one's own potentialities. But under inner stress one becomes estranged from the real self and protects oneself by creating and protecting a false, idealized self, based on pride, but threatened by doubts, self-contempt, and self-hate" (1992, p. 103). We encourage you to develop what Haney calls "an exceptionally

realistic self-image" (p. 104). It is unrealistic to assume that one cannot improve in speaking ability from instruction and practice. Change and growth are risky, but rewarding.

   c. Your intrapersonal processes about risk-taking are influenced by your past experiences and interaction with others. Your decisions about whether you should, or how you will, choose to interact with others are major areas of your internal or intrapersonal communication processes.

E. *Cognitive Patterns*. Each person structures and interprets messages in his or her own unique way. The process of measuring your thinking patterns is called cognitive mapping.

   1. Your cognitive map identifies the senses you use for obtaining data and the typical patterns of thinking you employ for understanding data.

      a. Each person also comes to rely on his or her senses differently. Perhaps you know someone who decorated his or her house with bright colors that you find visually interesting. Assume that someone else you know decorated with many textures, and you enjoy "the feel" of the home. These differences in taste reflect the use of different senses for processing information.

      b. Some people understand things more easily if the information is compared to something familiar through an analogy. (There is, for example, a popular statistics professor who teaches through parables, and his stories make statistics understandable for many students who normally have difficulty with statistics.)

      c. Think for a moment about a teacher you really liked, who was easy to understand, and from whom you received a high grade. Maybe things went easily for you in that class because you and the teacher had similar thinking or processing patterns. Perhaps you know someone who disagreed with you and did not think very well of the same teacher. Because different individuals come to rely on different cognitive structures in their analysis of messages, perhaps that other student's cognitive map was simply too different from the teacher's.

   2. As a speaker, you will most likely use thinking patterns and appeals to the senses that fit your own cognitive map. If you find that you have difficulty communicating your ideas clearly, your map may not be compatible with the cognitive map of your listeners. For this reason, we encourage you to use a variety of forms of support and appeal to a variety of senses.

II. **The Process of Listening.** An area of communication about which most individuals receive little formal education is listening. The majority of most persons' communication time, however, is spent listening. Researchers (Barker, et al., 1980) have found that we spend approximately 42–53% of our communication time listening, 30–32% speaking, 15–17% reading, and 11–14% writing. The purpose of listening is to receive and interpret a speaker's message appropriately. Our success in this process, however, is generally poor. Most of us actively listen to little of the messages we hear. We understand almost none of the "feeling part" of a message. We forget much of what we hear immediately and nearly all of what we hear after several days. We do not take notes, yet are surprised when we learn that we have forgotten important details that we heard orally. We think we listen and remember better than we actually do, because our frame of reference plays tricks on us. We seldom own up to our listening failures, and instead bluff with nods and "uh-huhs."

A. ***Learning Effective Listening Skills.***

1. Listening is much more than hearing. Hearing refers to the physiological process of detecting the frequencies, duration, and volume of sound waves. Listening refers to the psychological process of attaching meaning to the sound waves we detect. Often when someone speaks to us the message doesn't really register. You may even be able to parrot back the words despite the fact that the words have failed to "sink in." As one cartoon illustrates, we often think we are listening when we aren't. The cartoon shows a wife and husband sitting in the living room "talking." The wife says to her husband: "You couldn't have been listening. If you had been listening, you'd be mad."
2. There are some understandable reasons for poor listening habits: a lack of training, the difference between speaking and listening rates, and the tendency to hear what is expected.
   a. The first reason is the lack of training. Few colleges offer courses in listening skills. Although there seems to be a growing awareness of the importance of learning effective listening techniques, most of us never have received formal instruction in listening. At some point, you have probably been chastised for not listening and told you need to listen, but you probably never have been told how to listen better. That fact puts an important responsibility on your study of listening in this course. This may be the first and last time that you seriously explore ways to improve your listening skills.
   b. The second reason for poor listening habits stems from the difference between the rates of speaking and listening. Most people talk at a rate of 125–150 words per minute, but most people think and listen at a rate of over 300 words per

minute. If you consider the way you think, however, you know that you do not think in complete sentences. Words, phrases, images, and feelings, all flash through your mind at an incredible rate. So what do you do with the time difference between the speaking and listening rate?

(1) Ineffective listeners use the available time to daydream or attend to distractions. Each of us is constantly bombarded by many distracting stimuli. As you read this book, for example, your mind wanders to a memory of the past, you hear a dog barking outside, a hunger pain distracts you, and on and on. You must expend energy to focus your attention on one single stimulus. Think for a moment about a time recently when you totally concentrated on a job you had to do. Maybe your intense concentration lasted for only an hour or a few hours, but you probably felt tired afterward.

(2) Effective listeners use the extra thinking time to concentrate on the message, interpret meanings, look for hidden meanings, analyze nonverbal aspects such as facial expression, and so on. Because concentration is hard work, effective listening is hard work. When a person really concentrates on listening, it is an energy-consuming task. Effective listeners use their energy and spare time well.

c. Finally, listeners have a tendency to see and hear what they expect to see and hear. Certainly at some point, a friend has told you in a matter-of-fact way a surprising piece of information. Because of the friend's tone, you nodded in a matter-of-fact way and said "uh-huh." But as the message registered, you realized that it was not what you expected, so you asked the friend to repeat the message. You checked your perception. Unfortunately, because we often fail to check our perceptions, we hear only those parts of a message that we expect or want to hear.

3. Effective listening is an important skill to learn. "Listening" and "active listening" are used interchangeably here to indicate serious involvement in the process. Good listening can translate into better relationships with coworkers, increased understanding of the perspective of other people, a perception of caring, and more.

B. ***Types of Listening:*** We must adapt our listening behaviors to our purpose for listening. Some common types of listening include passive listening, selective listening, listening for pleasure, listening for therapy, listening for comprehension, and listening for evaluation.

1. Passive Listening. Passive listening occurs when you don't exert effort in the listening process, but just let the messages "wash over" you.

a. The process is more one of hearing than listening. Perhaps you are doing homework while listening to the radio. You are not actively listening to the radio, but you are aware that music is coming from the radio. You may have jotted notes during a professor's lecture while you were really thinking about something else. Now, the notes make no sense. Perhaps you have had the realization while driving that you were concentrating on something other than driving and could not remember passing the last several buildings.
b. These instances demonstrate ways we can function on a very low level of awareness. Being a passive listener when you need to respond to important information can have devastating consequences.

2. *Selective Listening*. Selective listening occurs when you select out or choose to pay attention to some things while ignoring others.
   a. A typical example occurs in the parent–child interaction. The parent gives a string of commands: "After you do your homework, pick up your room, take out the trash, then you can go down to Julia's to play." The child listens selectively and never hears that she was supposed to do homework, clean up her room, and take out the trash before playing. She simply hears the permission to go to Julia's to play because she selects out what she wants to hear.
   b. This selective listening may be unintentional. You may hear selectively because your experiences, attitudes, and/or attention makes you perceive selectively. In the workplace, colleagues seldom respect individuals who typically engage in selective listening.
3. *Listening for Pleasure*. Sometimes you listen for fun or pleasure. In this case you are not worried about solving the problems of the world or even the problems of your own life.
   a. When you listen to David Letterman's monologue at the beginning of his show, for example, you are simply listening for pleasure. You are not worried about whether he is doing the best job he should, whether he is using sound logic, or whether you will be tested over the material.
   b. While listening to Letterman, you have no purpose except wanting to smile or laugh at what he says. You probably won't remember much about what he said the next day. You probably won't think about Letterman's monologue again because it's a one-time occurrence and you experience it simply for pleasure or entertainment.

   c. While a graduate student, an individual had a professor who had an excellent voice that he used with great effectiveness. The student would listen with pleasure to the artistry of the professor's voice. Unfortunately, the graduate student could not remember what the professor had said. The classroom is no place for listening for pleasure. Similarly, students in a public speaking class frequently respond with enthusiasm to a classmate's effective style of delivery. Often these students fail to recognize deficiencies in the classmate's content.
4. *Listening as Therapy*. Therapeutic listening is the form you use when a friend has a problem and needs to talk. The friend may ask for advice, but really needs for you to help her or him think through a situation.
   a. The effective therapeutic listener seldom passes judgment on things that are said, but instead uses encouraging listening behaviors.
   b. When you want to help others to solve their own problems, you should nod frequently, use an expressive face, restate the speaker's ideas in your own words responding to the feelings the friend expresses, and ask probing and leading questions so the speaker is encouraged to speak his or her mind.
5. *Listening for Comprehension*. Listening for comprehension is the kind of listening you do in class while you listen seriously to a professor's lecture. Actually, it is the kind of listening you should do, but may or may not do.
   a. Listening for comprehension is listening to learn and remember.
   b. Listening for comprehension requires heavy concentration and comparison of new information to previous information and experiences. Effective retention of material may require your taking and reviewing notes.
6. *Listening for Evaluation*. Evaluative listening is important to your functioning effectively and responsibly. In this case, you evaluate the truth or falsity of the message. Evaluative listening is critical and discriminative listening. In this case, you do not simply accept everything the speaker says.
   a. You attempt to listen objectively to the speaker's message.
   b. You avoid responding emotionally to the speaker's word choice or supporting material.
   c. You avoid becoming distracted by the speaker's mannerisms or other elements of delivery. Instead you focus on content.
   d. You critically evaluate the evidence and reasoning of the speaker, judging the adequacy of the support and the logic of the argument.

III. **Improving Listening Skills.** As with any skill, active listening is a learned skill. You can do much to improve your listening skills. There are specific behaviors you can employ to improve your listening.

A. *Note-taking.* Note-taking can help you to listen and remember more effectively.

1. The sheer process of note-taking requires you to engage your body more actively in the listening process.
2. Note-taking gives you something to do with the extra thinking time and involves your eye–hand coordination in the process. The use of additional senses may help you to retain material.
3. Because you cannot write down everything the speaker says you must summarize in your own words. Your summary process structures your thinking and gives you a concrete product of the listening process.
4. Some people find note-taking distracting, especially in a one-on-one situation. If you are talking to your boss about your year-end evaluation, for example, you may not want to take notes while you listen. In most situations, however, you can prepare notes immediately afterward. By sitting and thinking about the things that were said, you can jot down important ideas in your own words for future reference.
5. In most public speaking situations, note-taking is appropriate and valuable.

B. *Preview-Review.* Previewing and reviewing makes listening more effective.

1. By learning and thinking about the topic in advance, you preview or prepare for the listening situation.
   a. If you know your professor will talk about "principles of organization" in class on Wednesday, reading the chapter on organization before Wednesday will increase the effectiveness of your listening.
   b. If your boss talks to you at a staff meeting once a month, you may want to keep a list of questions, ideas, and concerns you have had throughout the month. Then before the meeting, you can read over your list and preview issues that will be discussed.
2. Anticipation and thought about the upcoming communication event can be helpful. In addition, while a speaker is talking, the effective listener can add focus by trying to anticipate what the speaker will say next.
3. Review is important to help you synthesize and remember a message from a listening situation.
   a. How many times have you looked at your class notes just before a test and been unable to read or understand them?

b. The most effective method is to review your notes (or ideas) right after a message. If you have notes, you can elaborate and make corrections as you review.

C. *Concentration*. Concentration is essential to active listening. When you notice your attention wandering, you can refocus on the message in appropriate ways.

1. You may decide to pay more attention to the speaker's nonverbal messages, for example.
2. However, avoid becoming distracted. If, for example, you find yourself wondering why he selected that tie to go with that shirt... wondering if his wife bought the tie for him for Christmas...wondering if he actually has a wife...wondering what their home life must be like...and so on, refocus your attention on the message.
3. Random associations can flash through ours mind so quickly that we can suddenly find ourselves in fantasy land.
4. We must concentrate on the intended messages and their potential meaning. By using your spare thinking time well, you will be far more effective in receiving and remembering messages.

D. *Interaction*. The interactive process can be essential in listening effectively.

1. One semester while in a large section course, a professor talked to a student—one of a dozen who rushed up to ask a question after class. In trying to deal with the large number of students, she must have answered one student too quickly, gruffly, or incorrectly. At a later date, the student came to her office to talk individually, and said, "It upsets me that you don't like me, and that's why I'm not doing well in your class." The professor was shocked and apologized: "I'm sorry, but I don't even know who you are. Have we talked before?" There was no way the professor could have a negative attitude toward the student, because the professor didn't even remember seeing her before. Fortunately, the student decided to increase the "interactive process" by talking about her problem with the professor. In the case of a large class, the teacher may never speak directly to some students and never associate names with all the faces. This lack of direct interaction causes serious problems in understanding because of the lack of feedback.
2. When you are in a large audience, however, you can increase the interaction and the accuracy of the sending and receiving process. If you ask questions when you don't understand, if you make comments about your opinions, if you nod your head, if you catch the speaker's eye with your own eye contact, if you use one of many methods to interact with the speaker, then you become more involved in the communication process and increase your chances for effective listening.

3. Interaction is not only helpful to the listener, but it helps the speaker as well.
    a. After giving an oral report in class, a student came in to see the professor. He was surprised by the teacher's positive written comments saying that she thought his was the most creative and interesting project of the class. "While I was talking, no one seemed interested. After I finished, not one person asked a question or made a comment. They all just sat there and looked at me. I felt like a failure."
    b. The teacher explained that the class may have been deep in thought, that he may not have allowed enough time for questions, that his apparent frustration may have sent a message to the audience that he didn't want them to ask questions, or that because his report was the last one of the day, maybe the class was simply eager to go to lunch.
    c. But regardless of the reasons for the class' reaction, the whole process would have been much easier on the student if the class had responded to him with verbal and nonverbal interaction.

E. *Consider the Context.* You can improve your listening by considering social relationships and contexts. Usually within a matter of seconds after you see someone who is going to give a speech, you make a variety of assumptions about the person and decide whether you will like that individual. As it turns out, your initial impressions may or may not be correct. Your perceptions may, however, be affected by the context.
    1. You may know individuals very well yet be surprised by their behaviors in a certain context. You may have a friend, for example, who talks and behaves one way around you at home and another way up in front of a group giving a speech.
    2. By taking social relationships and contexts into account while listening, you can interpret messages more accurately.

F. *Observe nonverbal cues.* Because the majority of the social meaning of a message comes nonverbally, a good listener must "read between the lines."
    1. A facial expression, a pause, vocal stress on a word, a change in rate or pitch, movement forward, a gesture, and other nonverbal cues are as important as the words the speaker uses.
    2. By examining the words and non-word messages carefully, an effective listener can better find the intended or actual meanings.
    3. Reading between the lines provides a positive focus and can increase concentration and effectiveness.

G. *Listen for Ideas.* Listening for main points can be a helpful way to improve listening.
    1. Most speakers will give approximately three to five main points.

2. Regardless of the length of a speech, most trained speakers will give an overall structure that can be divided into a few key ideas. The listener may be able to identify the same main points easily, especially if the speaker says something like, "Today I want you to be able to identify the three most important ways you can obtain more effective college advising." Even if the speaker doesn't give signposts such as "First...Second...And finally..." you should be able to identify key ideas. You can quickly write down the key ideas during or just after a speech, for example, or, as you reflect afterward, you might try to restate the main points.
3. Sometimes you may become so engrossed in examples and details that you fail to see the overall picture of the speech. By listening for ideas, you will come away from the speech with the major concepts.

H. You can engage in a variety of additional behaviors to improve your listening. You can pay closer attention to the actual physiological and psychological process. You can avoid details as barriers and avoid distractions. Too often, you may think the responsibility for communication is on the sender or speaker. Not so. As the listener you have an equal or greater responsibility than the speaker. You need to listen actively and responsively if you want more effective communication.

IV. **Speech Analysis.** In this course we are primarily concerned with the improvement of your public communication. We shall provide you with the principles of public communication typically followed by those who wield political, social, and economic power in the United States. As you pursue your career and social life, you will observe that effective presentations will demonstrate techniques that vary from co-culture to co-culture in the United States. Similarly, you will learn what doesn't work with particular audiences. By analyzing the presentations you hear in different settings, you will constantly discover new ways to adapt to a variety of audiences. Should your career take you abroad, you will discover minor to radical departures from the principles of organization, support, language, and delivery described in this text. Because your effectiveness as a communicator will be enhanced if you analyze the presentations you hear in a variety of circumstances, we encourage you to analyze the speeches of your classmates. By doing so, you will establish a habit that will serve you well in your lifelong learning of public communication.

A. In this course you will have opportunities to speak publicly and opportunities to listen to public speakers. As you improve your speaking skills you should also improve your critical listening skills.

B. Speech analysis requires that you pay attention to a variety of factors.
   1. As a listener, you should be able to understand the message (including the speech purpose and main points), evaluate the types of support for those points, and critique the logic used in the speaker's reasoning process.
   2. Analysis of self (you, the listener) is important from the standpoint of recognizing the effects of your frame of reference on reception of the message.
   3. Analysis of the speaker is important from the standpoint of determining the speaker's ethics, motivation, and expertise.

C. In this course, you may use various methods of speech analysis. We provide one here, however, that provides a relatively comprehensive set of suggestions for preliminary speech analysis.
   1. Identify the purpose of the presentation.
   2. Identify the main ideas of the message (thesis, main points, and subpoints). Evaluate their clarity and appropriateness in light of the speaker's purpose.
   3. Analyze and evaluate the organization of the message (to what degree did the speaker accomplish the goals of an introduction and conclusion; to what degree did the speaker use appropriate patterns of organization to arrange main points and subpoints; to what degree did the speaker use effective transitions?).
   4. Analyze and evaluate the supporting material (to what degree did the supporting material clarify ideas, provide proof, hold attention, promote retention?).
   5. Analyze and evaluate the language (to what degree was the language clear, appropriate, memorable?).
   6. Analyze the effectiveness of bodily activity (e.g., posture, gestures, movement, facial expression, eye contact).
   7. Analyze the effectiveness of vocal elements (e.g., volume/projection, rate/pausing, pitch/inflection, quality).
   8. Evaluate the audience adaptation (how did the speaker relate the presentation to the needs, beliefs, attitudes, values, and expectations of this particular audience?).
   9. Analyze and evaluate speech attitudes (to what degree did the speaker demonstrate confidence, respect for the audience, and ethical behavior?).
   10. Analyze and evaluate the general effectiveness (to what degree did the presentation accomplish the specific purpose?).

D. While you are listening to a speech, you may decide to concentrate on one, some, or all of these factors of analysis. Your critical listening will provide good practice to improve your listening skills, and your constructive critical evaluation for the speaker will provide valuable information for the speaker's self-analysis and improvement.

Closing Remarks

Your public speaking and listening skills are affected by your intrapersonal processes. That internal communication depends on your frame of reference, creativity, willingness to take risks, and thinking patterns. You probably have seldom talked about your intrapersonal communication and have received little training to improve your listening. This course offers the opportunity to consider both. Depending upon the people involved or the situation you are in, you may have many different purposes for your listening, such as listening for pleasure, for therapy, for appreciation, for understanding, and for evaluation. By applying effective listening skills—note-taking, previewing and reviewing the message, concentrating on the ideas, interacting with the speaker, considering the context of the speech, and observing the speaker's vocal and bodily aspects—you can improve your success. In this course, you will be giving and listening to speeches. Begin now to listen more carefully and to consider factors relating to the message content, the situation, the delivery, and the audience in your speech analysis and evaluation.

References and Suggestions for Further Readings

Barker, L. R., Edwards, R., Gaines, C., et al. (1980). An investigation of proportional time spent in various communication activities by college students. *Journal of Applied Communication Research*, *8*, 101–109.

Bostrom, R. N., & Waldhart, E. (1988). Memory models and the measurement of listening. *Communication Education, 37(1)*, 1–13.

Cotzias, C. G. (1996). How to develop advertising concepts and demystify the creative process. *Journalism and Mass Communication Educator, 51*, 80–85.

Csikszentmihalyi, M. (1996). *Creativity: Flow and the psychology of discovery and invention.* New York: HarperCollins.

Floyd, J. J. (1985). *Listening: A practical approach.* Glenview, IL: Scott, Foresman.

Goss, B. (1982). Listening as information processing. *Communication Quarterly, 30*, 304–307.

Haney, W. V. (1992). *Communication and interpersonal relations: Text and cases.* (6th ed.). Homewood, IL: Irwin.

Hulbert, J. E. (1989). Barriers to effective listening. *The Bulletin of the Association for Business Communication, 52*, 3–5.

Lodhi, S., & Greer, R. D. (1989). *The speaker as listener. Journal of the Experimental Analysis of Behavior, 51*, 353–359.

Lustig, M. W., & Koester, J. (1996). *Intercultural competence: Interpersonal communication across cultures.* (2nd ed.). New York: HarperCollins.

Roberts, C. V., Watson, K. W., & Barker, L. (1989). *Intrapersonal communication processes.* Scottsdale, AZ: Gorsuch Scarisbrick, Publishers.

Rubin, R. B. (1982). Assessing speaking and listening competence at the college level: The communication competency assessment instrument. *Communication Education, 31*, 19–32.

Sternberg, R. J., & Lubart, T. I. (1995). *Defying the crowd.* New York: The Free Press.

Von Oech, R. (1990). *A whack on the side of the head: How you can be more creative.* New York: Warner.

Wolvin, A. D., & Coakley, C. G. (1992). *Listening.* Dubuque, IA: Wm. C. Brown.

Wolvin, A. D., & Coakley, C. G. (1993). *Perspectives on listening.* Norwood, NJ: Ablex.

CHAPTER 3

Analyzing Your Audience and Occasion

COMM 210

Objectives

After reading this chapter, you should be able to

1. apply principles of psychological and demographic audience analysis in the preparation of your presentations;
2. use analysis of the situation and occasion to maximize the effectiveness of your presentations;
3. adapt to circumstances and reactions during your presentations; and
4. identify ways to improve your speaking based on the experience gained from your presentations.

Topical Outline

Analysis of the Multicultural Audience and Key Concepts

Analysis after the speaking event
Analysis before the speaking event
Analysis during the speaking event
Apathetic audience
Attitude
Audience expectations
Audience feedback
Audience-centered speaker
Belief-attitude-value (BAV) system
Belief
Boomerang effect
Closed questions
Demographic analysis
Distractions
Friendly audience
Hostile audience
Instrumental values
Interview
Mixed audience
Mood
Neutral audience
Observation
Occasion
Open-ended question
Physical environment
Psychological analysis of the audience
Questionnaire
Scaled question
Self-centered speaker
Size of the audience
Surrounding events
Survey
Target audience
Terminal value
Types of audiences
Value

Occasion

PERSPECTIVE (Values of analysis of the audience and situation)

I. The fundamental skill of an effective communicator is the ability to create a message that is appropriate for the listener.
   A. The purpose for giving a presentation is to get a desired response from the audience.
   B. In order to offer the most valuable information, make the most effective appeals, and present the most appropriate image, you must understand your audience.
      1. What do they value?
      2. What do they know?
      3. How do they feel?
      4. What do they expect?

II. A fundamental challenge for many students of public speaking is to move from being self-centered to being audience-centered.
   A. Ineffective speakers are self-centered.
      1. Self-centered speakers focus only on issues that are important to them.
      2. Self-centered speakers act as though everyone has had the same experiences.
      3. Self-centered speakers lack respect for diversity among human beings.
      4. Self-centered speakers focus on their speaking performance.
         a. They may be self-conscious, worrying that they'll make a mistake.
         b. They may be arrogant, acting as though the audience is privileged to be hearing them.
   B. Effective speakers are audience-centered.
      1. Audience-centered speakers look at their goals in terms of the goals of the audience. The audience-centered speaker asks:
         a. What does my audience want and need to hear?
         b. How does my message pertain to the audience?
         c. What will my audience get out of it?
      2. Audience-centered speakers try to understand the experiences of the listeners.
         a. Audience-centered speakers present material to which the audience can relate.
         b. Audience-centered speakers use words familiar to the audience.
      3. Audience-centered speakers respect diversity among individuals. The audience-centered speaker keeps in mind that she or he is talking to human beings, and that he or she can facilitate communication by treating them like friends.
         a. Audience-centered speakers understand and respect the values of the audience.
         b. Audience-centered speakers avoid attacking or insulting the audience.

4. Audience-centered speakers focus on feedback they receive from the audience.

III. Effective speakers use to their advantage the physical environment in which they deliver their presentations. Hence, you should be familiar with the place where you will deliver your presentation in order to plan ways to facilitate communication and reduce distractions.

IV. ***Purpose statement:*** The purpose of this chapter is to identify the ways a speaker should analyze the audience and the speaking situation in order to prepare and deliver an effective presentation.

V. ***Preview:*** First, we shall examine the analysis you should conduct before the speaking event. We begin this section by exploring the importance of understanding the psychology of your audience. Next, we present the advantages and dangers of a demographic analysis of the audience. Third, we look at the importance of considering the facilities where and the occasion when you deliver presentations. Fourth, we examine ways to gather needed information about the audience and occasion. We conclude this section on analysis before the speech with a discussion of ways to use the information you have gathered. The final section of the chapter presents suggestions for analysis during and after the speaking event.

Chapter Body

I. **Analysis before the speaking event.** Before you begin to plan a speech, you should obtain as much information as possible about your audience and the circumstances surrounding your presentation. Understanding the knowledge, feelings, and values of your audience will allow you to present information appropriate for your audience and increase your chances of attaining your goal. Understanding the circumstances surrounding your presentation will help you capitalize on the nature of the speaking facilities and avoid embarrassing yourself or irritating your audience.
   A. *Psychological Audience Analysis.* Psychological analysis of the audience involves considering the impact of beliefs, attitudes, and values on the behavior of listeners. Our *belief-attitude-value (BAV) system* accounts for the way we think, feel, and behave.
      1. An *attitude* is a person's emotional reaction to an idea, object, person, or behavior. By emotional reaction we mean that attitudes fall on a continuum from highly positive to highly negative. In some cases, an attitude is neither positive nor negative: The attitude is neutral. In other cases, individuals are apathetic, that is they do not care at all about the idea, object, person, or behavior. Attitudes of the audience are particularly important to a speaker.
         a. The way individuals feel toward something predicts the way they will behave toward it. For instance, we tend to behave

quite differently toward people we like than toward people we dislike.

b. Attitude change (making a listener more or less favorable toward an idea, object, person, behavior, or plan of action) is often an important goal of a persuasive presentation.

c. The attitudes of listeners also are important in situations where a presenter seeks to inform. The speaker often needs
   (1) to motivate listeners to learn new information,
   (2) to reduce their negative attitudes toward the material to be learned or the process or procedure to be mastered,
   (3) to build confidence in their ability to learn or use new information, and/or
   (4) to encourage listeners to use or apply new knowledge.

2. A *belief* is that which an individual considers to be a fact, or statement, about reality. Hence, beliefs express what we consider to be true or false.
   a. Our attitudes and beliefs tend to be consistent.
      (1) For example, if you like cats (positive attitude), you probably hold several positive beliefs (facts) about cats. You might think cats are clean, cats are intriguing pets, cats have fascinating personalities, and that people who own cats live longer. On the other hand, if you feel the only good cat is a dead cat (negative attitude), you can easily list the negative qualities of felines.
      (2) If you like a person, you will tend to attribute positive motives to their actions. If you dislike a person, you will tend to attribute negative motives to similar actions. On the other hand, if someone you like repeatedly acts in ways you dislike, the new beliefs you begin to hold about that person will result in a less positive attitude toward the individual.
   b. Often a speaker must change the beliefs of a listener in order to change the listener's attitudes.
      (1) In one-on-one situations, we often find ourselves trying to change the beliefs of others. Through selective description we emphasize those facts that support our position and minimize those that weaken it. We try to show others that their "facts" are wrong. Additionally, we provide evidence that is consistent with the "facts" we want others to consider true.
      (2) Similarly, effective presenters accurately identify the audience's beliefs that need to be refuted and the new beliefs that need to be developed in order to change attitudes.

3. At the core of an individual's BAV system (and personal identity) are values.

a. Our *values* are our general rules for living (instrumental values) and our basic goals in life (terminal values). We have fewer values than we have beliefs or attitudes. Our personal rules and goals govern our behavior in a variety of situations.
   (1) Some positive instrumental values might include such common "rules of proper behavior" as being ambitious, assertive, broad minded, capable, cheerful, clean, courageous, creative, dependable, friendly, forgiving, helpful, imaginative, independent, intelligent, logical, loving, loyal, obedient, polite, responsible, and self-controlled.
   (2) An individual's terminal values might include such common goals, or end states, as a comfortable life, an environment of beauty, an exciting life, a feeling of accomplishment, a long and healthy life, a loving relationship, and a world at peace. Other terminal values might include national security, personal security, personal happiness, pleasure, recognition, salvation, self-respect, true friendship, wealth, wisdom, and the list goes on.

b. Personal values provide an individual with a frame of reference for evaluating situations. Our values lead us to judge ideas or behaviors from good to bad, worthwhile to worthless, or ethical to unethical. Our values influence the way we perceive information and our willingness to accept new beliefs. Since "9/11," many have viewed "a safe environment" as more important than "complete freedom" or "personal privacy."

c. Values are deeply ingrained in individuals. Rarely can a communicator change listeners' values except over a long period of time.
   (1) A wise speaker will avoid trying to change or attack the values of the listener. Individuals usually perceive an attack on their values as an attack on them personally. Hence, listeners tend to become emotionally aroused, defensive, and resistant when they feel their values are under attack. Stimulating listeners to feel under attack can even result in a *boomerang effect*, or strong movement away from the speaker's goals. If you understand the values of your listeners, you will be less likely to insult them unintentionally.
   (2) A wise speaker will seek out and emphasize audience values that are consistent with the goal of the presentation. Often our values come into conflict on particular issues.
      (a) In a particular situation, for example, your desire for excitement, independence, and achievement may

come into conflict with your desire for safety and security. Your choice in that situation may depend on the values that your companions make sound more important and rewarding.

(b) During a sales presentation, for example, an insurance agent might say, "Yes, I know this costs. But think about your family's need for protection. Where will they be without you?" The agent does not tell you you're cheap (an attack), but shifts your attention to the value of protecting your family.

(3) An effective speaker uses, rather than tries to change, existing values of the listeners.

d. Sometimes the values of classmates as an audience create specific concerns. The key is to recognize these potential problems and adapt to them.

(1) The personal values of some of your classmates may result in counter productive behavior.

(a) Some students may feel in competition with each other and fail to be supportive audience members.

(b) Some students may get to know each other extremely well. Their value of friendship may result in overly supportive behavior and a refusal to provide constructive feedback.

(2) Certain prejudices may surface in oral comments or on feedback forms. We encourage you to resist defensive behavior and to devise positive ways to reach such individuals. Learning constructive ways to deal with all types of individuals can only help you in your career and interpersonal relationships.

B. *Demographic analysis.* The word "demographic" comes from two Greek stems that mean literally "a picture of the people." Demographic data provides statistics about the composition of the audience in terms of a variety of social categories.

1. A demographic analysis of the audience means the speaker considers the importance of such characteristics of the audience as: gender (sex), age, educational level, occupational experiences, economic class, religion, regional background, and ethnicity.
2. A demographic analysis can provide useful information about the probable beliefs, attitudes, and values of the listeners as well as their interests, experiences, and levels of knowledge.

a. Members of particular occupations, for instance, may have training and experiences that affect their knowledge and attitudes on a particular topic. Words that are meaningful to individuals of a particular age, educational level, or social class may be meaningless to other individuals. How do you respond to the following: "ice box," "hostile audience," "skirt"?

b. Members of particular political, civic, and social groups often share common ways of responding to topics and issues. A proposal to exempt low-income individuals from payroll (i.e., social security) taxes may mean "tax relief for the poor" to one group but "class warfare" to another.

c. The experiences of individuals raised in rural areas may be quite different from the experiences of individuals raised in the inner city or suburbs. Other differences may stem from an individual's religion, ethnic background, or regional upbringing.

d. Stories and illustrations that are relevant to the lives of individuals who belong to some groups may be inappropriate, even insulting or threatening, for others.

3. You should approach a demographic analysis with extreme care. A demographic analysis may lead to dangerous stereotyping if a speaker assumes that all members of a particular category are identical or if the speaker's preconceptions about members of a category are incorrect or demeaning. Sometimes an apparently "harmless" comment can offend members of the audience. Hence, you should take care to test your assumptions about social classifications and avoid comments that could be perceived as condescending or prejudiced.

C. *Analysis of the Situation and Occasion*. A speaker needs to take into account the size of the audience, the characteristics of the physical environment, and the nature of the speaking occasion.

1. Size. As the size of the audience increases, presentations generally increase in formality.

a. The audience for your classroom presentations will probably have 20 to 25 members, a moderately-sized audience. Moderately-sized audiences generally are suitable for a wide range in levels of formality.

b. A small audience of two to five individuals, however, may feel uneasy if the presenter stands behind a lectern and uses highly formal grammar, dramatic gestures, and an oratorical voice. The situation may appear absurd if the presenter speaks into a microphone.

(1) As audiences decrease in size, presenters usually become more conversational and informal.

(2) As audiences decrease in size, effective presenters usually plan for more audience participation and involvement.

c. When an audience is large, a speaker needs to help the listeners to see, hear, and remain attentive. The speaker must prepare to use a more formal style of language and delivery that the situation will probably require.

(1) Any visual aids the speaker plans to use must be large enough for all to see.
(2) The speaker should plan to use a more articulate, energetic, and animated style of delivery.
(3) The speaker may need to practice using a microphone.

2. Physical Environment. To avoid unpleasant surprises, you should analyze the physical environment where you will deliver your presentation. Any speaking location will have strengths and weaknesses. During your speech preparation, plan the ways you will capitalize on the strengths or opportunities of the environment. Identify the ways you will compensate for or minimize the weaknesses.
   a. If you are using electronically delivered visual aids, know your needs. For instance:
      (1) Will you need to provide equipment? Spare bulbs?
      (2) Will you need to provide extension cords?
      (3) Do you know how to use the equipment on the site? and
      (4) Do you know how to raise or lower the lights in the room?
   b. Consider the physical arrangement of the room. For instance:
      (1) Would it improve communication to change the seating arrangement of the audience?
      (2) How will you compensate for inappropriate seating arrangements that cannot be changed?
      (3) From what location(s) can you deliver the presentation for maximum effectiveness?
      (4) Where will you place any materials (including notes and visual aids) you must use? and
      (5) What obstacles might prevent the audience from seeing your visual aids?
   c. Plan ways to create an appropriate mood for your presentation. For instance:
      (1) Would refreshments lend the desired mood?
      (2) Would symbols such as flags, posters, pictures, models, professional garb, or equipment enhance the mood? and
      (3) Would changing the lighting enhance the mood?
   d. Plan for ways to deal with likely distractions. For instance:
      (1) If the room is too hot or cold, what will you do? and
      (2) If distracting noises are present, how will you control or compensate for them?
3. The Occasion. You will deliver presentations in a variety of circumstances. Each occasion will have unique characteristics for which you should prepare. During your analysis of the occasion determine the audience's expectations and the likely impact of the events that will precede and follow your presentation.

a. Audience expectations. Because situations vary widely, we provide a general question for you to consider: What do these listeners expect a speaker to do in these circumstances?
   (1) How long do they expect the presentation to last? What will be the likely effect of this presentation being longer or shorter than their expectations?
   (2) What will be the likely effect of violating audience expectations in this setting? For instance:
      (a) Will this audience be amused, distracted, or offended by use of slang, unusual attire, or off-beat humor? or
      (b) How can I violate some expectations in a way that will hold attention and make a point without reducing my credibility?

b. Surrounding events. The events that precede or follow your presentation may have a profound effect on the audience's reaction to your presentation. Take the time to consider what those events are likely to be and their probable impact on your goals. For instance:
   (1) Who will be speaking before and after you? Are they likely to oppose your goals?
   (2) How will the time of day or the position of your presentation in a program likely affect your audience? For instance:
      (a) Will the audience be just starting the work day?
      (b) Will the audience be eager for the program to finish? and
      (c) Will the audience have just finished a heavy meal?

D. *You can gain information about the audience and the occasion through observation, interviews, and/or surveys.*

1. <u>Observation</u>. Life is an experience of continual learning about the similarities and differences among people—in the vernacular, a process of learning "what makes people tick."
   a. Many of your "audiences" will be familiar to you.
      (1) From days to years of observation, you will come to know not only the beliefs, attitudes, and values of many individuals but also their habits.
      (2) You also will learn who are the most influential members of the audience and learn to anticipate and prepare for their expectations and their typical reservations or objections to new proposals.
   b. Through travel, reading, and a variety of other life experiences you will continually increase your understanding of the diversity and similarities among people. A broadened understanding can only help to increase the effectiveness of your communication.

2. Interviews. When in doubt about an audience or speaking situation, ask questions.
   a. A speaker can interview one or more audience members before preparing the presentation. If you do not already know the answers, ask such important questions as:
      (1) Why is this group gathering?
      (2) How large will the audience be?
      (3) Who will speak before or after me?
      (4) How much time will I have to speak?
      (5) What are the facilities like?
      (6) What does the audience know about the topic?
      (7) How has the audience responded to this topic in the past? and
      (8) What else about this audience may be important?
   b. You should be careful about making generalizations based on one or two interviews. The person to whom you talk may not be representative of the entire group or may not know the answers to your questions.
3. Surveys. You may be able to gather information from your audience using a questionnaire.
   a. Some instructors use a form to gather information about their class and distribute the results to their students. In other cases, instructors encourage individual speakers to create a questionnaire or ask questions orally to better understand the audience's specific attitudes about a given topic.
   b. A good questionnaire encourages a response to questions that will yield the desired information.
      (1) Individuals are more likely to respond to a questionnaire that is attractive, short, and clear and that preserves the anonymity of the respondent.
      (2) A useful questionnaire contains questions that yield the desired information. Questionnaires commonly contain one or more of the following types of questions.
         (a) Closed questions. Closed questions ask the respondent to provide a limited response to a direct question.
            i. You're familiar with the types of closed questions often used on examinations: the "true/false," "multiple-choice," and "fill-in-the-blank" formats.
            ii. Closed questions will permit you to gather limited, but useful information, quickly.
            iii. The following are examples of closed questions that could appear on a questionnaire:

Please fill in the blank with the information that applies to you:

Age: _____

Please place an "X" in the blank that best applies to you:

Are you a parent?

_____ yes
_____ no

I would vote for:

_____ Maria Camilo
_____ Beth Ellison
_____ Duane Kiedrich
_____ Glen Stampede
_____ None of the above

(b) Scaled questions. A particular type of closed question, the scaled question asks the respondent to select a point on a continuum.

i. Scaled questions are particularly helpful in inferring attitudes. They can, however, gather other types of information.
ii. The following are examples of scaled questions suitable for a questionnaire:

Please place an "X" in the blank that best applies to you.

In 1999, I earned:

_____ below $5,000
_____ $5,000 to $14,999
_____ $15,000 to $24,999
_____ $25,000 to $34,999
_____ over $35,000

How often do you donate when you receive requests by phone for charitable contributions?

_____ Always
_____ Frequently
_____ Rarely
_____ Never

How do you feel about the proposal to include "sexual orientation" in the university's affirmative action statement?

_____ Strongly Agree
_____ Agree
_____ Slightly Agree
_____ Undecided
_____ Slightly Disagree
_____ Disagree
_____ Strongly Disagree

(c) Open-ended questions. Open-ended questions resemble essay and short-answer questions on an examination. Respondents can write anything they wish.
   i. Because answering takes time, many respondents will ignore open-ended questions.
   ii. Respondents may provide an answer irrelevant to your purpose.
   iii. Unless you are asking for a short response to a highly focused open-ended question, the format probably will not help you gather the information you need. Informal conversation with audience members is likely to be more effective.

E. *The speaker should consider the audience during each step of the speech preparation.*
   1. The speaker should adapt to the knowledge, interests, beliefs, attitudes, and values of the audience that pertain to the subject and the speech purpose. The position of the audience in regard to the purpose of the speech provides a useful classification of audiences.
      a. A friendly audience is one that is positively disposed toward the speaker's purpose.
      b. A hostile audience is one that is opposed to the speaker's purpose.
      c. A neutral audience is one that is undecided about (neither for nor against) the speaker's purpose.
      d. An apathetic audience is one that has no knowledge of or interest in the speaker's purpose.
   2. A speaker may have a mixed audience, which makes it difficult to identify the target audience. In such cases, we recommend adapting to the segment of the audience (those individuals) who can best help you accomplish your goals.
   3. Stress the areas of agreement between you and the audience rather than the differences.

a. Show that you have common goals, interests, and needs.
b. Present your areas of agreement before you introduce your areas of disagreement.

4. Try to evaluate your material from the frame of reference of the audience.
   a. Consider what the audience wants to hear in light of what you want to say.
   b. Narrow and phrase your purpose in a way that won't offend or turn off your audience.
   c. Find subtle ways to suggest that you have the best interests of the audience at heart. Audiences tend to be (rightfully) skeptical of speakers who openly assert that they have the best interests of the audience at heart.

II. **Analysis during and after the speaking event.** The theme of this section is "It's never too late to use your head." Audiences provide useful information both during and after speaking events. A professor once accepted an invitation to speak at a local museum. During a telephone interview with the program chairperson, the speaker learned that the event was a monthly meeting of volunteers. The program chairperson described the event as "a one-hour, winter-doldrums meeting—an effort to motivate and stir up enthusiasm." The program chairperson, who expected about 30 in the audience, described it as primarily composed of recently widowed volunteers, most of whom had little experience with the public and needed to be shown how to assist visitors in a friendly and assertive manner. The speaker prepared five simple, colorful overhead transparencies focusing on developing assertiveness and confidence and projecting a positive, friendly attitude. Upon arriving at the meeting, the speaker noticed that the audience of 75 was far different than expected. Most appeared to be married couples. The audience included some of the most prominent business people and civic leaders of the community. These were hardly timid, nonassertive individuals. During the preliminary business of the meeting, the speaker quickly reinvented the presentation. He discarded four of the overheads (keeping the one pertaining to projecting friendliness), reworked the introduction to emphasize the value of selfless civic-minded behavior, and changed his focus to a humorous presentation on the dos and don'ts of nonverbal communication with clients. The audience laughed during the presentation, and most of the audience thanked and complimented the speaker before they left the social gathering at the close. A speaker must learn to expect and cope with the unexpected.

A. *Analysis during the speaking event.*
   1. Before your presentation, check out the environment to identify any last-minute adjustments you must make. Because the audience doesn't know what you are planning to do, don't apologize for changes to your plan.

2. During your presentation, use audience feedback to continue to adjust your approach. Watch for information from the audience members. Audience members always provide a variety of nonverbal messages and sometimes oral ones.
   a. By looking at their faces, you can receive some indication of how attentive the audience appears, whether they seem to understand your message, and if they agree with your ideas.
      (1) Positive nonverbal cues—such as a smile, direct eye contact, leaning forward in the seat, and head nodding-probably indicate that your audience is attentive and receiving your message. Continue with your plan.
      (2) Negative nonverbal behaviors—such as fidgeting, frowning, averting eye contact, leaning back and slouched, and jiggling a foot—probably indicate that your audience is inattentive, confused, or rejects your message. Alter your plan.
   b. Also, your audience may give verbal feedback in the form of questions, comments, or answers to your questions. If someone answers a question you had intended to be rhetorical, don't show shock—act as though you had intended it to be a direct question: "Yes, thank you" or repeat the answer.
   c. If your audience appears confused, summarize your material or restate the purpose of the current section of the presentation and clarify your point.
   d. If your audience appears resistant to your ideas, provide additional evidence or make your position less extreme.
3. The most important point to remember is to avoid panic. Calmly think of ways to improve the situation.

B. *Analysis after the speaking event.* You will increase your presentational ability if you take the time to evaluate and learn from your speaking experiences.
   1. Use the feedback you receive from your instructor and classmates to identify your stronger and weaker points as a speaker. Use audio or video taped records of your presentations to identify elements of your delivery that work well and those that need improvement.
      a. Before your next presentation, review your past performance and set resonable goals for improvement.
      b. Identify areas for improvement that are likely to pay the largest benefits in terms of your overall image as a speaker.
   2. Always focus on the strengths of and the potentials for your speaking. In public speaking, a presentation is never a failure; it's an opportunity to learn and grow.

Closing Remarks

Analyzing the audience and occasion will greatly enhance your chances of success when making a public presentation. Before you prepare your presentation consider carefully the beliefs, attitudes, and values of your listeners and their relevant demographic characteristics. You should make every choice regarding your presentation with the audience in mind. During the actual speaking event, be prepared to adapt to the situation and the reactions of the audience. After a presentation, evaluate your speaking strengths and your opportunities for continued development.

References and Suggestions for Further Readings

Aristotle. *The Rhetoric and Poetics of Aristotle.* Trans. by Roberts, W. R., & Bywater, I. NY: The Modern Library.

Asante, M. K., & Atwater, D. F. (1986). The rhetorical condition as symbolic structure in discourse. *Communication Quarterly, 34*, 170–177.

Axon, D. E., & Stine, R. L. (1993). *The public speaking process: Computer-assisted speech organization and development.* Fort Worth, TX: Harcourt Brace.

Bradley, B. E. (1991). *Fundamentals of speech communication: The credibility of ideas.* Dubuque, IA: William C. Brown.

Clevenger, T. (1966). *Audience analysis.* Indianapolis, IN: Bobbs-Merrill.

Coleman, R. (1983). The continuing significance of social class to marketing. *Journal of Consumer Research, 10*, 265–80.

Erikson, E. (1980). *Identity and the life cycle.* NY: Norton.

Gamble, T., & Gamble, M. (1994). *Public speaking in the age of diversity.* Boston: Allyn and Bacon.

Hirsch, E. D., Jr. Kett, J. F.., & Trefil, J. (1988). *The dictionary of cultural literacy.* Boston: Houghton Mifflin.

Youga, J. M. (1989). *The elements of audience analysis.* NY: Macmillan.

CHAPTER 4

Organizing Your Ideas

Objectives

After reading this chapter, you should be able to

1. explain the basic functions of the introduction, body, and conclusion of a speech;
2. recognize and use different patterns of organization;
3. choose the best pattern of organization for your specific speech purpose;
4. recognize and employ effective transitions; and
5. apply an organizational system for responding to questions from the audience.

Topical Outline

VALUES OF EFFECTIVE ORGANIZATION

LEVELS OF ORGANIZATION

THE MAIN COMPONENTS OF A SPEECH

- Functions of the body
- Functions of the introduction
- Functions of the conclusion

THE NATURE AND USES OF PATTERNS OF ORGANIZATION

- Topical or categorical order
- Chronological or time order
- Spatial or geographic order
- Causal order
- Problem–solution order
- The Motivated Sequence

RELATING SUPPORTING MATERIAL TO IDEAS

- Didactic or deductive method
- Implicative or inductive method

TRANSITIONS

ORGANIZING AN ANSWER TO QUESTIONS FROM THE AUDIENCE

Key Concepts

Action step (of Motivated Sequence)
Answering questions
Anticlimactic arrangement
Appeal for action
Attention step (of Motivated Sequence)
Audience participation
Body
Building credibility
Building interest
Categorical order
Causal order
Chronological order
Climactic arrangement
Conclusion
Didactic method
Emotional response
Familiar to the unknown
Goodwill
Inductive method
Interjections
Internal previews
Internal summaries
Introduction
Levels of organization
Method of implication
Mixed visualization (of Motivated Sequence)
Mood
Motivated Sequence
Need step (of Motivated Sequence)
Negative visualization (of Motivated Sequence)
Organization
Organization of supporting material
Overall organization
Patterns of arrangement
Patterns of organization
Pointing (of Motivated Sequence)
Positive visualization (of Motivated Sequence)
Preview
Primacy
Problem-solution order
Recency
Rhetorical question
Satisfaction step (of Motivated Sequence)
Sense of finality
Signposts
Spatial order
Special devices (transitional)
Structure of the event
Summary
Topical order
Transitions
Use of a key phrase
Use of a memory aid
Use of a theme
Values of organization
Visualization step (of Motivated Sequence)

Organizing Your Ideas

PERSPECTIVE

I. **Values of Organization.** Many of our students have told us that they wished we had placed the topic of "organization" earlier in the course. Hence, we have moved this chapter toward the front of this text. Let's begin with the values of organization.
   A. Something which is put into categories or built into a structure is easier for us to understand and remember.
   B. If our ideas are clearly arranged in a pattern that makes sense, our listeners will understand and remember them better.
   C. If our ideas are sequenced effectively, we have a better chance of persuading others.
   D. Most teachers of speech communication expect well-organized presentations from their students. A lack of organization is a good sign of a lack of preparation.
   E. Research in speech communication has demonstrated the overall importance of effective organization.

II. **Levels of Organization.** You can view organization from four different levels: how your speech fits into the structure of the event; the overall organization of your speech (introduction, body, and conclusion); patterns of organization used to arrange ideas within the body of the speech; and the way supporting material is presented to develop a point (the didactic method and the method of implication).
   A. First, you should consider how your presentation will fit into the structure of the event. A presentation is but a part of a communication event. What happens before and after your message will influence your listeners' reactions to your message.
      1. When several speakers speak on the same issue, research suggests that being first (primacy) or last (recency) is advantageous if the objective is persuasion.
         a. Apparently, if your message is first, you may be able to persuade the audience to your position.
         b. Subsequent speakers will have less effect, especially if you get a public commitment from the audience.
      2. Other evidence shows that the last person to speak has the advantage (Wenburg & Wilmont, 1973, pp. 166–167).
      3. Because the research results are mixed and because so many variables are involved, your preference is probably most important.
         a. Sometimes a speaker is excited and eager to go first.
         b. Other times the speaker wants to hear the ideas of others and adapt to those ideas.
   B. Once you have analyzed the situation, you should consider your organization within the speech.

1. Usually your overall organization will be an introduction, body, and conclusion.
2. You should determine how you will arrange the ideas of your message within the body of the speech for maximal effect.
3. On the most specific level, you need to determine whether to state your key ideas before or after you present supporting material.
4. Finally, you need to use transitions to make your organization clear to the listeners.

III. ***Purpose Statement***: This chapter reviews principles of organization and structure as they apply to effectiveness in presentational settings.

IV. ***Preview***: In this chapter, we will discuss the overall organization of a speech and the specific arrangement of ideas within the body, ways to relate support to an idea, ways to signal movement within a presentation, and ways to organize your ideas when you receive questions from the audience.

Chapter Body

I. **The Main Components of a Speech.** Most people divide their message into three main parts: the introduction, the body, and the conclusion.
   A. There's a popular saying that in a speech, "You tell them what you're going to tell them, you tell them, and then you tell them what you've told them." The idea behind the saying is that you give your audience a preview in the introduction, tell them your main ideas and support for those ideas in the body, and summarize in the conclusion. There are actually many different ways of arranging a message, but the introduction-body-conclusion arrangement is the most common.
   B. Below is an outline that illustrates the way the three parts of a presentation interrelate:
      Introduction
         I. Attract the attention of the listener.
         II. Establish relationship of the topic to the audience.
         III. Build speaker credibility.
         IV. Give purpose and/or thesis statement and/or preview the message [these are ways to prepare the audience for the speech to come].
      Body
         I. Give first main point.
            A. Developmental material.
            B. Developmental material.
         II. Give second main point.
            A. Developmental material.
            B. Developmental material.

III. Give third main point.
   A. Developmental material.
   B. Developmental material.
IV. Give final main point.

Conclusion

I. Summarize key ideas.
II. Use interest device to make memorable.
III. Make final appeal.

C. **Preparing for overall organization.**
   1. *Body.* The body should be first in your planning and your most important concern.
      a. The body of the message is the main content.
      b. When you plan your speech you need to begin with the body.
      c. The body is the largest and most important part of your speech.
         (1) The body of the message usually contains two to five key ideas, or main points, that develop your thesis or central idea.
         (2) In some cases, additional ideas or subpoints are needed to develop main points.
         (3) You can support your main points and subpoints with a variety of different kinds of support. You may explain your ideas, give examples, compare ideas, give statistics, quote authorities, and more (as presented in Chapter 9). Your support will make your main ideas understandable and believable.
         (4) According to the speech research of Jones and Goethals (1972), material presented first (primacy effect) or last (recency effect) is remembered better than information presented in the middle. Hence, consider placing your most important points first or last.
   2. *Introduction.* The purpose of the speech introduction is to provide a good basic foundation for leading into the message.
      a. The introduction sets up a favorable atmosphere for the body of your message.
      b. To prepare your audience for the body of your message, you must get its attention, interest it in the topic, establish yourself as a credible source, and prepare the audience for the speech to come. Often a single technique can accomplish two or more of the functions of an introduction.
         (1) One major function of the speech introduction is to gain the listeners' attention.
            (a) Stories enable the audience to use imagination and encourage the audience to remember the message. The vividness and interest value of the story can make it an effective way to lead into a speech.

(b) Sometimes the speaker asks a rhetorical question. A rhetorical question is one that the speaker asks for effect, not because he or she expects the audience to answer directly. Usually, a rhetorical question is somewhat abstract and is designed to encourage thinking on the part of the audience.

(c) The speaker can have the audience—especially a large audience—easily answer questions orally or by raising their hands.

(2) Another important function of a speech introduction is to strengthen the audience's interest in the topic. There are many ways to involve an audience in the topic of a message.

(a) You can involve the listeners mentally by showing them the way the topic affects them.

(b) You can involve the listeners physically by asking them to do something with or for you.

(3) A third function of the introduction is to strengthen the speaker's credibility.

(a) Effective speakers establish their knowledge of the subject early in the message. In some cases, you may not have expert knowledge of the topic, but chances are that because you have done research that you know more than most of your listeners. If you haven't done research, you may not be prepared to inform or persuade others.

(b) You should have an interest in the topic. If not, forget about trying to interest anyone else in the subject. However, it's not enough to have interest, you need to show it. As an effective speaker, you need to show your interest to stimulate audience interest. Doing so will build the audience's perception of your dynamism.

(c) Showing your goodwill toward the audience can increase your overall credibility and acceptance by the audience.

(4) A fourth function of the introduction is to prepare the audience for the content of the body of the speech.

(a) If your purpose is acceptable to the audience, state it clearly.

(b) If your purpose is unacceptable to the audience, state it indirectly.

(c) Previewing the content, that is, telling the listeners what you're going to tell them, prepares the audience for the content of the presentation.

c. Introductions usually take no more than 20 percent of a speaker's time or less than 5 percent.

3. *Conclusion* of the speech. The speech conclusion is the speech ending. After you have presented your main ideas and supported them, you will provide some concluding remarks.
    a. The conclusion provides your last chance to bring home the purpose of the presentation.
        (1) The conclusion will usually refocus attention on the key idea of the presentation.
            (a) A summary of the key ideas functions to tell the audience what you told them, thereby promoting clarity and retention.
            (b) An appeal for action helps to remind the audience of the relevance of your ideas and directs the audience's behavior.
        (2) The conclusion provides your last chance to create a mood or emotional response in your audience consistent with your purpose.
        (3) An effective conclusion creates a sense of finality or completion.
            (a) You may find it useful to make a direct balancing link between your introduction and conclusion. You might refer back to your opening technique, a piece of support, or the thesis statement of your introduction.
            (b) You may also want to think of something interesting or involving for your speech conclusion.
                i. You may ask a question.
                ii. You might refer to the upcoming speaker, the group leader, the person in the front row. Anytime you involve the audience you increase your chances of having them listen to, understand, and remember your message.
                iii. Particularly in a persuasive speech, the appeal for action is crucial. You might have a message which influences the audience's thinking, but what good does it do if you cannot influence the audience's behavior? The conclusion is a good time to tell the audience what you want them to do and ask them to make a public commitment to do it. You may have them sign a petition. You may have them fill out a postcard that you will mail to their elected official. If you are trying to motivate or change behavior, the conclusion is the time to put that behavior in motion.
    b. The conclusion usually comprises about 5 percent or less of a presentation.

II. **Patterns of Organization.** The patterns of organization allow you to arrange the main points of the body of your speech and the subpoints developing a main point in ways that will help you accomplish your goals. A specialized pattern, the Motivated Sequence, provides a way to organize an entire presentation. Patterns of arrangement help the speaker to plan effectively and help the listener to follow, understand, and remember effectively. As discussed earlier, we naturally like to categorize and arrange material for easier recognition and understanding. You can arrange your main points or the subpoints developing a point according to the five frequently used patterns of organization: topical order, chronological order, spatial order, causal order, problem–solution. A sixth pattern, the Motivated Sequence, provides a method for organizing an entire speech.

A. *Topical order*. Topical order (sometimes called categorical order) arranges ideas into appropriate categories.

1. Sometimes students say the categorical or topical pattern is the one we use when nothing else works. In a sense, that's a good explanation because the categorical approach is often more difficult for many listeners to understand, and probably less desirable, when other approaches can be used. Sometimes, however, although the subject matter just doesn't fit in any of the more concrete approaches below, similar ideas can be grouped together into categories.
2. When you are dealing with problems or policies, you might consider their implications in terms of common values of the audience. Then you may select the topical areas of importance to your specific listeners:
   a. aesthetic implications;
   b. economic implications;
   c. educational implications;
   d. environmental implications;
   e. personal or psychological implications;
   f. political or legal implications;
   g. religious or moral implications; and/or
   h. social implications.
3. Once you have chosen topics or categories, you may further order them in more precise ways:
   a. from the familiar to the unknown or the reverse;
   b. from the simple to the complex;
   c. from less important to more important—climactic arrangement;
   d. from most important to less important—anticlimactic arrangement.

B. *Chronological order*. Chronological order considers ideas over time. Usually, we start with events or conditions that happened the longest ago and trace their development to more recent events or conditions.

Occasionally, a presenter begins with the most recent events and then describes the events which happened earlier.

1. Whenever we deal with historical events or speeches about people, chronological order is one logical arrangement.
2. Usually demonstrations or explanations of processes use the chronological arrangement.

C. *Spatial order*. Spatial order arranges ideas according to location or geography.
   1. Spatial order provides a way to examine structures, such as building and objects.
   2. Spatial order provides a way to analyze conditions in relevant locales.
   3. Spatial order may be combined with chronological order to explain geographical development or migration over time.

D. *Causal order*. Causal order examines the causes and effects of a phenomenon or a problem.
   1. Examining effects first, then their probable causes, is useful in understanding problems or accounting for historical events.
   2. Examining existing causes first and then their probable effects is useful in predicting the future.

E. *Problem–solution order*. Problem–solution arrangement explains the nature of a problem and the way to solve it.
   1. Often a presenter explains the nature of a problem using a causal pattern. The speaker identifies the harmful effects of the problem and the probable causes. In the solution, the presenter offers a plan to eliminate or control the effects of the causes.
   2. You may discuss several possible solutions and show the advantages of your preferred solution.
   3. Research has shown that certain types of listeners respond negatively if they hear the proposal or solution before the speaker explains the problem or need. Thus, the best arrangement is to begin with the problem, then explain the solution.

F. *Motivated Sequence*. Monroe's Motivated Sequence takes a different approach to organization than the first five methods. The first five are commonly used for arranging main points or subpoints that develop a main point. The Motivated Sequence organizes the entire speech.
   1. The Motivated Sequence is particularly useful when your purpose is persuasive. It also may be used when your purpose is informative, especially when you are trying to encourage your listeners to use the material you are teaching.
   2. The Motivated Sequence presents the message in five steps: attention, need, satisfaction, visualization, and action.
      a. <u>Attention</u>. The attention step functions like the speech introduction. You gain the audience's attention in a way that relates positively to the rest of the message.

b. Need. The need step points out to the audience the way a problem applies to the needs or motives of the audience. Monroe emphasized that the existence of a problem will not necessarily motivate listeners. The listeners must perceive that the problem affects them. Hence, a speaker must usually engage in "pointing," the process of showing the ways the problem affects the listeners.
   (1) In an informative speech, you might illustrate that the audience needs to learn your information.
   (2) In a persuasive speech you might present a problem in a way that emphasizes how it affects or should affect the listeners.

c. Satisfaction. In the satisfaction step, you show a way to satisfy the need.
   (1) In an informative speech, you would present the material you desire that the audience learn.
   (2) In a persuasive speech, you would present the plan or product that would meet the needs of your listeners.

d. Visualization. In the visualization step, you help the listeners see themselves in the future.
   (1) Positive visualization describes the advantages of adopting your plan or using your information.
   (2) Negative visualization describes the consequences of not adopting your plan or using your information.
   (3) The combination method (mixed visualization) uses both negative and positive visualization.

e. Action. In the action step, you make a specific appeal for action.
   (1) In an informative speech, you might encourage the audience to apply the information you taught.
   (2) In a persuasive speech, you might appeal to the audience to act on your plan.

III. **Relating Support to Ideas.** As you develop main points or subpoints with forms of support, you should decide whether to provide the idea or the support first.

A. *The didactic method.* The word "didactic" refers to teaching or an instructive approach. If you state your idea, develop it with forms of support and then restate it, you are using the didactic method.
   1. Didactic method helps your audience to grasp your point immediately, to follow your approach in developing it, and to remember your idea.
   2. The didactic method is particularly useful when you are trying to inform your audience regarding a point.

B. *The inductive method.* The inductive method (also called the method of implication) presents the support first and then draws a conclusion from it.

1. The method of implication allows you to avoid starting with an idea the listener may reject immediately. By presenting support first, you can illustrate to the listener the validity of the idea.
2. The inductive method is particularly helpful in persuasive situations when the audience is likely to oppose your ideas.
3. The inductive method can help provide variety to constant use of the straightforward didactic method.

IV. **Transitions.** Transitions link together the parts of a message. The purpose of a transition is to help the audience move as smoothly as possible from one point or section to another.

A. Effective transitions help the listener.
   1. Transitions help listeners see the important relationships between the ideas. The presentation may be organized, but if the listener cannot easily grasp the organization, confusion may result.
   2. Transitions help the listeners remember and understand ideas.
   3. Transitions contribute to variety, interest, and a sense of steady progress.

B. Transitions may be nonverbal as well as verbal.
   1. You may use your voice and body as well as your words to signal changes and movement.
      a. You may signal a major change in the presentation with a pause and a movement of several steps.
      b. You may signal a minor change with a tilt of your head, a hand gesture, or a facial expression.
      c. You may signal a transition with a change in the pitch, rate, or quality of your voice. The voice of many speakers is more relaxed and conversational during transitions.
   2. The transitions between ideas may take the form of words, phrases, and sentences, or parts of sentences.
      a. Often, one-word transitions are too abrupt and will make the speech sound choppy. They may, however, be used sparingly for minor transitions.

accordingly	again	although
also	and	because
besides	but	finally
for	further	furthermore
however	if	indeed
moreover	nevertheless	next
now	since	still
then	therefore	thus
when	yet	

b. Simple phrases also can help the listener understand the relationships among your ideas.

of course	as a result
on the whole	on the other hand
in addition	more importantly
similar to this	in contrast to

c. Often sentences or clauses best express a movement in ideas.

Of one thing we can be sure.
What I'm proposing is not new.
What do the facts show so far? They show we need to change. So let's look at a good change.

3. Jeffrey and Patterson (1983, pp. 206–208) identified five useful types of transitions: signposts, internal summaries, internal previews, interjections, and special devices.
   a. *Signposts*
      (1) Signposts alert the listeners to a new idea or point. They are usually numbers (for instance, "first," "my second reason," and "my fourth step") but can include words such as "next" and "finally" that express sequence.
      (2) Signposts indicate exactly where the speaker is in the presentation.
   b. *Internal summaries and previews*
      (1) Internal summaries. Before moving to a new point the speaker stops to repeat or emphasize the major ideas already presented. The length and precision of the internal summary will depend on the complexity and importance of the material.
         (a) In a persuasive presentation a speaker may simply refer to the previous point, for example, "We have seen there are four major causes of child abuse."
         (b) If the speaker wants to be sure the audience remembers the four causes, the internal summary will be longer and more precise, for example, "As we can see, parents abuse their children for a variety of reasons. Some because [speaker restates the four reasons presented earlier]."
      (2) Internal previews. The speaker may follow up an internal summary with a statement indicating the way she or he will approach the next part of the speech.
   c. *Interjections*
      Interjections emphasize the important ideas by drawing attention to a point the speaker does not want the listeners to miss, for example, "Now this is central to understanding the rest of the problem" and "Now this is important."

d. *Special devices*
   A variety of stylistic devices can signal the audience to movement in ideas.
   (1) Use of a theme.
   (2) Use of a key phrase.
   (3) Use of a memory aid.

V. **Answering Questions.** Most speakers think the process of organization is over once the speech is planned. Most speakers, however, also need to organize their thoughts when they answer questions during or at the end of a presentation.
   A. Some questions are simply genuine requests for information. Other questions may sound like attempts to trap the speaker. Speakers should know the points they wish to make (and how to support them with evidence), and they should know opposing points of view (and how to refute them with evidence).
   B. If someone seems to attack you or your position, remain cool. Consider the question an opportunity to demonstrate your poise and to advance your own position.
      1. Let the individual know you understand the question by rephrasing it.
      2. Compliment the individual's positive motives.
      3. Provide a bridge, or transition, to the point you want to make.
   C. Whether the question is a sincere request for information or one you perceive to be a trap, restate the question you wish to answer.
   D. Provide your answer in a single sentence or two.
   E. Develop your answer with an explanation, example, statistic, analogy, or testimony.
   F. Restate the answer in a single sentence or two.

Closing Remarks

The principles of organization will help you not only in your speaking, but also in your writing. Individuals who can organize their messages have a much greater chance of informing and persuading others successfully.

References and Suggestions for Further Readings

Baird, J. E. Jr. (1974). The effects of summaries upon audience comprehension of expository speeches of varying quality and complexity. *Central States Speech Journal, 25*, 119–127.

Consigny, S. (1976). The rhetorical example. *Southern Speech Communication Journal, 41*, 121–132.

Jones, E. E., & Goethals, G. R. (1972). *Attribution: Perceiving the causes of behavior.* Morristown, NJ: General Learning Press, 27–46.

Haynes, J. L. (1973). *Organizing a speech.* Englewood Cliffs, NJ: Prentice-Hall.

Holtzman, P. D. (1970). *The psychology of speakers' audiences.* Glenview, IL: Scott, Foresman.

Jeffrey, R. C., & Peterson, O. (1983). *Speech: A basic text.* 4th ed. NY: Harper and Row.

McCroskey, J. C. (1982). *An introduction to rhetorical communication.* Englewood Cliffs, NJ: Prentice-Hall.

McCroskey, J. C., & Mehrley, R. S. (1969). The effects of disorganization and nonfluency on attitude change and source credibility. *Communication Monographs, 36*, 13–21.

Spicer, C., & Bassett, R. E. (1976). The effect of organization of learning from an informative message. *Southern States Communication Journal, 41*, 290–299.

Thompson, W.N. (1967). *Quantitative research in public address.* NY: Random House.

Tolchin, S., & Tolchin, M. (1974). *Clout: Womanpower and politics.* NY: Coward, McCann & Geophegan.

Wenburg, J. R., & Wilmont, W. W. (1973). *The personal communication process.* NY: Wiley & Sons.

Wilcox, R. P. (1967). *Oral reporting in business and industry.* Englewood Cliffs, NJ: Prentice-Hall.

CHAPTER 5

Delivering Your Presentations

Objectives

After reading this chapter, you should be able to

1. explain the nature and functions of effective presentational delivery;
2. identify the vocal and physical elements of delivery;
3. analyze the strengths and weaknesses of your own delivery;
4. identify ways to improve your delivery;
5. identify and adapt to relevant nonverbal forces in a setting where you plan to speak; and
6. practice your presentations in an effective manner.

Topical Outline

FUNCTIONS OF EFFECTIVE DELIVERY

METHODS OF DELIVERY

- Extemporaneous delivery
- Impromptu delivery
- Delivery from manuscript
- Memorized delivery

VOCAL ELEMENTS OF DELIVERY

- Volume
- Articulation
- Pronunciation
- Rate
- Pitch and inflection
- Vocal quality

BODILY ELEMENTS OF DELIVERY

- Posture
- Movement
- Gestures
- Facial expression
- Eye contact

ENVIRONMENTAL AND SITUATIONAL ELEMENTS OF DELIVERY

- Personal appearance
- Time
- Amplification
- Physical environment

REHEARSAL

Key Concepts

Amplification
Articulation
Delivery from manuscript
Dialect
Enunciation
Extemporaneous delivery
Eye contact
Facial expression
Functions of delivery
Gestures
Impromptu delivery
Inflection
Intelligibility
Memorized delivery
Mispronunciation
Monotone
Movement
Nonverbal communication
Note cards
Personal appearance
Physical environment
Pitch
Posture
Pronunciation
Rate
Rehearsal
Standard pronunciation
Stress
Substandard pronunciation
Time
Use of a microphone
Vocal quality
Volume

Delivering Your Presentations

PERSPECTIVE

I. Research suggests that neither students nor instructors should be too concerned with delivery early during training in public communication. Why? Most of us feel very uneasy if we are in the spotlight, doing something "new," or know we are being evaluated. That's only natural. And it's only natural for uneasiness to influence the ways we use our voice and body. Hence, your instructor will not count your delivery for much of the grade on your early assignments. We know that by the time of your informative presentation your experience will result in greater confidence that will result in better delivery.

   Many students, however, have told us that they wished we had provided information about delivery before their first graded presentation. They argued that they would have had more "tips" about delivery and that instruction regarding delivery would have reduced ambiguity. For such reasons, we are studying delivery now.

   When we communicate, we not only convey our ideas and feelings regarding topics, we also establish relationships with our listeners. In public speaking situations, for instance, our behaviors lead the members of our audience to think we like, dislike, or have mixed feelings toward them. Whether we intend to or not, our behaviors lead others to think we feel superior, inferior, or equal to the audience. We communicate whether we have our listeners' best interests at heart or care little for them. Often the positive relationships we establish will contribute more to our success as speakers than will our arguments and emotional appeals.

   A. The relationships you establish with your listeners usually depend more on your nonverbal communication than on the words you use. On the other hand, the content or ideas you communicate will depend more on the words you use than on your delivery—as long as the listeners can hear you and are not distracted by your delivery.
   B. Although there is no one best way to deliver a presentation, your chances of success will depend to a large degree on the ways you use your voice and body and the ways you manage the space and facilities during the speech.
   C. Even if you have had too little previous experience to have developed your unique public speaking style, you already have developed an interpersonal communication style.
      1. Normally your public style should be an extension of your natural self. Although conversation is less formal than presentational speaking, most effective public speakers have a conversational style. They tend to speak extemporaneously, adapt to the audience, and use delivery that does not draw attention to itself.

2. We encourage you to capitalize on the strengths of your delivery and experiment with ways to eliminate weaknesses.
    a. We encourage you to listen to the suggestions of your instructor and classmates with an open mind.
    b. We encourage you to evaluate your own performance according to principles of effective delivery presented in this chapter and set personal goals for self improvement.
3. An effective style of delivery can only raise your level of success in your professional and personal lives.

II. ***Purpose statement:*** We believe you can improve the effectiveness of your communication by diagnosing your ability to use effectively the vocal and bodily dimensions of nonverbal communication. Capitalize on your strengths and find ways to eliminate your weaknesses. Additionally, we seek to heighten your sensitivity to nonverbal influences that might exist in settings where you speak and increase your ability to manage nonverbal influences to promote success in your presentations.

III. ***Preview:*** First, we shall identify the functions of effective delivery; second, elements of vocal delivery; third, elements of bodily or physical delivery; fourth, some nonverbal elements of the environment and situation that may affect the outcome of a presentation; and finally, ways to practice for effective speech delivery.

Chapter Body

I. **Functions of delivery.** We reiterate that the best delivery is the least noticeable delivery. Delivery becomes noticeable if it is too good or too bad. Delivery that is "too good" draws attention to itself. Listeners may even stop listening to a message to admire the speaker's beautiful use of the voice and masterful use of the body. Delivery becomes noticeable if listeners can't hear you (or cringe from your loud voice) or are distracted by other vocal or bodily mannerisms. Although delivery should not draw attention to itself, effective delivery will accomplish several communicative goals. Effective delivery will help you emphasize and reinforce your ideas and feelings, direct the audience through the structure and development of your presentation, hold the attention of the audience, and create an appropriate relationship with the audience.
    A. *Emphasis and reinforcement.* Effective delivery will emphasize key ideas much like italics, bold type, and effective layout emphasize key ideas in written communication.
        1. Effective delivery can reinforce your ideas and feelings and create meanings in ways unavailable to a writer. For instance, a pause, an inflection, or a gesture can add meaning that goes far beyond that of the words you choose.

2. Additionally, speakers can not only qualify, but even reverse the meaning of the words they use. For instance, your words may say "I really mean it," but a roll of your eyes or your tone of voice can communicate that you don't mean it at all.

B. *Direction.* Effective delivery helps the audience to follow the structure of your speech and the relationships among your ideas. For instance a change in rate or volume or a movement of your body can signal that you are beginning a new segment of your speech or introducing a story to support your point.

C. *Attention.* Effective delivery helps hold the attention of an audience.
   1. For instance, lowering your volume, slowing your rate, and hunching your shoulders forward can extend considerably the sense of suspense created by your words.
   2. Additionally, the energy and enthusiasm you display in your delivery can stimulate the audience to become enthusiastic and involved.

D. *Relationships.* Effective delivery helps a speaker develop appropriate relationships with members of the audience.
   1. By speaking fluently and authoritatively, you can increase the listeners' perceptions that you are a person they can rely on for knowledge and expertise.
   2. By showing your self-control and sincerity you can increase perceptions that you are a person of good judgment your listeners can trust to act in their best interests.
   3. By showing enthusiasm and displaying a friendly demeanor, you can increase perceptions that you are an attractive person.

II. **Methods of delivery.** A speaker can deliver a presentation in four different ways: the extemporaneous method, the impromptu method, the manuscript method, and the memorized method. Circumstances usually dictate the appropriateness of a particular method. However, you also should consider your individual style and skills in order to select the most effective method for a particular situation.

A. *Extemporaneous Speaking.* Most dictionaries define the word "extemporaneous" as unplanned or impromptu. In this course, however, we make a clear distinction between extemporaneous and impromptu delivery.
   1. The extemporaneous speaker carefully prepares the presentation but delivers the material in a spontaneous, conversational manner that highlights natural interaction with the audience.
      a. Extemporaneous speakers word the key ideas of the presentation to maximize clarity and impact, but do not write the entire speech word for word.
      b. Extemporaneous speakers select the actual wording of supporting material as they deliver their presentations.

c. Extemporaneous speakers sometimes memorize the speech introduction and conclusion, but carefully adapt to the audience during the body of the speech. Although some words and sentences may be misspoken or spoken less eloquently than possible, the advantages of natural spontaneity, audience adaption, and attention value outweigh the disadvantages of this method.
   (1) If the audience appears confused or skeptical, extemporaneous delivery will allow you to provide additional support to clarify or substantiate your ideas.
   (2) If the audience appears to readily understand or accept an idea, extemporaneous delivery will allow you to omit some of the support you were prepared to use. Instead, you will be able to expand subsequent portions of your presentation, if needed.
   (3) If an interruption occurs, extemporaneous delivery will allow you to deal briefly with the distraction and proceed with your prepared material. Additionally, extemporaneous delivery will allow you to adapt to comments or events that occurred before your presentation.

2. Because extemporaneous delivery is the most effective method of delivery in the majority of presentational settings, most basic public speaking courses emphasize mastery of this style.

B. *Impromptu Speaking.* When you talk "off the top-of-the-head," you are using impromptu delivery. Situations requiring impromptu remarks are quite common. In decision-making meetings you may find yourself explaining or arguing for positions. In interviews or after a presentation, you may find yourself providing an extended answer to a question. From time to time, you will find yourself "saying a few words" at an organizational event. Occasionally, you will find yourself explaining a problem with a product or service to a representative of a company or professional organization.

1. In one way, a lifetime of experience and the resulting knowledge you possess comprise your preparation for impromptu speaking.
2. Your success in impromptu situations can be enhanced if you apply the public speaking principles and skills appropriate in any presentational setting.
   a. Even on the spur of the moment you can quickly review the goals of a speech introduction and attempt to meet them.
   b. You can limit your comments to clearly stated and organized points that you develop with supporting material.
   c. You can incorporate transitions to signal the logical flow of your ideas.
   d. You can summarize your points or choose another closing technique.

3. Seemingly impromptu situations sometimes result in extemporaneous speaking.
    a. Effective communicators usually prepare extensively for an interview by anticipating likely questions and preparing concise, purposeful answers and selecting appropriate supporting materials to develop key points.
    b. When members of the print or electronic media ask questions, politicians and representatives of causes and institutions frequently use the questions as springboards for making the points they wish to convey to readers, listeners, or viewers.
    c. Similarly, you can anticipate likely questions and prepare effective answers before interviewing for a position or responding to questions on behalf of an organization to which you belong.

C. *Speaking from Manuscript*. When you write out a presentation fully and deliver it word-for-word, you are speaking from manuscript.
1. Speaking from manuscript may be the most appropriate method of delivery when the speaker must be very careful about what is said.
    a. Speaking from manuscript is often appropriate whenever poorly worded ideas or misstatements may have serious negative consequences for governments, businesses, or even individuals.
    b. Speakers frequently use manuscripts when they must observe strict time limits, such as in hearings or on television.
    c. Because of the need for coordination at complex or formal events, such as a college graduation, an entire ceremony may be delivered from manuscript.
2. Speaking from manuscript poses major challenges for speakers.
    a. The speaker should read the manuscript enthusiastically and expressively to enhance its meaning.
    b. The speaker should be familiar enough with the manuscript to maintain appropriate eye contact and to gesture freely.
    c. The speaker should write the manuscript in effective oral, not written, style.
3. The speaker should prepare the actual manuscript in a way that makes it easy to use and easy to deliver.
    a. Choose a font size that is easy to read. Double or triple space the lines if that will help you read the manuscript.
    b. Decide on an appropriate binder or method to change from page to page.
    c. Number the pages to prevent getting them in the wrong order.
    d. Include comments to yourself (in bold type or colored writing) about the ways to deliver the presentation in the most effective way.

D. *Speaking from Memory*. Speaking from memory involves delivering a manuscript without notes.

1. Seldom does a speaking situation warrant the time and effort necessary to memorize a presentation.
    a. A common reason for memorizing a presentation is that the speaker plans to deliver the speech several times (for example, in a political campaign or a sales promotion).
    b. Speakers frequently memorize short, formal speeches such as eulogies, introductions of speakers, toasts, and acceptance speeches.
2. Through memorization, many novice speakers attempt to pass off a manuscript speech as an extemporaneous speech. This practice can be dangerous.
    a. Memory lapses can result in long silences that prove uncomfortable for the speaker and the audience.
    b. As when speeches are recited, the language of a manuscript can sound stilted and the delivery can sound nonconversational.
    c. Usually speakers who are fighting to remember the exact wording of their speeches seldom have the energy to perceive the reactions of their audiences let alone to adapt to audience reactions.
    d. If the instructor judges the presentation as lacking in extemporaneous quality, the speaker's grade may suffer.

III. **Vocal elements of delivery**. Perhaps your primary tool as a speaker—not counting your mind—is your voice. When individuals read, they find the process easier if the typeface is of an appropriate size and of a style pleasing to their eyes. Furthermore, readers find it easier to recognize key ideas when they appear in bold or italics type and the page layout helps to identify the progression of ideas in the text. When you communicate orally, you should strive to use your voice in ways that facilitate listening. First and foremost, you should make your words intelligible, that is, easy to understand. Additionally, through effective use of the voice, you should communicate fine shades of meaning, provide emphasis, and make listening a pleasant experience. Because of the physical noise, lessened verbal feedback, and added distance involved in public speaking, your use of the voice needs to be better than it normally might be in daily conversation.

Below you will find a list of vocal elements and suggestions for their effective use. We encourage you to assess your abilities in these areas. Frequently, with a little extra concentration, you will be able to implement any suggestions your instructor or classmates may make. Occasionally, a speaker's vocal behaviors will justify some extra effort to eliminate a specific problem. Seek your instructor's help in making a precise diagnosis of any special challenges you might face. Most libraries contain a variety of texts and workbooks with titles such as *Voice and Diction* or *Voice and Articulation*. These texts will contain not only descriptions of the causes of various vocal problems, but also suggestions and drills for eliminating them. Locate the specific exercises and drills that address your goals. Spread out your practice of these drills rather than try to do several at one sitting. Just a few minutes, three or four times a week, may be all the time you need. Try recording then reviewing your drills. Learn to recognize the way your muscles feel when you are speaking with and without the problem. You will probably be surprised to see how quickly the sound of your voice improves. A little investment of time and energy can pay large dividends in terms of an improved overall image.

A. *Volume.* The public speaker needs to talk loudly enough to be heard easily without becoming overbearing.
    1. For most presentations, you will need to talk more loudly than you would in a conversation. If you are having trouble sensing an appropriate level of volume, ask a friend or acquaintance to sit in the back of the audience and signal you (in a subtle way) if you need to increase or decrease your volume.
    2. For interest and emphasis, you should vary your volume. Yes, sometimes the best way to get someone's attention is to whisper. However, guard against dropping your volume so low that you lose intelligibility or raising your volume so high that listeners cringe in shock.

B. *Articulation.* Articulation, or enunciation, refers to the manner in which an individual uses the lips, tongue, jaw, and soft palate to produce the vowel and consonant sounds of a language.
    1. Clear articulation will help listeners grasp your words easily.
        a. Many stage and film actors warm up before a performance in which they must articulate clearly by quickly reciting tongue twisters or difficult passages.
        b. If you receive feedback that you are "swallowing your words," tension or habit may be leading you to pull your lower jaw back toward your throat. By concentrating on pushing your lower jaw forward slightly, you may increase significantly your ability to articulate and project sounds.
    2. The delivery of a speaker who adds, omits, substitutes, or distorts specific speech sounds can easily become distracting and confusing unless the listener can recognize and adjust for the speaker's patterns of articulation. For example, one professor consistently substituted a "t" sound for a "k" sound (hence, "back" sounded like "bat" and "car" sounded like "tar"). When a word normally ended in "t," the same professor would simply drop the sound and draw out the final vowel (hence, "cast" sounded like "Cass," and "beat" sounded like "bee-e-e"; and "caught" sounded like "caw-w-w-"). The professor's students had to exert considerable energy to avoid becoming confused during lectures. Most of the students did not enjoy the experience.

C. *Pronunciation.* Whereas problems of articulation pertain to patterns of sound production that occur throughout one's speech, problems of pronunciation pertain to specific words. Correct pronunciation means presenting the appropriate sounds of a word in the accepted order, without additions or omissions, and with stress on the appropriate syllable or syllables. Clearly words such as "correct," "accepted," and "appropriate" refer to value judgments. Pronunciations accepted by one group of speakers may be "errors" to another. Substandard pronunciations are ones that are seldom used by educated individuals. Other mispronunciations may stem from lack of exposure to the way knowledgeable and experienced individuals pronounce a name, place, or specialized term.

1. Mispronunciations may reduce your listeners' perceptions of your credibility.
   a. Because words that have two or more consonants next to each other may be difficult to say, a speaker may fail to articulate each (for example, saying "winner" for "winter"; "hunerd" for "hundred"; or "liberry" for "library").
   b. On the other hand, mispronunciations may involve adding a sound to separate two consonants, the most common example being "athalete" for "athlete."
   c. Another common problem is substituting "-in" for "-ing" (for example, saying "goin" or "gon" for "going"). While such substitutions may be acceptable in informal conversations or presentations, they tend to stick out as errors in professional or formal settings.
   d. Some mispronunciations involve reversing sounds (for example, "revelant" for "relevant").
   e. Mispronunciation may result from relying on the spelling of a word (for example, pronouncing the "th" in "posthumous" as a "t" and an "h" rather than as a "ch"). Some of these "spelling" mispronunciations have become so common that they are widely used by educated people and hence are no longer considered substandard, except by zealous speech instructors (for example, pronouncing the silent "t" in "often"; or the silent "l" in "calm," "almond," or "psalm").
   f. Regarding stress, some words have two acceptable pronunciations (for example, "ad ver TISE ment" and "ad VER tise ment). Other stress shifts are seldom used by well-educated individuals (for example, "pre FER able" for "PREF er able"; "CE ment" for "ce MENT"; or "the A ter" for "THE a ter").
2. While it is difficult for individuals to know if they are mispronouncing a word, we recommend that you notice how newscasters and educated individuals in your community use pronunciations

that differ from your own. Additionally, if someone corrects your pronunciation, jot the word down, look it up, and learn the preferred pronunciation. One student continued to mispronounce the word "compromise" (the student pronounced the first syllable correctly but the second and third exactly like the word "promise." Although her classmates frequently corrected her, she continued to mispronounce the word. During her last presentation of the term, most of her classmates shouted out the correct pronunciation when she used (yet again) her unique mispronunciation.

3. Sometimes a person's dialect accounts for problematic articulation and pronunciation differences. We encourage you, as a listener, to attempt to recognize the patterns used by individual dialects different from your own. We encourage you who speak a dialect substantially different from standard U.S. English to make every effort to make your pronunciations understandable to your audience.

D. *Rate.* Vocal rate refers to the number of words a speaker utters in a minute.
   1. Most public speakers deliver 120 to 175 words per minute.
   2. If you are nervous and excited, you will probably speak faster than if you are relaxed. If you speak too slowly, you will probably lose the attention of many of your listeners.
   3. You should attempt to match your rate to the needs of the audience. When covering simple material, speed up. When dealing with complicated material, slow down. Additionally, identify ways to use rate to emphasize your ideas.
   4. Sometimes, silence (that is, pausing) is appropriate.
      a. Many beginning speakers are afraid of silence.
      b. A pause can add emphasis, regain attention, or provide a dramatic effect in a presentation.
   5. Often speakers find it helpful to write reminders in their speaking notes concerning the rate (including pauses) appropriate to a section of the presentation.

E. *Pitch.* Pitch refers to how high or low you speak during your message.
   1. Your pitch should be pleasing to the audience.
      a. As speakers wait to begin their presentations, they often develop tension in their throats. Sometimes, owing to the excitement of the presentation itself, throat tension will increase. Such tension may raise a speaker's pitch to an unpleasant level.
         (1) Often a discrete yawn before you begin will help you reduce neck tension.
         (2) You may find it helpful to write a reminder in your notes to check your pitch.
         (3) Try to relax and lower your pitch level if it appears that it's getting too high during your presentation.

b. On the other hand, forcing your pitch level so low that your voice sounds raspy can seriously damage your vocal cords.

2. *Inflection* refers to changes in pitch that influence meaning. We often signal a question with a rising inflection and the end of declarative sentence with a falling one. Changes in inflection can create just the right shade of meaning for words you wish to emphasize.
3. Repetitive, meaningless, patterns of pitch change are particularly distracting to listeners.
    a. A monotone delivery is one in which few inflections are used to emphasize meaning.
    b. A "whining" delivery is one characterized by pitch and rate patterns that are all too familiar.

F. *Quality.* Vocal quality refers to the unique (musical) characteristics of a speaker's voice caused by a variety of elements including one's manner of breathing, level of tension in the throat, use of the soft palate to close and open the nasal passage, and condition of the sinuses and their affect on resonating cavities. A complete discussion of quality problems would be of little interest or value to most speakers.
1. If your instructor or listeners describe your voice with terms such as "full," "resonant," "rich," and "pleasant," you need have little concern with vocal quality. You have probably already learned ways to control your breathing and tension levels when giving presentations.
2. If your instructor or listeners describe your voice with terms such as "nasalized," "denasalized," "strident," "harsh," "breathy," "guttural," "throaty," "thin," or "unpleasant," we recommend you seek your instructor's help in diagnosing your specific challenges and identifying ways you can locate exercises and drills that will help you control or eliminate the distracting qualities of your voice.

[Parting thoughts on vocal delivery: Most individuals find it relatively easy to improve the use of their voices. Some experimentation, feedback from your instructor and classmates, and self-recording on audio or video tape should give you insights into your current practices and potential areas of improvement. A self-directed program of improvement using drills and exercises from voice and diction texts available in most libraries may yield dramatically positive results. Many colleges and universities offer helpful classes and services to students who want to improve some specific aspect of vocal delivery. Students who plan to enter a career in broadcasting, for example, often seek out a voice and diction class or use the speech screening and therapy services at their schools to help them remove regional dialects and improve articulation and vocal quality.]

IV. **Bodily Elements**. Effective delivery consists of many nonvocal elements. Particularly important is your use of the body. The ways you stand or sit, move and gesture, and use facial expression and eye contact will influence your listeners' perceptions of you and your presentation. Although there is no one way all speakers should use their bodies in presentations, whatever you do should add, rather than distract, from your presentation.

A. *Posture.* The way you stand (or sit) before, during, and after a presentation will influence the perceptions of your listeners.
    1. Even before you begin to speak, listeners have made judgments about you from seeing your actions during preceding presentations, the manner in which you set up your materials, and the way you took the position from which you will speak. An erect but relaxed posture can contribute significantly to their perceptions of your credibility.
    2. During a presentation, your posture will continue to send messages about you.
        a. Effective speakers usually plant both feet a comfortable distance apart and distribute their weight on the balls of their feet.
            (1) With weight distributed on the balls of your feet and your posture erect but not stiff, you will signal your alertness, attention, and poise.
            (2) With weight distributed on the balls of the feet, a natural balance will allow you to move smoothly and easily when necessary.
            (3) With weight distributed on the balls of your feet, you will avoid the distracting mannerisms of twisting or moving a foot, rocking on your heels, or noticeably shifting weight from foot to foot in a swaying motion.
        b. Effective speakers usually orient their bodies directly toward the audience.
            (1) Swaying your shoulders away and toward the audience may reduce the audience's perceptions of your poise.
            (2) Orienting your shoulders toward the door or window may suggest you are so uncomfortable you wish to escape from the speaking situation.
    3. After a presentation, maintain your posture as you assume a nonspeaking position in the room.
        a. Inexperienced speakers frequently drop their otherwise alert posture at the end of a presentation, signaling "Thank heavens that's over."
        b. Overly relaxing your posture at the end of a presentation may have an even more negative effect if you sigh in relief, roll your eyes, or slink back to your seat.

B. *Movement.* Purposeful movement during a presentation can help you to hold an audience's attention through variety, to emphasize important ideas, to make your relationship with the audience more personal, or to signal major transitions in your speech.

1. Random movement usually distracts from a presentation. Random movement usually signals a speaker lacks confidence and poise.
    a. Random movers act as though they don't want to be in one place long enough to become a stationary target.
    b. Because the speaker is constantly moving, the audience cannot readily distinguish movement meant to signal a transition or a change in mood.
2. Purposeful movement usually enhances meaning or affects mood positively.
    a. Doubling your distance from a listener will tend to make you appear four times farther away, psychologically, from the listener. Conversely, decreasing your distance from a listener by one half makes you appear to be four times closer.
        (1) Speakers may use distance and barriers, (such as a podium) to project greater formality and objectivity.
        (2) Speakers may decrease distance and eliminate barriers to project greater informality and to enhance the personal quality of a portion of the presentation.
    b. We encourage beginning speakers to master effective posture first before addressing purposeful movement. Until you have mastered distributing your weight and eliminating mannerisms caused by inappropriate posture, your efforts to move will look particularly awkward.

C. *Gestures*. In your speech, your gestures should reinforce your message. Most people gesture naturally in conversation, and this characteristic should be enhanced—not suppressed—in public speaking situations.

1. We do not encourage you to plan every gesture in a presentation.
    a. Often, planned approaches such as holding up fingers to count off subpoints or pointing at the audience at the beginning of each main point look awkward and phony, especially if the speaker's timing is off.
    b. Allow your arms to hang comfortably at your sides.
        (1) As you feel yourself gesturing, bend your arms at the elbow to raise your hands above your waist.
        (2) Hand gestures made from below the waist often look particularly awkward and pull attention away from your face.
    c. Try to avoid becoming defensive if your instructor or classmates point out distracting mannerisms in your delivery. Most speakers need to guard against developing awkward or repetitive gestures that distract audience members. In particular, we recommend you avoid putting your hands in your pockets (especially if they contain generous amounts of coin), holding

tightly onto a lectern (especially if you catch yourself picking it up and dropping it noisily), or clutching your notes in two hands (especially if your pose resembles a choir member in prayer). The three actions just mentioned, as well as others you have observed, will deny your hands the freedom to move and emphasize ideas naturally.

2. If you have not had much experience giving presentations, we encourage you to plan ways to use your notes effectively.
   a. Speakers vary in their comfort level with different types of notes.
   b. Whatever form your notes take—index cards or full sheets of paper—they should not draw attention away from your voice and body or inhibit your ability to gesture naturally. Notebook paper with torn edges and yellow lined paper look make-shift and shabby.
   c. Some speakers who use full sheets place them on a clip board or in a plain folder or notebook. These approaches give a substantial backing and protect the paper, particularly if the speaker chooses to leave or not use the lectern.
   d. For manuscript speeches, we suggest you use an easy-to-read typeface on white paper. Large margins and double or triple spacing will allow you to make additional notations on the paper should you decide on last-minute changes or need to add reminders about your delivery.
   e. Index cards that are neither too large nor too small often provide a good form of notes for novice speakers. Hold the cards in one hand at a level that allows easy reading while leaving the other hand free to gesture.
      (1) For variety, you can shift the cards to your other hand.
      (2) Always number your note cards so that you can easily check their order before you speak.
      (3) Avoid using so many cards they are awkward to handle.
      (4) Avoid writing on both sides of your cards.
         (a) Speakers who start flipping cards over to find their place look ill-prepared.
         (b) Additionally, the writing on the back of cards may distract your audience.
      (5) Avoid lowering your cards when you are not using them. A repetitious dropping of the head to read cards that you are raising simultaneously results in an awkward, often comical, effect.
      (6) Avoid gesturing with your notes cards. Use your free hand for that purpose.

D. *Facial Expression.* As with every other element of effective delivery, the speaker's facial expression should reflect the meaning of the message and help establish an appropriate relationship with the audience.

1. A deadpan, expressionless face seldom helps a speaker appear attractive and interesting to an audience.
2. On the other hand, inappropriate smiling or giggling, especially when discussing a serious or tragic event, often strikes listeners as a sign of nervousness and lack of poise.
3. Overly dramatic facial expressions also may lead listeners to negative judgments of the speaker.
4. Upon receiving feedback from their instructor or classmates, many novice speakers find it hard to understand the nature and effect of their facial expressions. By reviewing videotapes of your performances you will gain a greater understanding of your strengths and weaknesses in this area.

E. *Eye contact.* Most audience members (and importantly, most speech instructors) consider effective eye contact an important asset in presentations. Eye contact not only enhances your ability to create a more favorable image but also provides you with important feedback.
   1. Most individuals believe the ability to look a person in the eye is a sign of honesty and sincerity. Most individuals expect their friends and colleagues to maintain a comfortable level of eye contact.
      a. With smaller audiences, effective speakers usually hold eye contact with individual listeners. The amount of time one holds this eye contact should appear natural to the audience.
         (1) Rapidly moving from the eyes of one listener to another may look like "shiftiness" or uneasiness.
         (2) Holding eye contact with one member of the audience for too long may appear to be staring, aggression, or preference depending on the speaker's facial expression. In any event, other members of the audience should not feel "left out" or ignored.
      b. With larger audiences, effective speakers usually move their focus from one entire section of the audience to another.
   2. In the process of maintaining eye contact, watch for cues of understanding or confusion and cues of acceptance or rejection in order to help you adjust your presentation to the response of the audience.
      a. Some speakers, believing they will control their nervousness, look above or between the heads of audience members. Such a practice keeps a speaker from learning not only how to develop a positive relationship with an audience but also how to use audience feedback to enhance the success of a presentation.
      b. Similarly, looking out of a window or staring at notes can only misdirect audience attention and minimize success.

V. **Environmental and situational elements.** Numerous characteristics of the environment and expectations of the audience regarding the situation will influence the effectiveness of your presentation. We wish to draw your attention to but a few of these environmental and situational elements. Our purpose is to encourage you to consider the likely influences of the settings in which you deliver presentations and, where possible, to take action to increase your effectiveness.

A. *Personal Appearance.* A key consideration in the delivery of a speech is the appearance of the speaker. Within the first few seconds after observers look at you, they will come to a variety of conclusions about you simply based on your appearance.
   1. Choices in dress and grooming that help you meet the expectations of your listeners will tend to increase your effectiveness.
      a. An attractive appearance, for example, may increase your persuasiveness.
      b. Wearing or using symbols of a respected profession or organization (for example, uniforms, insignia, or equipment) may increase your credibility.
   2. Choices in dress and grooming that offend your audience will tend to increase listeners' resistance to your purpose.

B. *Time.* Audiences vary considerably in their expectations regarding "proper" use of time. Some situations call for rigid adherence to a known schedule for starting and ending. Other situations are more flexible. We suggest, however, that you follow some general rules of thumb regarding time and public speaking.
   1. For classroom presentations, always know and observe minimum and maximum time limits for presentations. Violations may affect your grade significantly.
   2. Most audiences appreciate presentations being as short as possible.
   3. Audiences tend to resent speakers who "waste" time on insignificant or tangential material while going overtime to "cover important material" toward the end of the presentation.
   4. Presentations longer than a half hour will require exceptionally effective factors of attention to hold the audience's interest.

C. *Amplification.* Speakers must be prepared for situations that require the use of a microphone. Ehninger, Gronbeck, McKerrow, and Monroe (1986, pp. 281–282) provided four helpful suggestions for using a microphone:
   1. Practice with microphones before the presentation to know what to expect.
   2. Begin with a slow rate in order to help you adjust to the echoing you will often hear from the electronic speakers.
   3. Decrease your volume and avoid wide variations in volume. Imagine you are talking in the ear of a person five or six inches away.
   4. Be sure to articulate your words clearly. Additionally, if you hear "pops" when you make "p" and "b" sounds, try to make them less forcefully.

D. *Physical environment.* Numerous characteristics of the location can influence the effectiveness of a presentation. Consider ways to make the environment as conducive to your goals as possible.
   1. When you have an opportunity to select the location of a presentation, select a facility that will promote your goals.
      a. Listeners tend to become more aggressive in hot, crowded environments. Hence, if the audience is likely to be hostile to your ideas, choose a spacious, cooler location to deliver your presentation.
      b. Listeners tend to be more persuadable and productive in attractive surroundings. Hence, it's wise to schedule sales presentations and workshops in pleasant locations.
      c. Listeners, particularly executives, may easily be distracted by work demands during presentations held at their job sites. Hence, consultants often schedule retreats in a pleasant environment away from the job.
   2. When the location of your presentation is out of your control, consider ways to adapt the site to your purposes. By way of illustration:
      a. different purposes (for example, instruction, discussion, or persuasion) may call for different seating arrangements;
      b. the use of audio/visual aids may be facilitated by rearranging the room;
      c. your goals may be facilitated by providing refreshments of some sort; and
      d. decorations and displays may enhance your impact and effectiveness.

VI. **Practicing your speech.** A public speaker will benefit from rehearsing a speech.
   A. There are several reasons for practicing your speech.
      1. You will feel more familiar with the material and discover portions where you are having difficulty presenting your ideas succinctly and clearly.
      2. You will have a chance to visualize the audience and speaking situation which should help reduce your nervousness.
      3. You will be able to test your plans for use of visual aids.
      4. You will find out how long your speech will take you to deliver.
   B. Your method of rehearsal should provide you with feedback that will allow you to adjust your plan.
      1. The inexperienced speaker should practice the speech aloud because oral speaking style is quite different from reciting mentally.
         a. You should attempt to get feedback about your performance. You don't want to make counterproductive behaviors a habit.
            (1) Ask someone you trust to time your performance and provide you with honest feedback.

(2) Videotaping your rehearsal can provide you the opportunity to compare what you thought happened to what actually happened.

b. Always practice with your visual aids. Their use may take far more time than you expected.

2. A rehearsal in the place where you plan to give the presentation will be particularly helpful.
    a. In this manner you will experience no unfortunate surprises about the nature of the facilities.
    b. Knowledge of the facilities will allow you to make additional plans to adapt the environment in ways that will increase your chances for success.

Closing Remarks

We encourage you to take advantage of your opportunities to develop your personal style of delivery. The ability to project an image of friendliness, competence, and poise is a major career asset. If you would like to study nonverbal communication in greater depth, the Department of Communication Studies offers COMM 370, Nonverbal Communication, each Fall semester.

References and Suggestions for Further Readings

Cavanagh, M. E. (1988). Make effective speeches. *Personnel Journal, 67*, 51–56.

Davitz, J. R., & Davitz, L. J. (1959). The communication of feelings by content-free speech. *Journal of Communication, 9*, 6–13.

Ehninger, D., Gronbeck, B. E., McKerrow, R. E., & Monroe, A. H. (1986). *Principles and types of speech communication.* Glenview, IL: Scott, Foresman.

Hall, E. T. (1982). *The hidden dimension.* Garden City, NY: Doubleday.

Hickson M. L. III, & Stacks, D. (1993). *NVC—Nonverbal communication: Studies and applications.* Madison, WI: Wm. C. Brown.

Knapp, M. L. (1980). *Essentials of nonverbal communication.* NY: Holt, Rinehart, & Winston.

Poyatos, F. (1988). *Cross-cultural perspectives in nonverbal communication.* Toronto: Lewiston.

CHAPTER 6

Outlining Your Presentations

Objectives

After reading this chapter, you should be able to

1. explain and apply the principles of outlining;
2. explain the uses and limitations of the word, phrase, and complete-content outlines;
3. explain the advantages and uses of the sentence outline;
4. prepare useful speaking notes; and
5. create an effective preparation outline.

Topical Outline

PRINCIPLES OF OUTLINING

TYPES AND USES OF OUTLINES

ELEMENTS OF THE PREPARATION OUTLINE

- Purpose statements
  - General purpose
  - Specific purpose
  - Central idea or thesis
  - Body of the presentation
- Introduction of the presentation
- Conclusion of the presentation
- Transitions
- Reference list or bibliography
- Title
- Special considerations
- Process for constructing the preparation outline

Key Concepts

Annotation
Bibliography
Body of the speech
Central idea or thesis
Citing sources
Claims
Complete content outline
Complete sentence outline
Conclusion
Consistent system
Coordination
Cues for delivery
Direct quotations
Forms of support
General purpose
Indentation
Instructor requirements, Sources
Instructor requirements,
    Preparation outline
Introduction
Item
Main points
Outline
Phrase outline
Preparation outline
Preparing a speech outline
Principles of outlining
Purpose statements
Reference list or bibliography
Speaking notes
Special considerations
Specific purpose
Structure of ideas
Subordination
Subpoint
Sub-subpoint
Thesis
Title
Topic outline
Transitions
Types and uses of outlines
Values of outlining
Word outline

Outlining Your Presentation

PERSPECTIVE

I. Whether it's the quick plan scratched out on the back of an envelope or the carefully outlined message of a strategic speech, a speaker will find outlining to be a practical tool in effective speech making.
   A. An outline provides a concrete tool to plan and deliver an effective presentation.
      1. The outline helps you organize your ideas to achieve your desired results.
      2. The outline helps you refine the phrasing of your key ideas to promote clarity and retention.
      3. The outline helps you identify where you need to develop and support your ideas.
      4. The outline helps you identify where you need to help the listener by providing transitions.
      5. The outline helps you prepare useful speaking notes.
   B. An outline gives the public speaking instructor a method for previewing and analyzing the student's speech.
      1. The outline helps the instructor understand your thinking processes and offer suggestions for improvement.
      2. The outline helps the instructor analyze the nature and assess the quality of your preparation.

II. Different speech teachers have different expectations about outlines.
   A. Many professors of public speaking consider effective outlining to be a principal set of skills taught in the basic course.
   B. Often, instructors establish unique requirements that they believe will help the student perform well and will help the teacher evaluate the student efficiently and fairly.
      1. Often instructors will require a complete sentence outline to be given to the teacher on an assigned day before the classroom speech is given.
      2. Some instructors may require students to complete a form as part of their outline preparation.
      3. Still others may require a phrase outline be used as notes, then turned in to the teacher after the speech.
   C. Please find out, remember, and follow your instructor's outlining requirements—we do not want you to lose points for failing to meet requirements.

III. ***Purpose statement***: Our goal is to provide principles of outlining that will help you prepare and deliver well-organized informative and persuasive presentations.

IV. ***Preview***: This chapter will present basic principles of outlining, examine the nature and uses of various types of outlines, explore the contents of a preparation outline, and provide a step-by-step process for constructing a preparation outline.

Chapter Body

I. An outline is a simple, clear, and functional blueprint or guide that identifies the ideas, structure, and support of a presentation. Below you will find two basic principles of outlining: each item should contain one idea or piece of information and the relationship of ideas (their coordination and subordination) should be expressed using symbols in a consistent manner.
    A. Each item in the outline should contain one idea or one piece of support.
    B. A consistent system of numbers and letters should represent the relationship among the ideas and between each idea and its development.
        1. The most commonly used symbols include roman numerals, letters, and numbers.
            a. Below is a typical arrangement of the most commonly used symbols:

                I. Main point
                    A. Subpoint (first-level subpoint)
                        1. Second-level subpoint
                            a. Third-level subpoint
                                (1) Fourth-level subpoint
                                    (a) Support
                                    (b) Support
                                (2) Fourth-level subpoint
                            b. Third-level subpoint
                        2. Second-level subpoint
                    B. First-level subpoint
                II. Main point
                    A. Support
                    B. Support
                    C. Support
                III. Main point
                    A. Subpoint
                        1. Support
                        2. Support
                    B. Subpoint

            b. Speakers can identify the introduction, body, and conclusion of the presentation in two different ways.
                (1) Label introduction, body, and conclusion and repeat the symbol system under each division. That is the format we are following in these outlines.

(2) Begin the introduction after "I," the body after "II," and the conclusion after "III." Some instructors use the convention of placing the thesis after "II" to identify the key idea of the speech immediately.

2. *Coordination* refers to the grouping of items of equal importance.
   a. The items may be complete ideas arranged in a pattern of organization.
      (1) If the ideas are well-phrased, the listener or reader should be able to create the meaning of the point they develop.
      (2) The items should be phrased in parallel language.
   b. The items may be forms of support that develop an idea.
3. Indentation signals the subordination of a set of items.
   a. A set of indented items develops the item that immediately precedes the indentation.
   b. The set of indented items must contain at least two items.
   c. The indented items should be coordinate with one another.

II. An outline may use words, phrases, sentences, or—for speaking notes—a combination of the three. For planning a presentation, the sentence outline is usually the most useful tool.
   A. *Word Outline.* The word (or topic) outline contains the key topics contained in a speech.
      1. A topic outline can be helpful in planning an overall organization pattern for the speech.
         a. The word outline can provide a basis for developing a complete sentence outline.
         b. We discourage use of a word outline as a preparation outline because it often gives the inexperienced speaker a false sense of security.
            (1) The word outline does not help speakers to test the clarity of their ideas.
            (2) The word outline provides less opportunity for speakers to consider the time they will need to present their ideas.
      2. The word outline may serve as speaking notes for an experienced speaker.
      3. The word outline may serve as a visual aid for the listeners.
         a. You may present your outline using a flip chart, overhead transparency, slide, or electronic medium.
         b. The visual can help the audience follow the organization of the presentation while functioning as your speaking notes.
   B. *Phrase Outline.* The phrase outline uses sentence fragments for an outline.
      1. The phrase outline provides slightly more information than the word outline.
      2. The phrase outline has uses and weaknesses similar to those of the word outline.

C. **Sentence outline.** A sentence outline contains a complete sentence for each point in the outline.
   1. A sentence outline provides a sound planning tool for extemporaneous, manuscripted, or memorized speaking.
   2. The complete-sentence outline helps you prepare and test the key ideas in your presentation.
      a. The outline will allow you to test whether your ideas are clear and definite.
      b. Especially if you have difficulty phrasing your ideas on your feet, the sentence outline will help you avoid fumbling for words.
      c. Clearly phrased ideas are easier for your audience (including your instructor) to understand.
      d. Sentence outlines contain your key ideas, not the entire wording of the presentation.
      e. Some instructors require that students identify supporting material with a full sentence. Others allow phrases. Know your instructor's expectations.

D. **Complete content outline.** A complete content outline is the manuscript of a speech written in outline form.
   1. By using the outline form, the symbols help the speaker to quickly identify relationships during the planning and speaking phases.
   2. A complete content outline is seldom used in a basic public speaking course unless it contains an assignment for manuscripted or memorized speaking.
   3. A complete content outline should not be prepared or submitted for a speech requiring extemporaneous delivery.

III. **Speaking notes.** Your speaking notes should help, not handicap, the delivery of your presentation.

A. We recommend that you use a combination of words, phrases, and sentences that help you remember the content of your speech.
   1. Usually words and phrases help you remember your points while allowing you to change your phrasing to fit the situation.
   2. Usually full sentences will allow you to deliver direct quotations without taxing your memory or creating unnecessary anxiety.
   3. Similarly, your notes should probably contain important statistics, names and other facts in an easy to read form.

B. Reminders about your delivery are particularly useful in your speaking notes.

C. The form and format of your notes should not only help you during the presentation but also impress the audience favorably.
   1. Speaking notes should be easy to read and handle.
      a. Make sure you can read your notes easily.
      b. Number your note cards or pages.

c. Highlight delivery cues or content you wish to emphasize.
d. Using the indentation developed in your preparation outline will help you remember where transitions are needed.

2. Speaking notes should not distract the audience or lower your credibility.

D. Be sure to consider your instructor's specific requirements for notes.

IV. **Content of the preparation outline.** While different instructors will vary in their specific requirements for the full preparation outline, many require the following elements.

A. *Purpose statements.*
1. General Purpose
a. The general purposes of speaking are to inform, persuade, and entertain.
b. Your general purpose will remind you to use techniques best suited to your general purpose.
2. Specific Purpose: The specific purpose of your speech is the response you desire from the listeners.
a. Phrase your specific purpose in terms of the behavior you desire from your audience.
b. Each choice you make should promote the specific purpose of the presentation.

B. *Central idea.* The central idea is the essence of the speech, that is the main idea the audience should agree with or understand at the end of the speech.
1. Most public speakers begin to construct the body of their presentation with (at least a preliminary) phrasing of a central idea.
a. Phrase your central idea carefully so that it is brief, to-the-point, and clear.
b. Usually one simple sentence is adequate for phrasing the central idea.
2. Some authorities distinguish between a central idea and a *thesis* in order to remind the speaker to select techniques appropriate to the speaker's general purpose. We shall use the terms interchangeably.
a. Some authorities apply the term "central idea" to the single key idea of an informative presentation.
b. Some authorities apply the term "thesis" to the single key idea of a persuasive presentation.

C. *Body of the speech.* The body of the speech contains the claims and forms of support that develop your central idea or thesis.
1. The main points are the major divisions of the body of your speech.
a. In general, your speech should contain two to five main ideas arranged in an appropriate pattern of organization.
(1) Sometimes two points indicate an insufficient division of ideas.

(2) More than five points probably indicate insufficient grouping of ideas and may make your speech more difficult for the audience to follow.
(3) Owing to the time limits imposed on most classroom speeches, you seldom will have sufficient time to develop adequately more than two or three points.

b. Use the following five guidelines to enhance the clarity and organization of your ideas in your outline:
(1) Write each idea, whether it be a main point or a subpoint as a single, complete sentence. Complete sentences will allow you to test the clarity and structure of your thoughts.
(2) Present only one major idea in each main point.
(3) Your main points should be of approximately equal importance.
(4) Make sure that the central idea of the speech would be clear to anyone reading your main points. In other words, your main points should not overlap or leave gaps in the development of the central idea.
(5) Write your main points, if possible, in parallel structure to promote retention.

2. You may need to develop your main points with additional organized ideas called <u>subpoints</u>. In some cases, you may even need to break subpoints down into additional organized ideas called sub-subpoints or even subpoints of the second level, third level, and so on.
   a. Your central idea, main points, and needed subpoints provide the structure of the ideas in your presentation.
   b. You should develop with forms of support ideas that are not developed by other ideas.

D. *The introduction.* The speech introduction should be planned after the body of the speech.
1. You should accomplish four goals in the introduction.
   a. You should grab the listeners' attention in the beginning.
   b. You should interest them in the topic.
   c. You should establish yourself as a credible source.
      (1) Establish that you are knowledgeable and competent.
      (2) Establish that you are trustworthy.
      (3) Establish your goodwill toward the audience. By goodwill, we mean that you have the audience's best interest in mind.
   d. Prepare the audience for the speech to come.
2. In most classroom presentations you will need to accomplish all four goals. In most business, professional, and civic situations, you will find that one or more of the goals may have been met already or may need special attention.

3. Some instructors suggest that speakers write the introduction word for word, while others suggest that speakers prepare the introduction in outline form for extemporaneous delivery.

E. *The conclusion.* You should prepare your conclusion after you prepare the body and introduction of the speech or in conjunction with the introduction.
   1. You may also choose to write the conclusion word for word, but your planning should contain purposeful organization.
   2. The conclusion normally serves three major functions. A single closing technique can accomplish two or all of these functions.
      a. The speaker refocuses the listeners' attention on the key idea of the speech.
         (1) You may summarize your key ideas.
         (2) You may refer to the structure of the body of your presentation.
         (3) You may restate your central idea.
      b. The speaker attempts to create a mood consistent with the purpose of the presentation.
         (1) You might describe the advantages of applying the material you taught in an informative presentation.
         (2) You might use a form of support that creates an appropriate emotional response from the audience.
      c. The speaker attempts to create a sense of closure or finality.
         (1) You might make a direct link between your introduction and conclusion by referring back to your opening technique.
         (2) You might use a technique that is interesting or involving.
            (a) You might ask a question.
            (b) You might refer to the upcoming speaker, the group leader, or a person in the audience.
            (c) You might end with a final appeal for application or action.

F. *Transitions.* In general, you should add transitions to the outline after you have prepared the introduction, body, and conclusion. You need to know what you will say and the relationship among these ideas before you can make effective transitions between ideas.
   1. Some instructors require that transitions appear in parentheses.
   2. Some instructors require that transitions be labeled in a particular manner.

G. *Reference list* or *bibliography*.
   1. Determine whether your instructor requires a reference list or a bibliography. Different style manuals define these terms differently.
      a. By reference list, we mean all sources cited in your presentation or outline.
      b. By bibliography, we mean all sources that you consulted in researching for your presentation.

2. For the sake of efficiency in comparing students' work, instructors often require a particular style for noting sources.
   a. Your instructor may have created a format for you to use.
   b. Your instructor may require that you use a particular style manual or select from specified options.
3. Take the time to understand any special requirements of your instructor.
   a. Your teacher may expect you to cite sources within the outline itself.
   b. Some professors require students to use an annotated reference list in which students briefly explain the way each source was helpful in the speech preparation.
   c. Some professors require students to submit the printouts resulting from searches of computer databases.

H. *Title.* Probably the last step of preparation is to select a title for your speech. You will want a title that arouses and directs attention while indicating the essence of your message.

I. *Special considerations.* Most instructors have developed a variety of requirements designed to increase speaking success and promote efficient evaluation.
   1. Recording cues for delivery can help you to present your material and help the evaluator to assess your understanding of principles of speech delivery.
   2. Legibility will help both you and your instructor. Most instructors require typed outlines that allow them to see relationships more quickly.
   3. Some instructors require that students identify the introduction, body, and conclusion with the symbols I., II., and III., respectively. Others require students to label the three main divisions as the introduction, body, and conclusion and to begin the development of each division with roman numerals.
   4. Your instructor may have a preferred format for presenting supporting material.
      a. Some require that students identify supporting material in a complete sentence.
      b. Others call for labeling the support by name and referring to the content using a phrase.
   5. Study examples of outlines your instructor provides as models. Your instructor may have specific requirements about the length or format of outlines that influence grading.

V. **Preparing a speech outline.** Once you have completed your initial speech preparation including audience analysis and research, you should find the following step-by-step plan a useful guideline for creating a full-preparation outline.

Steps in Preparing an Effective Outline

Step 1: Write the topic, general purpose, and specific purpose for your presentation.

Step 2: Jot down all your ideas on a piece of paper or enter them into a computer file. You should use complete sentences to help you sharpen and clarify your ideas.

Step 3: Select out the key ideas and tentatively identify your central idea or thesis.

Step 4: Select an appropriate organizational pattern for the main points of the speech.

Step 5: Arrange the main ideas in your chosen pattern. Test and modify your arrangement until you are confident that a listener could state your central idea from hearing your main points.

Step 6: Identify the main points that must be developed with subpoints (and subpoints that must be developed with sub-subpoints).

Step 7: Arrange the sets of subpoints (and any necessary sub-subpoints) in appropriate organizational patterns and rephrase these ideas until from reading them alone you can phrase the idea each set develops.

Step 8: Choose forms of support to develop the ideas that you have not developed with other ideas.

Step 9: Identify the best way to introduce and conclude the body of the message.

Step 10: Add necessary transitional devices.

Step 11: Prepare the reference list or bibliography and note citations in the format required by your instructor.

Step 12: Examine and adjust the outline to meet any of your instructor's special requirements that you may have overlooked.

Closing Remarks

The purpose of this chapter was to provide instruction in principles of effective outlining for speech-making. Outlines can be helpful—even essential—to effective planning, organization, and delivery of a public message.

References and Suggestions for Further Readings

Brigance, W. N. (1952). *Speech: Its techniques and disciplines in a free society.* NY: Appleton-Crofts.

Ehninger, D., Gronbeck, B. E., Monroe, A. H., & Moore, L. (1984). *Principles of speech communication.* 9th brief edition. Glenview, IL: Scott, Foresman.

Grice, G. L., & Skinner, J. F. (1995). *Mastering public speaking.* Needham Heights, MA: Allyn & Bacon.

Hodges, J. C., Horner, W. B., Webb, S. S., & Miller, R. K. (1994). *Harbrace college handbook.* Ft. Worth, TX: Harcourt Brace.

Wagner, B. J. (1994). An easy outlining approach for producing solidly structured audience-directed reports. *Journal of Business and Technical Communication, 8,* 475–482.

CHAPTER 7

Beginning and Ending Your Presentations

Objectives

After reading this chapter, you should be able to

1. explain the four major functions of an effective speech introduction;
2. construct a speech introduction that accomplishes the four major functions of an effective speech introduction;
3. explain the three major functions of an effective speech conclusion; and
4. construct a speech conclusion that accomplishes the three major functions of an effective speech conclusion.

Topical Outline

RELATIONSHIP OF THE INTRODUCTION AND CONCLUSION TO THE BODY OF THE PRESENTATION

- Methods of preparation and delivery
- Behavior of the speaker before and after the presentation

CONSTRUCTING THE INTRODUCTION

- Goals of the introduction
- Length of the introduction
- Adaptation of the introduction
- Common weaknesses in introductions

CONSTRUCTING THE CONCLUSION

- Functions of the conclusion
- Adaptation of the conclusion
- Preparation of the conclusion

Key Concepts

Abrupt introduction
Adaptation of the conclusion
Adaptation of the introduction
Anecdote
Appeal for action
Audience participation
Balancing link
Challenge
Creating a mood or emotional response
Creating goodwill
Declaration of personal intent
Demonstrating competence
Demonstration or experiment
Developing interest
Direct question
Endorsement
Establishing credibility
Extended introduction
Final inducement
Functions of the conclusion
Gaining attention
Inappropriate attention grabbing
Irrelevant introduction
Length of the introduction
Length of the conclusion
Maintaining trustworthiness
Preparing the audience for the speech
Preview
Quotation
Reference to recent happenings
Reference to the speaker, the audience, or the occasion
Referring to the content
Refocusing attention
Relevant story
Rhetorical questions
Sense of finality or completeness
Startling statement
Summarizing key ideas

Beginning and Ending Your Presentations

PERSPECTIVE

I. After you have identified your specific purpose, the key points of the presentation, and your supporting materials, you are ready to write the introduction and conclusion. We stress that you should prepare the introduction and conclusion after you prepare the body.

II. As with any other part of your presentations, you should carefully plan the content and delivery of the introduction and conclusion.
   A. Especially for important presentations, some speakers prefer to write out the introduction and conclusion for delivery from manuscript or memory. Such speakers usually claim that a manuscript allows them to prepare and deliver effective wording for these important parts of the speech.
   B. Other speakers prefer to deliver the entire speech extemporaneously from an outline. Such speakers usually claim that an outline allows them to prepare effective wording while allowing them to adapt to the situation.
   C. Once you leave your speech course, you will probably select the method of preparation and delivery that suits your personal style and the situation.
      1. During this course, your instructor will likely make a specific recommendation or require a specific method.
      2. Whether you deliver your introduction and conclusion extemporaneously or from manuscript or memory, your delivery should be consistent with that of the body of the speech. A noticeable contrast in the style of your delivery or language may lead the audience to question your confidence, competence, or experience.

III. A presentation begins at the moment that the audience perceives the speaker and does not end until the audience's attention focuses on something or someone else. Remember the saying, "You cannot not communicate." When it comes to giving a speech, your delivery begins long before the words start and continues long after the words end.

IV. ***Purpose statement/Preview***: The purpose of this chapter is to provide a detailed description of the functions of and the techniques appropriate to the introduction and conclusion of a presentation.

Chapter Body

I. **Introductions.** A well-constructed introduction helps a speaker accomplish the specific purpose of his or her presentation.
   A. The introduction sets up a favorable atmosphere for the body of your message.

B. To prepare your audience for the body of your message, you must get its attention, interest it in the topic, establish yourself as a credible source, and prepare the audience for the speech to come. Often a single technique can accomplish two or more of the functions of an introduction.
   1. *Gaining attention.* Your first task in communicating is to get your listeners to focus their attention on you as the source of a message.
      a. Speakers commonly choose from a variety of techniques to focus the attention of listeners.
         (1) A reference to the speaker, the audience, or the occasion
            (a) Speakers often use references to themselves, the audience, or the occasion in formal and professional settings. These might include a formal greeting, a reference to past relationship with the audience or organization, and a (polite and/or indirect) request to pay attention.
            (b) A reference to recent happenings that relate to the topic, a genuine compliment to the audience, and a reference to oneself may work well in both formal and informal situations.
         (2) Audience participation
            (a) A question to listeners involves them directly in the presentation.
               (1) Rhetorical questions attempt to stimulate the audience to think about an issue without an oral response.
               (2) Direct questions ask for an oral or nonverbal response from the audience. A speaker may gather information about an audience using direct questions.
      b. You may ask the audience to participate in a demonstration or experiment.
         (1) A relevant story
            (a) Stories may be factual or hypothetical and include literary and historical illustrations.
            (b) A dramatic story can capture attention through suspense and other factors of attention.
            (c) A anecdote can capture attention through humor and other factors of attention.
         (2) A quotation
            (a) A quotation can provide an effective opening, especially in formal situations.
            (b) You may be able to find the words of a famous (or not so famous) person who eloquently captures attention.
            (c) The name of the source may cause the audience to pay attention and think.

(3) A startling statement
    (a) A startling statistic, event, or prediction can grab the attention of the audience.
    (b) You should repeat or restate the statement if it contains material important to the presentation. In that you did not already have the attention of the audience, the repetition will allow the information to "register."
(4) Use your creativity to devise other opening techniques for your presentation.

c. Use good judgment in selecting your opening device.
    (1) If listeners are over stimulated, they cannot pay attention to material that follows.
    (2) You can destroy your credibility with techniques that are excessive, irrelevant, or inappropriate.

2. *Developing interest and involvement.* Another important function of the speech introduction is to strengthen the audience's interest in the topic and involvement in the presentation.
    a. You should involve the listeners mentally by showing the way the topic affects them.
        (1) Make your purpose clear.
        (2) Let your listeners know how they will benefit from your presentation.
    b. You can involve the listeners physically by having them do something with the speaker.
    c. You should involve the listeners indirectly by explaining and demonstrating your interest in the topic.

3. *Strengthening credibility.* A third function of the introduction is to strengthen the speaker's credibility. Audiences view credibility from several perspectives: Is the speaker competent and knowledgeable? Is the speaker trustworthy? Does the speaker have the best interests of the audience at heart? Does the speaker care about the subject?
    a. Effective speakers establish their knowledge of the subject early in the message. In some cases, you may not have a great knowledge of the topic, but your research will allow you to know more than most, if not all, of your listeners.
    b. Effective speakers do nothing to bring into question their honesty and trustworthiness.
        (1) To paraphrase Aristotle, it's not enough for an audience to think you know the truth; the audience must believe you're willing to tell the truth.
        (2) Most listeners will assume you are honest unless you give them evidence to the contrary, such as attacking someone unfairly or using extreme material.

c. Showing goodwill toward the audience can increase a speaker's overall credibility.
d. Showing enthusiasm will make you more credible to the listeners.

4. *Preparing the audience.* A fourth function of the introduction is to prepare the audience for the content of the body of the speech.
   a. If your purpose is acceptable to the audience, state it clearly.
   b. If your purpose is unacceptable to the audience, state it indirectly.
   c. Previewing the content, that is telling the listeners what you're going to tell them, prepares the audience for the content of the presentation.

C. Without being abrupt, a speaker should accomplish the functions of an introduction in as short a time as possible.
   1. Rarely should the introduction require more than 20 percent of your speaking time.
      a. If some of the functions of the introduction have already been accomplished, you should shorten the introduction:
         (1) when listeners are already highly involved in the topic, and/or
         (2) when listeners already believe you are a competent and trustworthy person on this topic.
      b. If listeners are hostile toward you, the organization you represent, or your purpose, you should develop your introduction more fully.
   2. If your introduction lasts less than 5 percent of your time, it is probably too abrupt.

D. You must adapt your introduction to the unique nature of your purpose, audience, and occasion.
   1. Your specific purpose should guide the way you accomplish the goals of an introduction.
      a. In an informative presentation you will probably need to stress your expertise on the subject, motivate the audience to learn the material, and provide a definite and complete preview of the approach you will take.
      b. In a persuasive speech, you should probably emphasize the similarities between you and your audience.
      c. In a speech to entertain, you should make an extra effort to "warm up" to the audience.
   2. Early in the presentation, you may need to deal with certain strong attitudes or feelings held by your audience.
   3. You should be familiar with the expectations of your listeners and the nature of the occasion.
      a. Avoid violating the expectations of your audience.
      b. Consider the forces that will be at work when you deliver the presentation.

(1) What will precede and follow your speech?

(2) What needs of the audience will dominate the situation?

E. Avoid common weaknesses in speech introductions.

1. Especially in classroom speeches, avoid abrupt introductions. Often, we hear beginning speakers start their message: "Today I'm going to talk about...." We don't want you to announce your topic. We want you to arouse our attention and interest, then give us an indication of what you will discuss. That's why speakers usually explain the purpose or main idea of the speech toward the end of the introduction. At that point, preview your message. If your topic is not controversial, you might specifically tell your three to five main ideas. If your audience disagrees with your position, your preview will be more indirect and suggestive. But you should give your audience an idea of what is coming. Previewing your speech will increase understanding and retention.

2. Avoid unnecessarily long introductions. Occasionally, speakers will spend so much time on the introduction that they have little time for the body or exceed their time limit.

3. Avoid excessive or inappropriate attention grabbing techniques that over stimulate the audience or lower your credibility.

4. Avoid including material irrelevant to your topic or purpose.

II. **Conclusion of the speech**. After you have presented your main ideas and supported them, you will provide some concluding remarks.

A. The conclusion may provide your last chance to have an effect on the audience. Often, a single closing technique can accomplish more than one of the three major goals of a conclusion.

1. *Refocus attention*. The conclusion should refocus attention on the specific purpose of the presentation.

a. Avoid introducing new ideas or information in the conclusion.

b. You may review the body of your presentation by summarizing your key ideas or referring to the content of the major divisions.

(1) A summary of the key ideas functions to tell the listeners what you told them, thereby promoting clarity and retention.

(2) If retention of the wording of the specific main points is not necessary, you may refer to the topics covered in your main points.

c. An appeal for action helps to remind the audience of the relevance of your ideas and direct audience behavior.

2. *Establish an appropriate mood*. The conclusion provides your last chance to create a mood or emotional response in your audience consistent with your purpose.

a. A positive mood is generally preferable to a negative one.

b. Few speakers use humor in a speech conclusion, but if used appropriately, it can help to make the speech memorable.
c. A vivid illustration, dramatic statement, or interesting quotation can also help to create an emotional response from the listener.

3. *Provide a sense of finality.* An effective conclusion should create a sense of finality or completion.
   a. You may find it useful to make a direct balancing link between your introduction and conclusion.
      (1) You might refer back to your opening technique, a piece of support or the central idea of your introduction.
      (2) You might mirror the preview in your introduction with a review in the conclusion.
   b. You may find it useful to involve members of the audience. Anytime you involve the audience you increase your chances of having them listen to, understand, and remember your message.
      (1) You may ask a question.
      (2) You might refer to the upcoming speaker, the group leader, the person in the front row.

B. Your specific purpose should guide the way you accomplish the three goals of a conclusion.
   1. In an informative presentation you might end by telling the audience ways to proceed in the future.
      a. You may encourage the listeners to apply the information you provided.
      b. You may distribute a list of additional resources or a summary of your information.
   2. Endings that direct the listener's behavior are particularly appropriate for a persuasive presentation.
      a. You may declare your personal intent to address a problem, thereby providing a model for your audience.
      b. You may provide an endorsement of your proposal by a source the audience respects.
      c. You may provide a final inducement to act in a particular manner.
      d. You may challenge the audience.
      e. You may appeal for action.
         (1) Facilitate immediate actions such as signing a petition, signing a contract, or making a public commitment.
         (2) Facilitate future actions by identifying the exact action to take and providing necessary materials.
   3. The conclusion of a speech to entertain usually stresses the positive mood developed during the body of the presentation.

C. Preparing the conclusion.
   1. You should prepare the conclusion after, or along with, the introduction. As you gather support, look for material that can help you link the introduction and conclusion.
   2. Speakers often signal the listeners that the message is going to end.
      a. Transitions such as "And finally...." or "Before I leave you tonight...." tell the audience that the speaker is finishing.
      b. No speaker should be so self-involved that the most exciting part of the speech is the information that the speech is nearly over.
   3. Conclusions are usually shorter than introductions. They rarely exceed 5 to 10 percent of a speaker's time. Audiences usually become irritated if the speaker continues and continues after signaling the conclusion has begun.
   4. As popular wisdom tells us, "End with a bang, not a whimper."

Closing Remarks

Effective introductions and conclusions can go a long way toward making or breaking a presentation. Review the goals and techniques we have outlined for you and let your reasoned creativity loose.

References and Suggestions for Further Readings

DeVito, J. A. (1986). *The communication handbook: A dictionary.* NY: Harper & Row.

Grice, G. L., & Skinner, J. F. (1995). *Mastering public speaking.* Needham Heights, MA: Allyn & Bacon.

Knapp, M. (1978). *Social intercourse: From greeting to goodbye.* Boston: Allyn & Bacon.

Lucas, S. E. (1995). *The art of public speaking.* NY: McGraw Hill.

Plavetich, R. G. (1992). How to be an effective public speaker. *Training and Development, 46*, 17–20.

Presentations that pack a punch. (1994). *Managing Office Technology, 39*, 61–67.

Rafe, S. C. (1990). *How to be prepared to speak on your feet.* NY: Harper Business Publications.

Sprague, J. & Stuart, D. (1992). *The speaker's handbook.* Ft. Worth, TX: Harcourt Brace.

Townsend, M. A. R., Hicks, L., Thompson, J. D., Wilton, K. M., Tuck, B. F., & Moore, D. W. (1993). Effects of introductions and conclusions in assessment of student essays. *Journal of Educational Psychology, 85*, 670–678.

CHAPTER 8

Planning and Researching Your Presentations

Objectives

After reading this chapter, you should be able to

1. Develop an organized and effective method for planning a presentation;
2. Locate, from a variety of appropriate sources, information suitable for a presentation;
3. Plan and conduct an interview to gather information;
4. Develop an effective system for taking notes when researching for a presentation; and
5. Cite sources effectively in a presentation.

Topical Outline

MAKING A PLAN

- Classroom assignments
- General purpose of the presentation
- Checklist for preparation

RESEARCH NOTE-TAKING

- Expectations
- Bibliographic style

CITING SOURCES OF IDEAS AND INFORMATION

SOURCES OF INFORMATION

- Using the library
- Sources of print information
- Interviews
- Surveys

Key Concepts

American Psychological Association (APA)
Atlases and geographical dictionaries
Bibliographic style
Bibliography
Biography
Citing sources
Closed question
Coding system (for research notes)
Collection of quotations
Dictionary
Encyclopedia
Expectations (of instructor)
Forbidden topics
General purpose
Government documents
Index
Index cards
Interlibrary loan
Interview
Library databases
Magazine
Modern Language Association (MLA)
Newspaper
Note-taking
Open-ended question
Paraphrase
Periodical
Place of publication
Plagiarism
Planning a speech
Professional and trade publication
Publisher
Reference area
Reference librarian
Reference list
Reference works
Research notes
Scholarly journal
Source
Speech collection
Statistical compilation
Survey
Textbook

Planning and Researching the Presentation

PERSPECTIVE:

One of the key purposes of a college education (and a specific goal of your University Core Curriculum) is to help you learn how to teach yourself. If you know how to use a library effectively, you will have a nearly infinite resource to help you learn and solve problems.

I. Whenever you give a speech, you'll find the process easier and probably more successful if you discuss a topic about which you have knowledge and interest.
   A. No matter how well you know a topic, it is important to plan your presentation and research your topic carefully.
   B. We encourage you to develop a personal filing or organization system to help you save your time and increase the effectiveness of presentations you will be making in professional, social, and personal situations.
      1. Prepare clipping files on topics relevant to your career or interests.
      2. Prepare a file or document to collect and save interesting material that you might use in a variety of presentations.
         a. Add humorous and serious material that appeared in publications
            (1) When you find appropriate material in a magazine or other publication, write its page number on the cover.
            (2) When you are ready to dispose of the publication, cut out or scan the items and add them to your file.
            (3) Remember to note the source on the item itself.
         b. Carry a small notebook to record materials or approaches you have heard in other presentations.
      3. By creating project files for written reports and oral presentations, you may be able to use information from these files to save you time preparing future projects.

II. ***Purpose statement***: This chapter aims to help you prepare oral presentations; specifically we will stress ways to take advantage of the most valuable resource on Ball State's campus, the University Libraries.

III. ***Preview***: First we present a method for preparing presentations; next we offer suggestions for organizing your research; third we provide guidelines for citing sources during a presentation; we close by discussing the various types of sources you may wish to consult in the research process.

Chapter Body

I. **Planning for the oral presentation.**
   A. Like any project, a speech is one that requires careful thought and planning. If you try to cram that planning into the evening before you must give the speech, you will have less success than if you spread the work over a week or two.
   B. The exact process for planning a speech may be a rather personal approach.
      1. Thus, you may want to make some modifications to the suggested plan.
      2. Unless you have considerable experience in giving public speeches, you should try to follow this basic plan.
   C. Classroom assignments often provide you a plan.
      1. For the classroom, you must meet the expectations, or requirements, of the person(s) who will grade your performance.
         a. Record your instructor's requirements, read them carefully, and ask appropriate questions for clarification.
         b. No matter how impressive your speech is by some standards, if it fails to meet expectations for the particular assignment, your speech—and probably the evaluation and grade—will disappoint you.
      2. Below are some key suggestions in preparing public speeches for classroom assignments.
         a. Most instructors will insist that you meet all basic requirements of the assignment in order to earn a grade of "C" or better.
         b. Avoid topics that are exceedingly controversial or on an instructor's list of "forbidden topics."
         c. Select a topic of interest to you about which you have knowledge or a desire to learn.
         d. You could also select a topic you are studying in another course.
         e. Review your instructor's written and oral instructions for the speech.
            (1) Be sure to incorporate any specific requirements for the assignment, such as the use of certain kinds of support, the number of main points or references, etc.
            (2) Once your research is nearly complete, you might need to narrow the topic significantly, remembering the instructor's time limits.
         f. Know exactly when you will give the speech, then don't procrastinate, and make a plan with that date in mind.
            (1) Unless you are giving an impromptu speech, prepare the speech well in advance.
            (2) You should complete your outline at least one class meeting before you deliver your presentation to allow for practice time and final adjustments.

D. General Purpose for the Assignment: Your instructor may give you an assignment in which your general purpose should be "To Inform," "To Persuade," or "To Entertain." These general purposes should be your overall guide.

E. Checklist for preparation; each speech should go through a process of careful preparation.
   a. To help guide your preparation so that you sufficiently plan and narrow your topic, we provide a checklist below.
   b. You should find the checklist helpful in the process of planning your next speech.

Checklist for Speech Preparation

___1. Carefully consider the specific requirements of the assignment.
___2. Analyze the audience.
___3. Select a topic.
___4. Determine a specific purpose, and central idea.
___5. Reevaluate the topic and purpose in terms of the audience, occasion, and assignment requirements.
___6. If you have sufficient knowledge, write down three to five main ideas for the speech.
___7. Do research to collect data and support.
___8. Prepare the body of the speech by phrasing your main points and outlining their development.
___9. Organize your ideas by writing an outline of the body of the speech.
___10. After you have created the body of the speech, determine the best way to lead into and conclude your message by planning the speech introduction and conclusion.
___11. Create transitions to help distinguish main points and help the audience follow along with the presentation.
___12. Recheck your outline to refine your organization, support, and wording. You may ask your instructor to review the outline in advance of the speech date.
___13. Prepare presentational aids if appropriate.
___14. Prepare your speaking notes.
___15. Practice your message.
___16. Make appropriate adjustments to your speech, presentational aids and outline.
___17. Make sure you time your presentation multiple times to assure it fits the time requirements.
___18. Deliver the presentation.
___19. Evaluate your success. Consider the responses of your instructor and peers and your own impressions of the speech. You are often your harshest critic, thus it is can be advantageous to engage in a self-evaluation for further improvement.

II. **Making research notes.** Effective note taking will allow you to accomplish two goals: (1) to prepare your outline as quickly as possible and (2) to link your researched information to its source.
   A. The two key principles of taking effective research notes are:
      1. Using an efficient system.
      2. Maintaining accuracy and completeness.
   B. Most people record research notes on index cards, sheets of paper, or computer files.
      1. Many students simply photocopy materials they cannot check out, or borrow.
         a. This method not only is costly but also tends to make speech construction inefficient and to encourage plagiarism.
         b. A cheaper alternative is to electronically download the material; however this can also encourage plagiarism, **DO NOT** illegally download materials for a speech.
         c. Many news websites, as well as the library databases, will allow you to email articles to yourself.
      2. If you use index cards, use a size that will help you construct the speech quickly.
         a. Using cards with a spiral binding will allow you to keep your notes together until you are ready to sort them.
         b. Recording one piece of information on a card will allow you to sort the ideas quickly.
      3. If you record information on sheets of paper, use a coding system that allows you to cut the pages to use the information in the appropriate part of your presentation.
      4. Some prefer to record and arrange their notes using a computer or word processor.
         a. Similar to when using sheets of paper to organize research notes, when using an electronic system you will need to use a system of coding that allows you to link the source to the information you are placing in the presentation.
         b. Additionally, you will need to be careful not to "cut and paste" sections from an electronic file created by someone else without using quotation marks.
      5. Using post-it notes can also be an effective method of note taking.
         a. When using post-it notes each piece of information should be placed on its own note.
         b. If you print out a paper copy of research materials the notes can be stuck directly where information was found.
         c. Post-it notes could also be placed on a hard surface in the order the information will be used in presentation.
         d. This will allow you to remove and replace them in a different order making for easy restructuring of a presentation.

e. Further post-it notes are relatively cheap and thus using a large amount of them will not require large amounts of money.
f. It may also be advantageous to have a large board to stick the notes to so the entire presentation can be easily seen and transported.

C. Regardless of the system you use, make sure you record a complete reference citation.
   1. Some teachers require the use of a specific style manual (for bibliographic style and citation format) such as the style manual of the Modern Language Association (MLA) or the American Psychological Association (APA).
      a. We typically request that you use the *APA Manual*, unless your instructor chooses another.
      b. This is because in the social sciences, in which communication studies falls, APA is the most commonly used style.
   2. You will need to create a reference list at the end of assigned papers or on the outline of speeches.
   3. References give credit to the source and provide sufficient information to locate a source.
      a. Thus, the more information about the reference you give, the easier it will be for someone else to find it.
      b. Hence, references typically include the following elements:
         (1) The author.
         (2) The date of publication.
         (3) The title of the work.
         (4) The name of the periodical or book.
         (5) The volume number of periodicals,
         (6) The publisher and place of publication,
         (7) The pages of an article or chapter, and
         (8) The complete web address and date accessed.
   4. While you are recording notes, you may want to include the library location (for example, "Reference," "General Collection") and call number of your sources in case you need to find them again.

III. **Citing sources of ideas and information**

A. The *Merriam-Webster Collegiate Dictionary* (2004) defines plagiarism as the act of stealing and passing off of (the ideas or words of another) as one's own: using (another's production) without crediting the source; To commit literary theft: presenting as new and original an idea or product derived from an existing source.
   1. Ball State University has a policy regarding plagiarism.
      a. Presenting as one's own work the ideas, representations, or words of another person without proper acknowledgment.

   b. Submitting an assignment purporting to be the student's original work, which has been wholly or partly created by another (this includes working with one or more other students in the course to create essentially the same paper or presentation).
2. You risk failing your assignment, or the course, if you plagiarize the work of another student or speaker, fail to cite the sources of the information you use in the speech, or prepare with other students together a single speech or paper.
   a. Hence, we suggest that you cite your sources, even if you are paraphrasing the ideas of your source.
   b. Additionally, citations will let the audience know that you have researched your topic adding to your credibility.
   c. Even in a business or professional presentation, you should be ready to tell your listeners the source of your information.
3. Professors vary in their requirements for citing sources in outlines and in presentations.
   a. If your teacher requires a reference list, this means you should include all the sources that you cited in your speech.
   b. If your teacher requires a bibliography, in this you should also include all the sources you used in your presentation.
   c. Copies of various citation manuals (such as those of the MLA and APA) are available at the reference desk in Bracken Library, first floor west.

B. Complete citations could sound awkward in a presentation; however with practice you can include the information in many interesting ways.
   1. Create elegant ways to cite your sources.
      a. "In 1986, the noted researcher Michael Neer wrote that..."
      b. "When reading a *Time* magazine article from March 27th, 2013, I was surprised to find that eighty-five percent..."
      c. "To paraphrase Thomas Jefferson from August 4th 1780..."
      d. "Last week, when I was reading the *Wall Street Journal* from January 14th, 2013, I discovered that..."
   2. By using such techniques, you can give credit to your sources and add to your own image of competence in the eyes of your audience.
   3. You can provide the complete citation if the members of the audience question your sources.

C. When you start early and take notes carefully, you not only build your sense of professionalism but also avoid ethical temptations.

IV. **Sources.** Consulting a variety of sources to locate supporting materials will increase your chances of success. In addition to using materials available in any of the campus libraries (Bracken Library, the Architecture Library, the Science-Health Sciences Library), consider gathering materials through interviews, surveys, or requests.

A. The University Libraries provide a major source of supporting materials for public speakers.
   1. The competent communicator avoids the tendency to use only familiar materials, while ignoring the wealth of other sources. You will find it helpful to examine a variety of up-to-date, relevant sources.
   2. The lists of the materials owned by the library are available under the databases link on www.bsu.edu/library.
      a. Databases may be searched by a variety of fields, including subject, title, and author.
      b. Use the guides supplied at the Internet stations in the reference area of Bracken Library if you are unsure how to use the databases.
   3. If you cannot find what you need contact a reference librarian.
      a. The reference librarians at the branch libraries and at the reference desk on the first floor west of Bracken Library are excellent resources.
      b. Their job is to help others find information.
      c. Additional help is available through the "ask a librarian" service that can be accessed through email, by phone, or in person.
      d. Another service is the chat service; until 1am a librarian is available to speak with students about research problems over the phone.
      e. There is also a librarian available at the reference desk on the first floor of the library until 1am and on call after.
   4. The library also offers research workshops on various databases often announced through the library Facebook page.
   5. If the library does not have the specific materials you need, you may be able to obtain them from another library through an interlibrary loan system.

B. There are several general types and sources of *published* information.
   1. Varying the types of sources used in your presentations can assist in finding different types of information and increase your credibility.
      a. A *newspaper* is a paper that is distributed usually daily or weekly and that contains news, articles of opinions, features, and advertising.
         (1) Information found in a newspaper is typically considered credible as it goes through a peer review or editing process prior to publication.
         (2) Newspapers are often considered relevant based on how updated the article, a year old article is considered less relevant than an article one week old.

(3) Newspapers can sometimes be viewed as biased based on the ownership of the paper, as certain papers support a specific political view and thus papers from different perspectives should be sought out.
(4) In-text citations should include the author, and year of the article.
(5) Where verbal citations should include author, full date and the paper's title; "Mathew Wald reported in the *New York Times* of March eighth 2013…"
(6) In the reference list newspaper articles should reflect this APA format; Wald, M. (2013, March 8). Solar cells may supplement smart phone batteries. *New York Times*, pp. A1, A4.

b. *Scholarly journals* typically publish articles quarterly (4 times per year) that are written by experts reporting the findings from their research.
   (1) These are considered the most credible of sources as they go through intensive peer review and are written by scholars considered experts on that topic.
   (2) Articles in scholarly journals often contain a large amount of information about a specific topic including the most recent findings on that area and each journal typically has a specific focus.
   (3) These articles can often be extremely long and difficult to comprehend for someone not an expert in the field, however non-experts can still gather valuable information from these sources.
   (4) In-text citations for these articles include the author's last name and year of the publication.
   (5) Verbal citations should include the full name of the author and year of publication.
   (6) A full citation in the reference should follow APA format; Vik, G.N. (2004). Breaking bad habits: Teaching effective powerpoint use to working graduate students. *Business Communication Quarterly*, 67, 225–228.

c. *Magazine articles* are similar to those of newspapers, however magazines are more specialized in a specific area, and published less often.
   (1) The specialty of a magazine can often offer more credibility than a newspaper because the authors are more likely to be knowledgeable in their topic area, in addition to the extensive editing process previous to publication.
   (2) However the writers are still staff writers and not experts in their field, thus they are not as credible as scholarly journals.

(3) Not all magazines are the same, and it is necessary to be able to tell the difference between credible magazines and tabloids, which typically lack the use of primary sources within articles.
(4) Much like newspapers, magazines often present a biased perspective based on the political slant they take, thus it is important to seek out multiple perspectives to account for that bias.
(5) Magazine citations would be the same as that of a newspaper.

d. Articles in *professional and/or trade publications* can be a good source when seeking information on a professional topic or field.
(1) Because these articles are often written by members of the given field they will provide relevant and valid information.
(2) These are often considered credible because they offer up-to-date information from the perspective of an expert, though it is also important to remember that they are not scholarly sources.
(3) The citations for professional and/or trade publications would reflect the format of a scholarly journal article.

e. *Government publications* cover a wealth of information published by the executive, legislative, and judicial branches of the federal government.
(1) These sources are considered extremely credible as they come directly from the government.
(2) The federal government publishes more information than any other source, becoming a valuable source of information.
(3) Some of these publications may be difficult to decipher as they may be filled with legal jargon.
(4) You can also find sources published by state governments and municipalities.
(5) The full citation format for these often depends on the type of document being cited, though verbal citations should include the title of the document, the date it was created, and where it was found.

f. *Web sources* are any source found on the Internet.
(1) The credibility of web sources can vary on the type of website; .org and .gov are almost always preferred over .com or .net.
(2) It is also important to understand who is sponsoring the website as the group who created the site could increase or decrease the credibility of that source.

(3) This is most obvious when looking at newspaper websites.
(4) NYtimes.com is the electronic version of the *New York Times* newspaper and thus holds a great deal of credibility despite being a .com.
(5) On the flip side, Wikipedia.org holds little credibility as anyone can edit a page on that website, though the footnotes can provide a good starting point for your own research.
(6) If you are unsure about the credibility of a website check with your instructor to assure its quality.
(7) When citing a web source verbally state the website but also the organization that produced the website and the date the website was last updated.
(8) The full citation in the reference list varies based on the type of source, blogs for example are different from a standard web page.
(9) For specific questions ask your instructor or visit the Purdue Owl website (http://owl.english.purdue.edu/owl), a free website produced by Purdue University designed to answer citation questions.
(10)If citing a web source that has a hard copy equivalent, such as the *New York Times*, cite the source as you would the hard copy and add the URL (the full web address) at the end.

g. *Textbooks* are often a good starting point for research.
   (1) If you have a topic that interests you, find one or more textbooks on the topic, and then review them.
   (2) By looking at the subjects within the textbook, you may find just the right idea for a narrowed topic.
   (3) Because it takes years to write and publish a textbook, you should question if the textbook contains up-to-date information, instead use it as a starting point and then do further research to go beyond what you find.

2. The reference collection is located on first floor west of Bracken Library. A reference librarian will help you locate reference works appropriate for many classroom presentations.
   a. Most of us have used general encyclopedias such as the *World Book* or *Encyclopedia Britannica*.
   b. Other specialized encyclopedias may be even more helpful. Examples include *Encyclopedia of Multiculturalism*; *Encyclopedia of Energy, Technology, and the Environment*; and *The Concise Blackwell Encyclopedia of Management*.
      (1) Encyclopedias are also a helpful starting point for your research, providing a general overview of your topic, people and terms related to your topic, and a chronology of events surrounding it.

(2) Be sure to consult the index of the encyclopedia to determine if you located all the entries for your topic.

c. Dictionaries are particularly helpful when you come across the jargon and new language in scholarly research.

d. Biographical collections provide details about the lives of individuals.

e. Biographical information can help you establish the credibility of your sources by providing their credentials as experts.

f. Atlases and geographical dictionaries provide facts about geographical areas ranging from cities and municipalities to nations and continents. The map collection in Bracken Library, second floor east, also is a valuable resource.

g. Collections of quotations provide material that will make your speech more interesting or impressive.

(1) You may be able to find websites that provide famous quotations, but it is important to ensure the accuracy of such websites.

3. A bibliography is a list of books or other materials that are available on a given topic.
   a. It can help you to find relevant material easily.
   b. Bibliographies often can be found at the end of an encyclopedia or journal article or a book chapter.
   c. On some topics, an entire book may be a bibliography.
4. The Bracken Library provides several indexes and databases that will help you find information in a variety of sources.
   a. These indexes and databases can be found on the library webpage (www.bsu.edu/library) under the research tools tab.
   b. Under this tab you will find a databases link which will take you to a list of databases Ball State provides to all students.
   c. To the right side of the screen you can locate information icons that will provide you with information on individual databases including types of sources searched, topics covered, and the typical use of the database.
   d. At the top of the database link page you will see a list of "most commonly used"; these are the best choices for beginning researchers.
   e. A good place to start when conducting research is the Academic Search Premier database.
      (1) This provides access to information from over 8000 sources that include academic journals, newspapers, and magazines.
5. If the library does not have the book you need you can request an interlibrary loan.
   a. This is a process through which the library requests materials from other libraries.

b. Interlibrary loan a free service that can be located on the library home page under the services menu.
c. Unfortunately, sometimes the library is forced to pay for access to certain materials.
   (1) In this case you are given the option of paying the fee or canceling your request.
   (2) If you select that you are willing to pay for materials when submitting the request the charge will be applied to your BSU account, however, the library will not complete the loan and charge you if you have not indicated that you are willing to pay.

C. *Interviews*. Interviews may give you specific, up-to-date information for your speech and lead you to other excellent sources.
   1. Interviews usually add perspective, interest, and credibility to a presentation.
   2. Effective interviewers prepare for the interview.
      a. Interview an individual who is likely to have and share the information you need.
      b. Decide whether a face-to-face or telephone interview is more appropriate.
      c. Learn as much as you can about the person you will interview.
      d. Prepare a set of questions.
         (1) It is often helpful to prepare an interview guide.
            (a) An interview guide consists of a list of topics and questions that can be asked but does not dictate the order allowing for flexibility in interviewing.
            (b) This will help guide the interview but allow the interviewer to adapt questions in order to expand on interesting findings.
         (2) A combination of both open and closed questions will help you get the information you need.
            (a) Closed questions call for a short answer such as "yes" or "no" or the statement of a fact. Closed questions allow you to gather specific information quickly.
            (b) Open-ended questions, ones that call for elaboration or explanation, allow you to gather in-depth information.
         (3) Highlight your most important questions to give you direction should a lack of time become a problem.
      e. Decide how you will record your information.
         (1) You will find it helpful to take notes or tape record the interview so that you can remember and use accurate information.
         (2) However, be prepared for an interviewee to say, "No," when you ask for permission to record.

f. Identify ways to project an appropriate image that will meet the expectations of the individual you will interview.
g. Whenever conducting an interview you should act and dress in a professional manner.
h. Always have your questions typed rather than written out on notebook paper for example.

2. Effective interviews have an opening, body, and closing.
   a. Your first task is to establish rapport and clarify the purpose of the interview. (Include in developmental material, for example: Introduce yourself, let the individual know how the information will be used, respect requests for confidentiality, ask for permission if you are recording the interview, and determine if the interviewee requires to review the information you use.)
   b. During the body of the interview, ask your prepared questions.
      (1) Listen carefully.
      (2) Ask additional questions if you need clarification.
      (3) Politely redirect the conversation if the person you are interviewing strays from the topic.
   c. At the end of the interview, you may need to summarize your thoughts to check their accuracy. Always thank the person for the interview before you leave.
3. Effective interviewers follow up on the interview as soon as possible.
   a. Summarize your information in writing before you forget it.
   b. Send a thank you note to the individuals you interviewed.
4. Another option for conducting research is a focus group.
   a. Focus groups are small groups of people with a particular characteristic or characteristics convened for a focused discussion of a particular topic.
   b. Focus groups are similar to interviews to the point that many consider focus groups a form of interview.
   c. These often result in a "chaining" or "cascading" effect where each group member's contribution stems from that of another which is less likely to occur in traditional one-on-one interviews.
   d. As a result focus groups can often lead to varied findings from a traditional interview providing further insight about a topic.
   e. A focus group is often a better choice than an interview. If you want to gather multiple perspectives in a shorter period of time—the downside is that you may not get as in-depth information.
   f. You will want to secure a professional space for the focus group as well; this must be arranged in advance as to assure the space will be available.

   g. You will also want to make sure the space is large enough for all participants.
   h. While it is not a bad idea to record an interview as well, it is essential that a focus group be recorded, so make sure to get permission from participants prior to recording.

D. *Surveys*. When conducting a survey to gather reliable information, researchers follow demanding guidelines and procedures.
   1. You must recognize that without valid survey research techniques, you should not consider your survey an accurate measure of reality.
   2. Unscientific surveys can, however, stimulate thought and interest.
      a. Therefore, student surveys are helpful as one type of support to provide a particular perception or an interest device.
      b. Also, surveys of your peers provide a good source of peer testimony.
   3. Survey questions can be either quantitative or qualitative in nature.
      a. Quantitative survey questions look for statistical data, typically numbers that can be averaged.
      b. For example, if you were conducting a presentation on a particular music group you could gather quantitative data on how many people listen to that group as well as how much they like them, and then use those numbers in your speech.
      c. Questions to gather this data would often be classified as closed-ended, seeking answers such as yes no, frequencies, or strength of ideas.
      c. Qualitative survey questions seek data indicating feelings or perception.
      d. For that same speech you could ask open-ended questions about people's opinions of the group and then quote some of the responses in your speech.

Closing Remarks

Although there is no room in this textbook to fully explain every type of source of information for your speech, you should be aware of the multitude of possible sources of supporting materials for a speech. Many students find their public speaking course to be the first college course to directly involve them in learning to use their college library. You can use your valuable research skills throughout college and in your career and personal activities.

References and Suggestions for Further Readings

Frey, L. R., Botan, C. H., & Kreps, G. L. (2000). *Investigating communication: An introduction to research methods*, (2nd ed.). Needham Heights, MA: Allyn and Bacon.

Gibaldi, J. (2009). *MLA handbook for writers of research papers*. (7th ed.). Modern Language Association of America, New York, NY.

Goad, T. W. (2010). *The first-time trainer: A step-by-step quick guide for managers, supervisors, and new training professionals*, (2nd ed.). New York, NY: AMACOM.

Hult, C. A. (1990). *Research and writing: Across the curriculum*. (2nd ed.). Belmont, CA: Wadsworth.

Lindlof, T. R., Taylor, B. C. (2011). *Qualitative communication research methods*. (3rd ed.). Thousand Oaks, CA: Sage.

Metter, E. (1995). *The writer's ultimate research guide*. Cincinnati, OH: Writers Digest Books.

Metzler, K. (1989). *Creative interviewing: The writer's guide to gathering information by asking questions*. Englewood Cliffs, NJ: Prentice Hall.

N.A. (2004). *Merriam-Webster's Collegiate Dictionary* (11th ed). Springfield, MA. Merriam-Webster Inc.

Pyrczak, F. (2011). *Writing empirical research reports: A basic guide for students of the social and behavioral sciences*. (7th ed.). Glendale, CA: Pyrczak Publishing.

Rubin, R. B., Rubin, A. M., & Piele, L. J. (2000). *Communication research: strategies and sources*. (5th ed.). Belmont, CA: Wadsworth.

VandenBos, G. R. (Ed.). (2009). *Publication manual of the American Psychology Association* (6th ed.). Washington, DC: American Psychology Association.

Whitely, S. (Ed.). (1994). *The American Library Association guide to information access: A complete research handbook and directory*. New York, NY: Random House.

CHAPTER 9

Supporting Your Ideas

Objectives

After reading this chapter, you should be able to

1. explain the difference between developing ideas with additional ideas and developing ideas with supporting material;
2. identify supporting material appropriate for developing your ideas;
3. use supporting material effectively in your presentations;
4. recognize factors of attention in supporting material;
5. incorporate factors of attention into your presentations; and
6. recognize fallacious use of supporting materials.

Topical Outline

THE DEVELOPMENT OF IDEAS
- The nature of claims
- The development of ideas with other ideas
- The development of ideas with supporting material

THE NATURE AND USES OF SUPPORTING MATERIAL
- The functions of support material
- Using supporting material
- Types of supporting material

FACTORS OF ATTENTION
- Using factors of attention
- Attention-grabbing qualities

FALLACIES

Key Concepts

Activity
Analogy
Anecdote
Argument by analogy
Argument by example
Argument by testimony
Audio-visual aid
Authority (Testimony)
Bandwagon (Popular opinion)
Bias
Central idea
Central tendency
- Mean
- Median
- Mode

Claim
- of fact
- of policy
- of value

Cliché
Comparison
Conflict
Jargon
Literal analogy
Main point
Measurement
Metaphor
Mixed metaphor
Name-calling (*Ad hominem*)
Parable
Paraphrase
Percentage
Contrast
Definition
Development of ideas
Direct quotation
Evidence
Example
Expert opinion (Testimony)
Explanation
Factors of attention
Fallacy
False cause (*Post hoc, ergo propter hoc)*
False division
Familiarity
Figurative analogy
Hasty generalization
Humor
Hypothetical example
Ideas
Illustration
Important information
Indirect quotation
Induction
Repetition
Restatement
Simile
Specific instance
Statistics
Story (Narrative)
- Climax, of narrative
- Closing, of narrative
- Complication, of narrative
- Scene, of narrative

Proverb
Proximity
Quantification
Quotation
Range
Real example
Reality
Reluctant witness
Supporting material
Surprise
Suspense
Testimony
Thesis
Typicality
Visual aids
Witness (Testimony)

Supporting Your Ideas

PERSPECTIVE

I. We begin by repeating the theme of this project: To communicate effectively we must always keep in mind the nature and expectations of our audience.
   A. Never forgetting the audience, our first stage in preparing for a presentation usually calls for our completing a cycle of four steps:
      1. assess the need for our presentation;
      2. set reasonable goals for the presentation;
      3. inventory our knowledge and feelings on the topic; and
      4. locate needed information on the subject.
   B. These steps are indeed a cycle, because once we have researched the topic, we often must reassess the need for our presentation and adjust our goals.
   C. Once we feel confident with our preparation cycle, we are ready to begin construction of the presentation.
      1. Many individuals prefer to list all of their ideas on the subject and then attempt to arrange the most important ones into a meaningful structure.
      2. Others visualize a structure immediately and rephrase their ideas to fit the pattern.
      3. We examine strategies of structure, or organization, in other chapters.

II. ***Purpose statement***: We believe you can develop important communication skills by first practicing your ability to develop the basic building block of a presentation—an idea plus its development. In the process, we shall focus not only on the ability to use supporting material well, but also to evaluate the supporting material of other speakers.

III. ***Preview***: First, we shall examine the basic building block of a speech; second, ways to develop ideas with supporting material; third, ways to make material an interesting listening experience for the audience; and finally, fallacies to avoid in idea development.

Chapter Body

I. **The Basic Unit of a Presentation.** The basic unit, or building block, of a presentation is an idea plus its development.
   A. An *idea* is a complete sentence that claims or denies that something is true or desirable.
      1. We can develop broad, complex ideas with other ideas.
      2. We can develop narrow, specific ideas with techniques we call forms of support.
   B. Ideas, or *claims*, have different names based on their importance to the structure of a presentation.
      1. The single unifying claim of a presentation is called the thesis or central idea.
      2. The thesis or central idea is developed by additional claims, the main points. To test the clarity and relevance of your main points apply this simple test.
         a. Recite your main points orally.
         b. Ask yourself, "Would a member of my audience be able to capture the thought and feeling of my thesis from hearing only these points?"
         c. If you find no one could identify the thesis, then you need to revise your main points. Why? Because expressing yourself clearly can only put you ahead of those who can't.
      3. Complex or controversial main points may require development with additional ideas called subpoints. Just as main points should develop a thesis, subpoints should develop a main point.
      4. Sometimes it is difficult to find a balance between simplicity and definiteness. But the time spent phrasing key ideas will increase your effectiveness as a communicator by allowing you to state your ideas easily and clearly, thereby helping your listeners grasp your intended meaning immediately.
   C. Ideas or claims may also be classified into three functional categories:
      1. Claims of fact, value, and policy.
         a. A *claim of fact* either (1) asserts or denies that something exists (present), existed (past), or will exist (future) or (2) defines what something is or is not.
         b. A *claim of value* answers the question, "Of what worth or morality is something?"
         c. A *claim of policy* answers the question, "What should be done?"

(1) A speaker who feels the audience would resent a direct request or order sometimes chooses to imply a policy claim in the actual presentation.

(2) Hence meaning, rather than absolute form, best categorizes policy claims.

2. The three claims each place different demands on the speaker. We shall explore these demands in the chapter on persuasive speaking.

D. Ultimately, we must use the second type of development. We must develop our specific ideas with forms of support, techniques that function to prove, clarify, or promote retention of our ideas.

II. **Supporting Material.** Developing our ideas with forms of support is a process of choosing and using techniques that help us better accomplish our goals. (This text provides "bare-bones" concepts and principles related to supporting material. Please refer to the "Encyclopedia" located on the Hayden-McNeil Web site for additional detailed explanation and examples.)

A. *Functions of support.* The use of support will play a major role in determining whether a listener understands, accepts, enjoys, and remembers the message.

1. For communication to occur, we need to be sure that our audience, be it one individual or many, is listening to us. Hence, we must get and hold the individual's attention.
2. When our goal is to inform, we need to help the listener to understand and remember our ideas.
3. When our goal is to persuade, we also need to change or intensify the listener's views of reality and reactions to the world.
    a. We must reach individuals on a more personal and emotional level.
    b. We will enhance our credibility if we use sound supporting materials and valid reasoning to back up our ideas. Responsible speakers test their evidence to make sure it is up-to-date, consistent, reliable, and valid.
4. Certainly there are many times in public speaking when we will give our opinions, but backing our opinions with facts will enhance their informative and persuasive value.
5. Providing interesting support to back up our ideas will enhance the enjoyment value of our presentations.

B. *Using support.* When developing ideas, we must find a balance between detail (a.k.a., accuracy) and brevity (a.k.a., simplicity).

1. Examine your support from the point of view of your listeners. If you had the experiences of these listeners, would you understand? Would you be feeling the appropriate emotions?
2. Choose details that stimulate the audience's senses to help your listeners experience the called for thoughts and feelings.

3. As the various types of support run through your head, you may feel lost about which to use. To guide your decisions, pay close attention to the functions of the various support forms. Note the ways in which they can provide proof, clarification, and/or retention of your ideas. Additionally, note the ways you can increase their effectiveness in a presentation.

C. Types of supporting materials.
1. *Examples.* The example is a versatile and powerful way to develop ideas. Well-constructed examples can make abstract ideas more concrete, understandable, persuasive, and memorable. Real examples are usually more meaningful to the audience members than hypothetical examples, but a carefully constructed hypothetical illustration can provide the specific support called for in a given situation. Examples may be brief or extended.
   a. Functions of examples.
      (1) Examples serve as the evidence in the reasoning process known as induction. We reason by induction when we draw general conclusions from specific cases.
      (2) When reasoning by example, we can increase the persuasiveness of our messages by showing that our examples are **typical**. When possible, back up your examples with a statistic or testimony that shows that your examples are **typical**. Similarly, think about ways you might use statistics or testimony to refute the negative examples that are likely to be in the minds of your listeners.
   b. Types of examples
      (1) <u>Specific instances</u>.
         (a) Speakers frequently use brief examples, also known as specific instances, to clarify an idea.
         (b) They present one specific example after another to make their point.
            i. Although this technique, through the sheer number of examples, can create an impression of typicality, good listeners will evaluate the typicality of each instance.
            ii. If they find fault with one instance, they may question your credibility and disregard the remaining examples.
      (2) <u>Stories</u>. Stories—also known as extended examples, illustrations and **narratives**—can be one of the most involving, enjoyable, and memorable ways to support your speech.
         (a) The story provides an effective contrast to the scientific nature of numbers and statistics.

(b) The story may have happened to you or others. It may be hypothetical. The story may be an anecdote, that is a brief amusing story that arouses interest or curiosity. It may be a parable, a story designed to illustrate a doctrine or moral. Whatever form it takes, the story must make a point.

(c) Like a good play, movie, or TV story, the fully developed story progresses through the appropriate stages of scene, complications, climax, and closing.

  i. The story begins by setting the scene in an interesting way that captures the attention of the listeners. To do this, we use words that paint a mental picture.

  ii. As the character or characters face complications, the story holds the attention of the audience, through suspense.

  iii. The complications are resolved in the climax (which may be a punch line in the humorous story).

  iv. In a presentation, the speaker usually ends by showing the typicality of the story or its relevance to a point of the speech.

(d) You will benefit from developing your ability to use stories. You will experience a strong sense of satisfaction from holding the attention of your audience while making your point.

(e) In a presentation, you must create an appropriate atmosphere for your story with your voice, body, and words.

(3) <u>Hypothetical Examples</u>. Real examples, brief or extended, focus on the past: They illustrate what has already occurred. Hypothetical examples emphasize conjecture, possibility, and probability—not certainty.

(a) The hypothetical example can illustrate what might have happened in the past, may be happening now, or could happen in the future.

  i. When we try to understand a current problem, we form hypotheses, that is guesses or hunches, about what may be happening or may have happened to cause the problem.

  ii. Considering the future, we often use hypothetical examples to predict the ways persons might respond to our or others' actions.

(b) Although hypothetical examples are products of the imagination, if we think they have occurred or are likely to occur, they influence our beliefs, attitudes, and actions. Lawyers often try to create possibilities that would exonerate their clients.

i. Hence, in presentations, your listeners must find your hypothetical examples realistic.
ii. Examples that are far-fetched may damage your credibility.

(c) You may use hypothetical examples when you want your listeners to experience a situation personally.

(d) You also can use the hypothetical example to help an audience understand your meaning. Throughout this text, you have seen many hypothetical examples used to clarify meaning.

(e) When you are the listener, watch out for hypothetical examples that make mere possibilities seem like probabilities or realities—especially examples that exploit ignorance, prejudice, or fear. In particular, beware of negative hypothetical scenarios regarding minorities, women and the disadvantaged that promote racism and discrimination.

(f) Be they real or hypothetical, brief or developed, examples can help you accomplish your goals as a communicator. Look first at your own experience for specific instances and stories. Most of us enjoy listening to others' experiences. And don't forget that your experience includes stories you remember from literature, history, and other speakers. Finally, while you are researching your topic, look for appropriate real examples and information you can blend into hypothetical examples.

2. *Quantification*. We live in the information age, and much of that information is numerical. Numerical data, or quantification, can give you the precision you need to clarify a point or the evidence you need to prove a point. Additionally, numerical data can enhance your credibility by demonstrating to your listeners the thoroughness of your research and the thoughtfulness of your analysis. Measurement and statistics are two quantitative tools for supporting our ideas.
    a. <u>Measurements</u>. Measurements of quantity, distance, length, and time are frequently helpful when informing an audience. You can help your listeners bridge the gap between the known and the unknown and the gap among individuals' experiences by using the precision of numerical measurement.
    b. <u>Statistics</u>. Statistics provide numerical information about an entire set of measurements.

(1) Speakers frequently find useful such statistics as the average (the mean, median, and mode), the range, and the percentage.
  (a) The mean, median, and mode, technically known as measures of central tendency (3 types of averages), allow us to identify the typical or average score among our measurements.
    i. The *mean*, also known as the arithmetic average, results from adding up the measurements and dividing by the total number of measurements.
    ii. The *median*, or middle score, involves arranging the scores from lowest to highest and finding the score in the middle.
    iii. The *mode* identifies the most frequently occurring score among the measurements. We could have multiple modes, if two or more scores tie as the most frequently occurring scores.
  (b) The *range* identifies the difference between the lowest and highest scores among the measurements.
    i. The range may be expressed by providing the end points of the range or the mathematic difference between them.
    ii. While both methods express the same range, their impact on listeners may differ.
  (c) The *percentage* expresses a portion of the entire set of scores as a part of 100.

(2) We may damage our credibility if listeners perceive we are using statistics carelessly, unfairly, or manipulatively. Hence, when we compare statistics, we must consider exactly what was measured and the way the measurements are expressed.

c. Quantification is sometimes difficult to understand when heard. Speakers have found that three techniques tend to increase the effectiveness of statistics presented orally.
  (1) Avoid overusing measurements and statistics. Consider using a visual aid in the form of a chart or graph to avoid losing your listeners in a series of hard-to-follow numbers.
  (2) Round off your statistics.
  (3) Consider ways to make important statistics meaningful to the audience.
    (a) Where appropriate, help the audience to visualize the meaning of the statistic.
    (b) You might help the listeners to respond more emotionally to the statistic by asking them to participate in a demonstration that illustrates the meaning of the statistic.

(c) Showing the way a statistic will affect your listeners, or the groups to which they belong, will almost always make the statistic more meaningful.

3. *Testimony*. The word "testimony" brings to mind the courtroom where attorneys call witnesses to share their observations or expert opinions for the jury to assess. In addition to testifying to your own experiences, you can support your ideas with the experiences, beliefs, or words of other individuals, be they lay persons or experts.
   a. The testimony of experts, or authorities on the subject, can be particularly useful in building credibility for your ideas.
      (1) When using testimony as evidence (argument by testimony) to try to prove a point, you should keep in mind, however, that eyewitnesses and even authorities can be wrong.
         (a) When witnesses are emotionally involved, their perceptions and memories can vary considerably from the facts.
         (b) Even experts can be wrong or misguided by self interests.
      (2) If listeners are to accept the conclusions of an authority, they must believe the authority is credible. When citing the opinions of experts, try to apply as many of the following suggestions as appear appropriate:
         (a) Be certain your material is up-to-date. It can be humiliating and disastrous to your credibility to cite authorities who have changed their minds.
         (b) Avoid extreme positions that have been attacked by other authorities. If you believe that your authority is correct, show how she or he arrived at the conclusion. Try backing up the opinion with other authorities, examples, statistics, and/or literal analogies (the 4 forms of support that function as evidence, or proof).
         (c) Share with the audience, in as few words as possible, the authority's special qualifications or special competencies. If they do not appear in the article, or other source that you are using, try looking up the name of the authority in the relevant biographical collection.
         (d) Show that your source is reliable and free from bias in this matter. Listeners tend to be particularly impressed by "reluctant witnesses" who speak against their own self interests.
   b. Often, you will find it necessary to paraphrase testimony to avoid long direct quotations that could bore the audience. Paraphrased quotations also are known as <u>indirect quotations</u>.
      (1) At other times you will judge a person's words so effective

that you cannot improve upon them. You may choose to use the exact words as a direct quotation.

(a) You may find eloquent material to quote in literature such as a famous story, play, or piece of poetry.

(b) A proverb, that is a short familiar sentence that expresses an accepted truth or moral, usually is picturesque, simple, and memorable.

(c) Several books of quotations allow speakers to locate quickly an appropriate and memorable quotation.

(2) On the other hand, you may choose to quote directly, not because of eloquence, but because someone expressed an idea with exceptional clarity, usefulness, or authority.

c. Although you will occasionally hear individuals begin and end direct quotations with phrases such as "quote" and "end quote," most public speaking teachers consider the practice old-fashioned. We encourage you to signal the beginning and ending of direct quotations with more subtle techniques such as by changing your tone of voice or by lifting and lowering your notes containing the quotation.

4. *Analogy*. One of the ways we try to understand, predict, and control our world involves our looking for similar patterns of form (the way things are built or shaped) and function (the way things act or operate, benefit or harm us). In search of similar patterns, or analogies, we compare and contrast. A comparison shows the ways two or more things are similar, while a contrast shows the ways two or more things are different. Specialized types of comparisons and contrasts include the literal analogy and the figurative analogy, including the simile and the metaphor.

a. Comparison and contrast.

(1) From hearing important similarities and differences among a set of people, places, or ideas listeners can better understand the nature of each.

(2) When as speaker you compare or contrast new information or ideas to ones the audience already knows, you will be using a valued approach to understanding and agreement.

b. Literal analogies. The literal analogy is a comparison most often used as evidence to convince or persuade a receiver.

(1) An argument by analogy assumes that what is true in a known situation should also be true in another situation, if the two situations are adequately similar.

(2) If you are speaking to a listener who supports your claim, the listener may accept a literal analogy uncritically.

(3) On the other hand, if your listeners oppose your claim, you will need to demonstrate that the situations are similar and that you have accurately portrayed both situations.

(4) Hence, to develop a literal analogy for an argument, you will probably need to use other forms of support such as real examples, statistics, and testimony to show that the situations you are comparing are similar.

c. Figurative analogies. The figurative analogy is a comparison of unlike things that share a common characteristic. For example, you might compare insurance to an umbrella that provides protection when situations go badly.

(1) The common element highlights the speaker's point, often making it more memorable.

(2) *Metaphors and similes*. We use a metaphor when we call a person, animal, object, or event something it is not in order to imply a comparison. We use a simile when we use words such as "like" or "as" to compare the two items.

(a) Many metaphors and similes are so familiar that they have become *clichés*. Hence, look for fresh comparisons for your metaphors and similes.

(b) Avoid *mixing metaphors*.

i. We mix metaphors when we shift, during a single comparison, from one comparison to another. "It's water under the dam"; or is it "water over the bridge"? Got the picture?

ii. The listener, who has been trying to grasp the implications of the original metaphor must now devote energy to understanding the shift in perspective. Confusion or irritation is the likely result.

5. *Explanation*. When you provide more detailed information to clarify your meaning, you are explaining. Hence, you can explain your ideas with all forms of support, except for repetition.

a. By the support form labeled explanation, we refer to those segments of the presentation that describe the characteristics, functions, or parts of an object, process, event, or idea.

(1) Explanations provide answers to such questions as What? How? and Why?

(2) Definitions are explanations of the meaning of a word or idea. Definitions are necessary when you use specialized terms or jargon unfamiliar to the audience. Jargon is the language used by a particular field of study or professional work.

b. Long and complicated explanations quickly confuse an audience and create disinterest.

(1) Use simple, but vivid, language.

(2) Present details and ideas in an orderly fashion.

   c. You should **avoid overusing abstract explanations** at the expense of more concrete forms of support such as examples, statistics, and comparisons.
6. *Repetition and restatement.* When we say a word, phrase, or sentence again, we repeat. When we put an idea into new words, we restate.
   a. Repetition and restatement help reinforce the ideas we wish to communicate.
   b. Repetition and restatement promote learning.
      (1) In order for the audience to understand and remember an idea, usually the speaker must present the idea several times.
      (2) You do not want to become boring and tedious by using the same words over and over. Hence, by changing the wording of your statements and using different forms of support, you can restate your ideas to provide emphasis and promote clarity and retention.
   c. Repetition can serve additional functions in a presentation.
      (1) One such purpose is to emphasize a movement from one point to another. In the process of repeating a phrase in a series of points, the speaker adds emphasis to the theme of the points.
      (2) Repetition also can serve as a powerful tool in persuasion. Speakers may repeat striking slogans or phrases to reach an audience emotionally.
7. *Audio-visual aids.* Maps and globes, models and real objects, recordings, posters, chalkboard drawings, flip-charts, projections, and computer-generated graphics are just a few of the audio-visual aids that presenters commonly use.
   a. Audio-visual aids can increase the audience's understanding, interest, and retention.
   b. Audio-visual aids should enhance and reinforce the ideas in your presentation.
      (1) Perhaps one of the most common errors in presentations is using either too few or too many audio-visual aids.
      (2) Use visual aids that promote understanding and retention or that emphasize a point. But remember that emphasizing everything results in emphasizing nothing.
   c. Before you prepare or select your aids, try to visualize the way you will use them.
      (1) Your aids must be large or loud enough for your audience to see or hear them.
      (2) They must be simple or clear enough for your audience to grasp them.
   d. Once you have prepared or selected your aids, you should practice with them in advance. From doing a trial run, you can anticipate your needs during the actual presentation.

(1) You might need an extension cord, an assistant to uncover or remove aids or to help you with equipment, or far more time than your presentation permits.
(2) Failure to anticipate your needs may result in awkward or embarrassing actions that could reduce your credibility or increase your tension.
(3) Plan and practice ways to avoid distracting your listeners with aids when they are not in use.
   (a) Decide when and how you will turn on and off an overhead projector, uncover and cover a model, expose and remove charts.
   (b) Be familiar with the equipment and software if you plan to use computer-generated graphics.
   (c) Generally, visual aids should not be passed among audience members if the aids will draw attention from your words.
      i. Some speakers distribute at the end of a speech printed copies of materials they projected or displayed during the speech.
      ii. If the listeners must work with equipment you are teaching them to use, you will need to adjust to the potential distractions involved. You might need to allow more time for your explanations or practice ways to draw back the full attention of the audience at important points in the presentation.
   (d) Practice will increase your confidence in your presentation.
   (e) Should something go wrong, adjust your use of the audio-visual aids naturally, drawing as little attention to the problem as possible. Your audience will admire your ability to keep problems in perspective and solve them without apparent panic or effort.

III. **Factors of Attention.** Factors of attention are qualities of ideas and supporting materials that encourage a desire to listen to the speaker.
   A. Using factors of attention.
      1. As you review your experiences and research your topic, look for supporting materials that will hold your listeners' attention.
      2. After you construct your outline, review the following factors of attention and attempt to incorporate them into the support you have chosen.

B. Types of factors of attention.
   1. *Activity* attracts attention. Activity, or movement, may be physical or mental.
      a. The speaker who stands rigidly in front of the audience generates less attention than the same speaker who moves naturally and with purpose by gesturing, walking in front of the audience, and handling visual aids.
      b. Similarly, content that moves forward mentally rather than devotes too much time to minor or irrelevant points helps listeners remain involved.
   2. *Conflict* can also arouse attention, whether it is a conflict of ideas, a conflict of "facts," or a conflict among people.
   3. *Familiarity* draws attention because people feel comfortable (or perhaps uncomfortable) with those things they know and have experienced. You know you are using this factor if your listeners smile and groan with recognition as they hear of certain types of physical examinations or other common experiences.
   4. *Humor* can be an effective attention device in public speaking, if used appropriately.
      a. Humor should pertain to the topic of the speech.
      b. Humor should not offend the audience.
         (1) Speakers will generally enhance their image by making themselves, rather than the audience, the object of the humor.
         (2) A speaker should consider the consequences of humor that the audience might consider as stereotyping or attacking a group of people.
         (3) Speakers should not be surprised if the audience takes literally humor meant to be figurative.
   5. *Important* information is that which the audience finds relevant and motivating. Such information relates to the health, happiness, security, and well-being of the listeners or individuals important to them.
   6. *Proximity* arouses attention because people are more interested in that which is close to them in space or time than that which is distant.
   7. *Reality* can be an effective attention device because the audience is more interested in actual people, events, and problems, than hypothetical ones.
   8. *Surprise* arouses attention because it is unexpected. Some business researchers indicate that surprise is one of the best techniques for holding the attention of an adult audience.
   9. *Suspense* captures the attention of listeners who desire to know what the outcome will be.

IV. While a speaker may use interesting forms of support that may seem to "prove" ideas, both as a speaker and as a listener, individuals must be able to identify fallacies. Fallacies are intentional or accidental mistakes in the use of reasoning or support that lead the speaker or listener to incorrect conclusions. Kahane (1976) advances the definition by explaining that "... a fallacy is an argument that should not persuade a rational person to accept its conclusion" (p. 2). While Kahane (1976) identifies nearly 50 types of fallacious arguments, we shall examine only 5 common fallacies: the hasty generalization, the false division, the appeal to popular opinion, the false cause, and name-calling.

A. A *hasty generalization* draws a conclusion based on insufficient evidence. For instance, because a particular employee in a department store appeared incompetent, it would be fallacious to conclude that all employees are incompetent. To make a generalization from specific examples, a speaker needs to show that the examples are relevant and typical.

B. The *false division* occurs when a speaker divides or categorizes an issue in an artificial or arbitrary way. A speaker who says, "There are three solutions to the problem of pollution in our society," is using a false division. The problem of pollution is an extremely complex one. Depending upon your point of view, the solutions may vary from none to many.

C. The *appeal to popular opinion*, or *bandwagon*, occurs when a speaker attempts to rally support by claiming "everybody thinks so" or "everybody is doing it." Perhaps all of us remember when we told our parent(s) or guardian(s), "All my friends are going to..." In all likelihood those responsible for us said, "But I'm not responsible for them; I am responsible for you. And in this house..."

D. The *false cause* (also known by its Latin name of *post hoc, ergo propter hoc*) occurs when one asserts that because $event_1$ occurred before $event_2$, $event_1$ is the cause of $event_2$. Just because you washed your car before the rain doesn't mean washing your car caused the rain. Or did it?

E. A speaker who finds it difficult to attack an opponent's arguments may attack the opponent on personal issues. The personal attack is labeled *name-calling* (also commonly known by its Latin name of *ad hominem*). An ethical speaker will focus on the issues rather than demean an opponent.

Closing Remarks

You can increase the effectiveness of your communication if you develop your ideas with a variety of interesting forms of support. Additionally, developing a sensitivity to fallacies will help you develop your critical listening skills.

References and Suggestions for Further Readings

Brummett, B. (1984). The representative anecdote as a Burkean method, applied to evangelical rhetoric. *The Southern Speech Communication Journal*, *50*, 1–23.

Ehninger, D., Gronbeck, B. E., Monroe, A. H., & Moore, L. (1984). *Principles of speech communication.* 9th brief edition. Glenview, IL: Scott, Foresman.

Fisher, W. R. (1978). Toward a logic of good reasons. *Quarterly Journal of Speech, 64*, 376–384.

Gruner, C. R. (1993). Audience's response to jokes in speeches with and without recorded laughs. *Psychological Reports, 73*, 347–350.

Gruner, C. R. (1985). Advice to the beginning speaker on using humor—What the research tells us. *Communication Education, 34*, 142–147.

Irby, C. (1989, January 22). *The Kansas City Star*. p. 1–2G.

Kahane, H. (1976). *Logic and contemporary rhetoric: The use of reason in everyday life*. Belmont, CA: Wadsworth.

Kirkwood, W. G. (1985). Parables as metaphors and examples. *The Quarterly Journal of Speech, 71*, 422–440.

Miller, M. (1989). *You be the jury*. NY: Scholastic Inc., pp. 21–25.

Stewart, L. P., Cooper, P. J., & Friedley, S. A. (1986). *Communication between the sexes: Sex differences and sex-role stereotypes*. Scottsdale, AZ: Gorsuch Scarisbrick.

Van Til, W. (1986). *Writing for professional publication*. Boston: Allyn and Bacon.

CHAPTER 10

Developing and Using Your Presentational Aids

COMM 210

Objectives

After reading this chapter, you should be able to

1. contrast the advantages and disadvantages of using visual aids in a presentation;
2. identify the types of visual aids appropriate for a specific presentation;
3. prepare appropriate and effective visual aids for a presentation; and
4. use visual aids effectively during a presentation.

Topical Outline

VALUES OF VISUAL AIDS

- Increase comprehension
- Make ideas memorable
- Heighten interest

CHARACTERISTICS OF WELL-PREPARED VISUAL AIDS

- Useful
- Visible/Audible
- Comprehensible
- Professional

TYPES OF PRESENTATIONAL AIDS

- Not requiring electronic equipment
- Requiring electronic equipment

USING AIDS EFFECTIVELY

Key Concepts

Actual objects
Animals
Appropriateness
Audio aids
Bar graph
Boards
Chalkboard
Charts
Common errors
in the use of presentational aids
Computer-generated graphics
Diagrams
Dry-erase marker board
Effective use of visual aids
Electronic equipment
Emerging technologies
Felt, Velcro, or magnetic boards
Films
Flip chart
Flow chart
Graphics
Graphs
Handouts
Line graph
Maps
Objects
Overhead projector
Persons
Photographs
Physical models
Pie graph
Posters
Professionalism
Simplicity
Slides and slideware
Values of visual aids
Video aids
Visibility
Well-prepared presentational aids

Presentational Aids

PERSPECTIVE

I. Effective presentational aids enhance a speaker's message. Such devices include charts, posters, PowerPoints, pictures, objects, computer-generated graphics, video/audio recordings, and more. Rather than consider presentational aids an addendum to a speech, you should consider them an integral part of most presentations. You can use presentational aids to improve significantly the effectiveness of your messages.

II. ***Purpose statement***: The purpose of this chapter is to familiarize you with the advantages and disadvantages of using presentational aids. Our goal is to help you use presentational aids effectively in your presentations.

III. ***Preview***: First we present the values of using presentational aids; second we examine the qualities of a well-prepared presentational aid; third, we examine various types of aids; and we conclude with the discussion of their use.

Chapter Body

I. **Values of Presentational Aids.**
   A. A primary reason for using presentational aids is that they can *increase audience comprehension* by making the material more understandable.
      1. Presentational aids can give the audience a concrete representation of an abstract concept.
      2. When the audience is unfamiliar with a process that the speaker discusses, a presentational aid can help clarify the content for the audience.
      3. Presentational aids are especially helpful when the listeners are trying to imagine objects with which they are unfamiliar.
   B. Second, presentational aids make a speech *more memorable*.
      1. The aid serves as a visual restatement of the spoken word.
      2. Most individuals remember more of what they see than of what they hear.
   C. Third, presentational aids can create *interest*.
      1. Presentational aids can help you to gain and direct the listeners' attention.
      2. Aids can help you establish an appropriate mood for the presentation.
      3. Including aids can add variety to your speech.

II. **Characteristics of Well-Prepared Presentational Aids.**
   A. You should select and use presentational aids that will *enhance the presentation*.

1. One of the most common errors in the use of presentational aids is to use too few or too many.
    a. If you use too few aids, the audience may find it difficult to understand and remember your message.
    b. If you use too many, your aids will fail to emphasize your most important ideas, and you risk not emphasizing anything.
    c. For example a good rule for PowerPoint presentations is to have no more than one text slide per minute of presentation.
2. Presentational aids should be appropriate for the situation, as different situations will have different requirements for presentational aids.
    a. Certain types of presentational aids should be avoided or at least used carefully.
    b. For example, a speaker may find that animals can be unpredictable presentational aids.
    c. The reactions of the audience to shocking materials make them risky presentational aids.
    d. The presentational aid should also reflect good taste and sensitivity to the audience members.
    e. Avoid potentially insulting content, and conduct an effective audience analysis to account for potential allergies to objects introduced in the speech.
    f. The presentational aid should be accessible to all audience members regardless of abilities.
    g. An audience analysis could help you decide what types of presentational aids to use or which ones to avoid.
3. Presentational aids should be worth the time, energy and money required to produce them.
    a. You may use your time unwisely if you spend 10% of your speech preparation time on planning the speech and 90% of your time creating visual presentational aids.
    b. You may spend your money poorly if less expensive aids would be equally effective.

B. All members of *the audience should be able to see and/or hear your presentational aids.*
1. Presentational aids must be large enough for the audience members to see clearly.
2. If your presentational aid is too small, it may detract more from your speech than it adds.
3. If audience members are spending too much time trying to read or see your aid, they are not paying complete attention to your presentation.
4. Sound tracks must not only be clear and free from noise, but also the sound system must be appropriate for the size of the room.

C. Presentational aids should be *simple* enough for the audience to grasp the content immediately.
   1. If an aid is too complex, audience members may be forced to focus on the aid and not on the speaker.
   2. This could result in audience members missing key concepts of the presentation while attempting to make sense of the aid.

D. Presentational aids should look as *professional* as possible.
   1. Sloppy, ill-constructed presentational aids may lower your credibility rather than contribute to the effectiveness of the presentation.
   2. Before preparing poster boards, visit your local copy center to discover the services it can provide in preparation of such a presentational aid.
   3. If electronic equipment is not available one option is to convert a PowerPoint into a poster presentation by printing the slides and attaching them to a poster board
   4. At Ball State, the GIS Research and Map Collection (GRMC) on the second floor of the Bracken library offers large scale printing and laminating services.

III. **Types of Presentational Aids.** Only your imagination limits the variety of types of materials that you can use as presentational aids. Advances in computer-generated graphics, copying techniques, and video delivery systems provide the speaker with easy and effective opportunities for constructing presentational aids. Below are different types of aids you may find helpful during your presentations.

A. Even without the benefit of electronic equipment during a presentation, a speaker can use objects, handouts, graphics, and boards to enhance the spoken message.
   1. <u>Objects</u>. Physical objects, both animate and inanimate, can serve as effective presentational aids for the public speaker.
      a. Animate or living objects are sometimes used in speeches.
         (1) Many college speech instructors prohibit the use of animals in speeches because of previous negative experiences.
            (a) An animal may be unpredictable and disruptive not only during your speech, but during the speeches before and after you.
            (b) If you choose to use an animal, have a friend who is familiar with the animal accompany you.
            (c) The friend can bring the animal to the classroom and stay outside with it, and then bring the animal in at the moment you want to show it during your speech.
         (2) A person can also serve as a presentational aid.
            (a) The speaker is always the first presentational aid.

(b) The movements and dress of a speaker should always be considered in the same way as any other presentational aid.
(c) The speaker can be an effective aid when demonstrating a task or action, as they are already the focus of the audience's attention.
(c) If a speaker is demonstrating an action it is important for them not to turn their back to any parts of their audience or limit eye contact.
(d) If a demonstration is required it may be more beneficial to have a second person act as the aid allowing the speaker to maintain appropriate eye contact with all of the audience.

b. Inanimate objects, including materials, equipment, and physical models can help to illustrate a process or phenomenon or to create a mood.
(1) Actual materials and equipment are particularly helpful in teaching the listener the way to do something.
(2) Physical models are particularly helpful when the actual objects are either too large or too small for use in a presentation.
(a) Models can provide a concrete representation of an abstract idea.
(b) Models can simplify a complex process.
(c) If a pre-constructed model is not available, you should give yourself enough time to gather materials and build the model.
(3) Physical objects also can create an appropriate atmosphere, or mood, for a presentation (for instance, decorations and refreshments).

2. Handouts. Handouts allow the audience to take a useful record of information from the speaking situation.
a. A handout you made yourself or one designed professionally may enable you to continue your message after you stop talking.
b. Distributing a handout, or any object, during a presentation often causes problems for a speaker.
(1) As members of the audience pass the handout, they are likely to start reading and miss the words of the speaker.
(2) Once they have the handout, the audience members may read the handout, rather than pay close attention to the speaker.
(3) Unless the audience must follow complex material, as in a business or decision-making meeting, we suggest you distribute material to the audience at the end of your presentation.

(4) If audience members need the handout to follow the presentation always hand it out ahead of time to avoid the distraction of handing it out during the presentation.

3. Graphics. Graphics are two-dimensional representations of reality, probability, possibility, or imagination. Graphics may include graphs, photographs, diagrams, charts, maps, and others.
   a. Photographs provide a highly realistic representation of reality.
      (1) When using a projected image it is important to know how the image will look on the screen you will be showing it on.
      (2) We suggest asking your instructor to let you test your image in the classroom prior to your presentation day so that if it is blurry, too big, or too small, you can find another picture.
   b. Diagrams and drawings can be tailored to the specific points being made in the presentation.
      (1) When a physical model is not available, a diagram can provide an effective alternative.
      (2) Drawings can provide a simplified and inexpensive alternative for photographs.
         (a) Draw the picture as neatly as you can, or enlist the help of an artistic friend.
         (b) Be sure to provide appropriate labels so that your audience can easily make sense of the drawing.
   c. Charts and posters also provide useful presentational aids.
      (1) Charts can be as simple as a list of ideas you wish to reinforce.
         (a) The ideas may be words or phrases representing the main ideas of your presentation.
            i. To promote suspense, you should reveal each item on the list at the appropriate time.
            ii. You can increase the impact of lists of ideas by using a mnemonic, or memory, aid.
         (b) The ideas may be numerical or statistical data.
      (2) Flow charts show the breakdown of different steps in a process or parts of a system.
         (a) These help an audience follow stages or steps in a process over time.
      (3) Flip charts are large pads of paper mounted on an easel.
         (a) Flip charts are particularly helpful when recording ideas offered from the audience.
         (b) You can tape to the wall multiple sheets so that the audience can view all of the ideas for group reflection and discussion.

(c) When use of an overhead projector is not feasible, you can prepare a flip chart in advance so that you can reveal information at the proper time.

d. Graphs provide a specialized visual representation of numerical data that are generally easy to read and understand because they provide visual comparisons.

(1) Three common types of graphs are the pie graph, the bar graph, and the line graph.

(a) A pie graph divides the pie or circle according to percentages or portions of 100% highlighting the relative size of the parts that make up a whole.

(b) A bar graph expresses percentages or amounts by the height of bars located next to each other expressing the relationships among multiple variables over time, location, or topic.

(c) A line graph, which shows the distribution of categories through one or more lines placed next to each other, is well suited to showing trends or changes over time.

(2) All three types of graphs are relatively simple for the public speaker to prepare.

(a) Most computer graphics programs will allow you to enter the numbers and experiment with the format of your graph.

(b) Graphs will allow you to express numerical relationships in an interesting, understandable, and memorable manner.

(3) When using a projected graph, much like a picture, it is important to check how the image will appear on the screen you will be using to present.

(a) This will assure that the graph is easy to read from the distance the audience will view it from.

(b) It is important to make sure the type of graph you use is an appropriate choice for showing your data, if not your audience may not understand your point.

(c) Another risk with the use of graphs is that, if the information is more easily explained verbally, then the graph may be more distracting than helpful.

4. <u>Boards</u>.

a. The chalkboard can create special challenges for a speaker.

(1) The chalkboard is handy when you need to write or draw something quickly.

(a) If you have no experience with a chalkboard, a little practice will help.

i. Many people find it difficult to write neatly and in a straight line on a chalkboard.
ii. Speaking with your back to the audience may break the flow of your presentation.
iii. This could result in the audience missing important details leaving them confused.
iv. Material left on the chalkboard can distract the audience during the remainder of the presentation.

(b) If you have something that requires more than a few seconds to write, you should opt for a prepared presentational aid.

(2) Because of the potential problems in using a chalkboard, many speech teachers discourage its use in a classroom presentation.

b. Although they have many of the same disadvantages as do chalkboards, dry-erase marker boards offer more advantages.
   (1) The markers do not create the dust of chalk:
      (a) Their ink erases quickly (if you don't use a permanent marker that can ruin the board).
      (b) The markers come in a variety of bold colors that provide greater interest value and visibility than does chalk.
   (2) Additionally, the speaker can write with the marker more as he or she would with a regular pen.
   (3) Messy writing and turning their back on the audience are common mistakes with dry-erase boards as well as chalkboards.

c. Some speakers like to use felt, Velcro, or magnetic boards.
   (1) Teachers frequently use boards to display characters and scenes in a story.
   (2) These boards can result in an exhibit for display after the presentation.

B. Forms of electronic equipment provide ever-increasing ways to present graphics and other types of presentational aids.
   1. When using electronic equipment, you should take special precautions.
      a. First and foremost, you should know how to operate the equipment with ease and confidence.
      b. Additionally, you should be familiar with the facility in which you will give the presentation.
      c. You will avoid possible disaster if you know where the electrical outlets are, and if you have the needed extension cord, replacement bulb, appropriate screen, or other required items.
      d. Only by rehearsing with the actual equipment can you visualize the needs for your final presentation.

1. Video aids allow you to depict situations in action.
    a. Because of limited time in most speeches, you will probably use only a brief segment from the full video.
        (1) A variety of commercially produced films are available today in libraries and on the Internet.
        (2) You may also make your own videos using a video camera or recording a television broadcast.
        (3) When using commercially produced videos and videos of televised broadcasts, you should not violate copyright laws.
    b. When using videos, make sure you preview them in their entirety.
        (1) You will need to know the exact content to provide an appropriate introduction for the clip.
        (2) The video clip could be dated, boring, or contain shocking material, and the audience should know this previous to viewing.
2. Audio aids. While video clips usually appeal to the sense of sound as well as that of sight, sometimes, a sound clip itself can serve as an effective aid in a presentation.
    a. Religious and political organizations often use music to create an appropriate mood.
    b. Musical selections would certainly increase the effectiveness of a presentation dealing with a musical instrument or type of music.
    c. Segments of interviews may help to build your credibility or create an emotional response from the audience.
    d. When using audio aid, you will need to take basic precautions.
        (1) Be sure the audio clip is cued to the exact starting time.
        (2) Be sure that the sound system can provide adequate volume.
        (3) Be sure that the recording is distinct and free of irritating noise.
3. Slideware. Slideware is becoming a more and more commonly used technology.
    a. Computer enhanced presentations (such as PowerPoint) have become the baseline of persuasive communication especially in the business world.
    b. On the Bracken Library website under services the software locator link can help you locate software you wish to use and which library computers have that software.
    c. While it is not the only option of slideware technology, PowerPoint dominates the technical aid arena.
        (1) A general suggestion is that for PowerPoint you should include no more than one text slide per minute of speech.

(2) You also want to carefully choose your font; Times New Roman and Calibri are strong choices because they are professional in appearance and easy to read.
(3) Font size should also be considered, if it is too small the audience will struggle to see, if too big it will be distracting and equally difficult to read.
(4) A good font size for the slide titles is between 38 and 44, and for the text in the slide between 28 and 36.
(5) Always test your slides in the classroom previous to the presentation day in order to assure your choices were appropriate.

d. Another option for presentation software is Prezi.
(1) Prezi is a free online software which does not follow the standard linear presentation format.
(2) This software has many benefits because of its non-standard format including keeping the audience interested.
(3) However, this can often make a presentation difficult to follow.
(4) Whichever program is used, make sure the presentation is not confusing to the audience.

e. It is also important to understand the basics of graphic design principles to enhance effectiveness of slides.
(1) Contrast: Make sure the contrast is pleasing to the eye, and easy to see.
(a) Certain color schemes will clash, resulting in difficulty for the audience.
(b) For example, certain shades of red can be hard to see on a black background.
(c) Other color schemes make for easy viewings and may in fact create a positive mood in audience members.
(d) Yellow text on light blue for example can create a soothing mood in your audience, just make sure the contrast is appropriate.
(2) Alignment: There should be a consistent pattern of alignment between all the slides.
(a) Titles should be in a consistent location, and text should be placed in a standard pattern.
(b) A lack of consistency can cause a presentational aid to lose effectiveness as audience members are trying to decipher a slide rather than listening to the speaker.
(c) This inconsistency can also result in the speaker losing credibility, as the presentational aid reflects on the speaker.

(3) Proximity: The presenter should be conscious of the size of the screen and how their slides will appear in the presentation space.
   (a) Whenever possible check the appearance of your presentational aid with the projector and screen you will be using in the final presentation.
   (b) This will also allow you to become aware of difficulties with the equipment you may face during the presentation.
(4) Repetition: Not only is repetition good for the memory of the audience, but consistency between slides adds to the feeling of a cohesive presentation.

IV. **Effective Use of Presentational Aids.** Effective use of visual aids can add much to a speech, just as ineffective use of presentational aids can detract from the speech.
   A. Visual aids are just that—aids—and they cannot compensate for a poorly constructed or researched speech.
   B. When constructing a visual aid one should consider the audience, practice using the aid, and use pathos effectively.
      1. *Audience Analysis* is important in constructing a visual aid.
         a. Always consider how an audience might react to the presentational aid.
         b. A presenter should be conscious of possible allergic reactions to animals or edible objects.
         c. Presenters should also be conscious of audience's cultural feelings towards images.
         d. Audience analysis also includes situational analysis; be sure the visual aid is appropriate for the situation.
         e. Also be aware of disabilities of audience members, presentational aids should be accessible to all; when necessary provide an alternative aid in order to accommodate to all audience member's needs.
         f. It can also be helpful to vary types of visual aids to account for the different learning types.
      2. *Practice* is essential when using a presentational aid.
         a. Many presentations fall short because of poor use of slideware.
            (1) The audience can easily be distracted by the background being too busy
            (2) An excessive amount of animation and sound can often result in reduced comprehension.
            (3) Be certain the graphics are clear and easy to understand

(4) Keep the text to a minimum, as the slides should not be able to present the information by themselves.
(5) Remember that slides cannot act as a substitute for transitions.
(6) Not practicing, especially how slides will be changed can often result in a sloppy presentation.

b. Do not sacrifice visibility of speaker for visibility of an aid.
c. Do not block the audience's view of you presentational aid (this is true for many forms of aid).
d. Murphy's Law states that anything that can go wrong will go wrong, but by practicing you can begin to account for some of these problems before they occur making them less noticeable in the final presentation.
e. It is also important to practice using a video clip or sound bite even though it may seem simple.
   (1) It is always necessary to know and preset the spot you want to start the video ahead of time
   (2) If using a video clip of the Internet be sure to load the clip and test it just before the actual presentation as well as when practicing.
   (3) Do not be afraid to skip the video if a problem emerges; do not struggle with technology during the presentation.
   (4) Never assume anything, have a backup plan in case the clip malfunctions.

3. As mentioned earlier certain color combinations on your presentational aids, especially slideware, can impact the emotions of your audience enhancing your use of pathos (emotional appeals).
   a. The color combination used, especially in slide presentations, can impact the mood of the audience.
   b. It is also important to consider how the text and background colors interact because setting the mood can influence the perception of the audience.
   c. Warm combinations include yellow on white, blue on white, or yellow on light blue.
   d. Harsh emotions can be emphasized through blue on black, yellow on black, and yellow on red.
   e. It is important to be conscious of the ease of seeing the text on the background; low contrast can be easily seen on a computer screen but when projected large scale it can be near impossible to see.

Closing Remarks

Presentational aids can yield major dividends to a speaker who knows how to use them effectively. Considering the situation, and audience can help guide your choices. By making appropriate choices with presentational aids you can create the maximum impact on your audience and give an effective presentation.

References and Suggestions for Further Readings

Cavanaugh, D. (2006). *Preparing Visual Aides for Presentations.* (4th ed.). Boston, MA: Allyn and Bacon.

Cyphert, D. (2004). The problem of powerpoint: Visual aid or visual rhetoric. *Business Communication Quarterly, 67*, 80–84. doi: 10.1177/1080569904671008

Cyphert, D. (2007). Presentation technology and the age of electronic eloquence: From visual aids to visual rhetoric. *Communication Education, 56*, 168–192. doi: 10.1080/03634520601173136

King, J. W. (1992). A primer on using visuals in technical presentations. *Food Technology, 46*, 157–164.

Mandel, S. (1987). *Effective presentation skills.* Los Altos, CA: Crisp Publication.

O'Malley, C. (1986). Driving your point home. *Personal Computing, 10*, 86–100.

Raines, C. (1989). *Visual aids in business.* Los Altos, CA: Crisp Publications.

Reynolds, G. (2008). *Presentation zen: Simple ideals on presentation design and delivery*. Berkeley, CA: New Riders.

Romo, R. & Boone, B. (1982). *How to make and use your own visual delights.* Rowley, M.A: Newburry House.

Seiler, W. J. (1971). The effects of visual materials on attitudes, credibility, and retention. *Speech Monographs, 38*, 331–334. doi: 10.1080/03637757109375727

Vik, G. N. (2004). Breaking bad habits: Teaching effective powerpoint use to working graduate students. *Business Communication Quarterly, 67*, 225–228.

CHAPTER 11

Your Informative Presentations

Objectives

After reading this chapter, you should be able to

1. explain the types, values, and challenges of informative presentations; and
2. apply the principles of simplicity, clarity, credibility, and interest to your own informative presentations.

Topical Outline

TYPES, VALUES, AND CHALLENGES OF INFORMATIVE SPEAKING

- Types of informative speaking
- Values of informative speaking
- Challenges of informative speaking

PRINCIPLES OF SPEAKING TO INFORM

- Simplicity
- Clarity
  - Language
  - Appropriate support
- Credibility
  - Competence
  - Trustworthiness
  - Dynamism
- Interest
  - Motivation
  - Factors of attention
  - Audience participation

CONSTRUCTING THE INFORMATIVE PRESENTATION

- Introduction
- Body
- Conclusion

Key Concepts

- Audience participation
- Clarity
- Comparison/contrast
- Credibility
  - Competence
  - Dynamism
  - Trustworthiness
- Didactic method
- Examples
- Explanations
- Factors of attention
- Figurative analogies
- Interest
- Internal previews
- Internal summaries
- Mnemonic device
- Motivation
- Preview
- Repetition and restatement
- Retention
- Seven-plus-or-minus-two Rule
- Simplicity
- Speaking to inform
- Understanding
- Visual aids

Informational Presentations

PERSPECTIVE

I. As college students, we have participated as receivers and senders in countless informative speaking events. Some of these events were highly successful; some were dismal failures. The most successful events were probably interesting, clear, and useful. We may even remember much (or at least some) of the information. The unsuccessful events were probably boring, confusing, and worthless. We probably remember little of the covered information.

II. ***Purpose***: The purpose of this chapter is to focus on techniques that promote success in informative presentations. Most of these techniques appear earlier in this text. We hope, however, that you find our summary and new material useful.

III. ***Preview***: First, we shall explore the nature of informative speaking. Next we shall present four major principles of speaking effectively to inform. We conclude with suggestions for structuring informative presentations.

Chapter Body

I. **Types, Values, and Challenges of Informative Speaking.** A presentation with the general purpose "to inform" helps an audience understand and remember information. An informative presentation may focus on understanding ideas (for example: concepts, rules, processes, and events) or building skills (that is, increasing the listener's ability to carry out a task or action).
   A. *Types of Informative Speaking*. The specific requirements of the situation may call for giving demonstrations, giving instructions, exploring a question of fact, presenting an oral report, providing everyday explanations, and devising speeches about concepts, events, objects, and processes.
      1. Providing a demonstration requires the speaker to show the audience how something is done.
      2. Giving instructions requires the speaker to teach the audience how to do something. Often listeners can best learn how to do something by also seeing how it is done (that is, receiving a demonstration as well as instructions).
      3. Exploring a question of fact requires the speaker to provide objective information about the truth of a situation.
      4. Presenting an oral report requires the speaker to present information in a relatively formal organizational, professional, or social setting.
      5. Everyday explanations are the kinds of informative messages we give in interpersonal situations, business meetings, the classroom, and other situations.

6. Informative speeches may be about concepts (ideas), events (situations that took place), objects (things), processes (a series or structure of events), conditions (circumstances, situations, or states of a person, place, or thing), places, or about people.

B. *Value of informative speaking.* Enhancing your ability to inform others should serve you well in your career.
   1. For instance, you may find yourself responsible for showing a client how to use a product, for explaining rules and procedures to other employees, for building the skills of employees, for making a report to a group of your superiors or subordinates, or for describing the operations of your department or business to the public.
   2. Additionally, during your college career, you frequently may find yourself giving classroom presentations.

C. *The challenge of informative speaking.* Most informative speakers face a challenge in limiting their goals. In most public speaking classes, you will have only several minutes to make an informative speech. Hence, you must carefully limit your goal, especially if you are dealing with a skill. For example, in 6 to 8 minutes, it's unreasonable to try to teach a listener how to make forehand, backhand, and volley strokes with a tennis racket. On the other hand, you might be able to increase the listener's appreciation of the strategies behind "down-the-line" and "cross-court" shots. Or, you might be able to increase the listener's ability to keep proper score of a tennis match.

II. **Principles of Informing.** When speaking to inform, effective presenters capitalize on the principles of simplicity, clarity, credibility, and interest.

A. *Simplicity.* You don't need for us to tell you that *simple material is easier to understand and remember than is complex material.*
   1. Ineffective informative speakers, however, often disregard the principle of simplicity. Please simplify the complexity of your material to a level the audience can grasp in the allotted time.
   2. One way to simplify your material is through the organization of your main points and subpoints. Human beings can remember organized material better than they can a long series of unrelated points.
      a. In fact, psychologists have reported what's called the "Seven-plus-or-minus-two Rule."
         (1) The rule states that most individuals can remember no more than 5 to 9 pieces of unrelated information.
         (2) Perhaps it's just coincidence that phone numbers have 7 digits, but it's a fact that most U.S. Americans have resisted using the 9-digit zip codes developed by the U.S. Post Office.

   b. When speaking to inform, limit your main points to the fewest number possible. If, for example, you want to explain a process that has 16 steps, try to group the steps under 2 to 5 main points that follow a pattern of organization. By way of illustration, if you want to teach the audience how to hang wallpaper, you might limit your main points to the following topics: gathering the necessary tools, preparing the surface, applying the adhesive, hanging the paper, and finishing up.

B. *Clarity. To inform an audience effectively and efficiently, we must phrase our ideas clearly and select appropriate forms of support.*
   1. Use language appropriate for the level of knowledge of the audience.
      a. Avoid technical language with a nontechnical audience.
      b. Don't try to impress the audience with your vocabulary.
      c. Don't make allusions to events, people, or other ideas that are apt to be unfamiliar to the audience.
   2. Select forms of support that promote comprehension and retention among the audience. Certainly you might use any form of support in an informative presentation. However, particularly helpful in informative speeches are examples, explanations, comparison/contrast, analogies, visual aids, and repetition and restatement (see Chapter 9 to review these concepts).
      a. Both real and hypothetical examples can help an audience understand and remember your information.
      b. Often, we'll need to explain our points to an audience.
         (1) Define any key term that the audience is not apt to know.
         (2) Avoid overusing explanation, however.
            (a) Often ineffective informative speakers do little more than explain their concepts in abstract terms.
            (b) Listeners learn best from concrete forms of support that appeal to their senses.
      c. Comparison and contrast are particularly effective in informative presentations.
         (1) Listeners tend to learn well from seeing how new information is similar and different from information they already have.
         (2) Appropriate figurative analogies are particularly effective in helping listeners remember new ideas.
      d. Visual aids are particularly appropriate in informative situations. A picture *is* worth a thousand words. Therefore, some instructors require their students to use visual aids in informative speeches.
         (1) Listeners learn best when they use more than one of their senses.

(2) The visual aid can serve as a real example of the ideas you present.
(3) Visual aids can promote retention by making ideas vivid.
e. Repetition and restatement promote retention.
(1) Often informative speakers concretely preview and summarize each main point to promote retention.
(2) You can restate your ideas through use of a chart or other visual aid.

C. *Credibility. A listener is more likely to pay attention to and learn from a source with high credibility.* Not only should the speaker demonstrate knowledge and interest in the subject, but the audience should perceive the speaker as trustworthy.

1. Competence. Listeners are more likely to spend the energy required to learn new material if they perceive the speaker is competent.
   a. You will likely find an informative situation uncomfortable if you as the speaker know less than the audience knows about a topic.
   b. Additionally, speakers appear less competent when they make errors in grammar and pronunciation or appear unorganized, even if they are experts on the subject.
   c. To strengthen your image of competence, follow these steps in preparing an informative speech.
      (1) Select a topic about which you have knowledge or a sincere interest in learning.
      (2) Analyze the knowledge and interest level of the audience.
      (3) Carefully research your topic and consult authoritative sources.
      (4) Select the ideas, organization, and support that appear most appropriate for the audience.
      (5) Demonstrate your connection to the topic by showing your knowledge or alluding to your experience.
      (6) Cite authorities during your speech.
      (7) Use a variety of support to increase your chances of reaching all audience members.
      (8) Practice with your visual aids until you feel prepared to use them smoothly and confidently.
2. Trustworthiness. Audiences generally assume the speaker is trustworthy unless the speaker violates that trust.
   a. Illustrating the value of the material to the audience can build your image of trustworthiness.
   b. Avoiding extreme language and illustrations can help to protect your image of trustworthiness.
3. Dynamism. Audiences are more likely to pay attention to speakers who demonstrate an energetic and responsive style of delivery.

a. Express your enthusiasm with your voice and body.
b. Respond to feedback from the audience during the speech. By paying careful attention to nonverbal reactions among the audience, you will notice the facial expression, posture, and eye contact of the audience members. From these cues you can decide whether the audience shows interest and understanding in the message. If not, adapt the message accordingly.

D. *Interest. Listeners learn more from presentations that interest them.* You can increase the interest of your listeners by showing them ways the presentation will benefit them, incorporating factors of attention, and having the listeners participate in the presentation.
  1. Assume that you must motivate your audience to listen and learn. Show the audience the significance of your topic. Help the listeners to understand how they will benefit from learning your material.
  2. Once you have planned the basic content of your presentation, ask yourself "How can I make this material more interesting and enjoyable?" Attempt to incorporate a variety of factors of attention into your material (see Chapter 9 if you need to review "factors of attention.")
     a. Activity
     b. Conflict
     c. Familiarity
     d. Humor
     e. Important
     f. Proximity
     g. Reality
     h. Surprise
     i. Suspense
  3. Listeners learn more from presentations that involve them mentally and/or physically. Hence, audience participation will usually enhance learning. Although classroom presentations seldom allow for enough time for listeners to practice a physical skill, practice and activities are widely used in effective training and educational programs. Despite the time limits of classroom speeches, you would be wise to devise ways to allow the audience to participate briefly in your informative presentations.

III. **Constructing the informative presentation.** The introduction, body, and conclusion of informative presentations should promote understanding and retention.

A. *The introduction*
  1. Secure the attention of your audience.
  2. Use subtle ways to build your credibility.
     a. You don't want to turn off the audience by appearing arrogant or condescending.

b. You do, however, want your listeners to recognize your interest in and knowledge and understanding of the topic. For example, if you have had firsthand experience related to the topic, you could refer to a situation in which you used your specialized knowledge.

3. Emphasize the relevance and importance of the topic to the audience so as to increase the listeners' motivation to learn new material.
   a. Usually an abstract comment such as "This information is important. You'll need to know this!" will fail to motivate a listener.
   b. You may want to list the reasons why the material is important or illustrate the advantages of learning the material.
4. Clearly preview the main points of your presentations. Your preview will function as one of your planned repetitions to promote retention.

B. The body of the informative speech should contain clearly phrased main points arranged in an appropriate pattern of organization. (See Chapter 4 if you need to review patterns of organization.)
   1. Speakers who fail to plan the phrasing of their main points often confuse their listeners. Such a speaker commonly laments, "I know what I wanted to say, but I just didn't know how to say it." Unfortunately, the speaker's discovery came too late.
   2. Look for an opportunity to phrase your main points in a way that promotes retention. Common mnemonic devices (memory aids) include phrasing main points in parallel language.
      a. For example: "To prevent food poisoning, keep your food cool"; "To prevent food poisoning, keep your food clean"; To prevent food poisoning, keep your food covered." These three main points not only use parallel language, but also use repetition of the "hard C" sound for each of the key words.
      b. Another common mnemonic device is to form a word or common expression from the first letters of the key words of the main points. [For instance, a speech on cardiopulmonary resuscitation (CPR) might contain the following main points: "Clear the **A**irway of obstructions," "Restore **B**reathing," and "Restore **C**ardio functioning." The three key words allow the speaker to present the "ABC's of CPR."]
      c. The keynote speaker at a conference developed his plan of action using letters (AVA) that form the abbreviation of the organization (American Volkssport Association): Remain **A**ctive; be **V**ocal, become **A**dvocates.
   3. *Internal previews and internal summaries.* Between your main points, summarizing the content of your previous point and previewing the content of your next point will provide yet another planned repetition or restatement to promote retention.

4. When relating supporting material to your main points, you probably will be more effective if you use the *didactic method.*
   a. The word "didactic" refers to something that is instructional.
   b. The method calls for stating your main point, providing the evidence that supports it, then restating your idea. The didactic method helps the audience follow carefully the development the speaker provides. In contrast, the inductive method, often appropriate in persuasive speaking, calls for the speaker providing support first, then drawing a conclusion.
5. Identify the material that you can best clarify or emphasize with visual aids. However, avoid overusing visual aids—if you emphasize everything, the result is nothing stands out as more important.

C. The conclusion of the informative speech provides a final opportunity to restate key ideas and encourage the audience to use the material.
   1. The summary of an informative presentation is usually more developed than in persuasive presentations.
      a. In informative presentations, a speaker who is trying to promote retention may review (that is, restate) the wording of each of the main points.
      b. In persuasive situations, speakers often refer only to the topic covered in each of the main points.
   2. The conclusion provides you with a final opportunity to build the confidence of the listeners to try to use your material.
   3. Try to end your presentation in a memorable way.

Closing Remarks

As the economy moves more toward service and away from manufacturing, the chances increase that all of us will find ourselves in numerous informative situations. By applying the principles of simplicity, clarity, credibility, and interest, you should be well equipped to meet the challenge.

References and Suggestions for Further Readings

Andrew, P. H., & Baird, J. E. (1995). *Communication for business and the professions*. Madison, WI: Brown & Benchmark.

Armentrout, B. W. (1993). Public speaking: A necessity for the '90s. *HR Focus, 70*, 17.

DeVito, J. A. (1986). *The communication handbook: A dictionary*. NY: Harper & Row.

Goss, B. (1989). *The psychology of human communication*. Prospect Heights, IL: Waveland.

Grice, G. L., & Skinner, J. F. (1995). *Mastering public speaking*. Needham Heights, MA: Allyn & Bacon.

Hanna, M. S., & Gibson, J. W. (1995). *Public speaking for personal success*. Dubuque, IA: Wm. C. Brown.

Moyer, P. E. (1990). *The ABC's of a really good speech*. East Hampton, NY: Circle press.

Powers, J. (1994). *Public speaking: The lively art*. NY: HarperCollins.

Sprague, J., & Stuart, D. (1992). *The speaker's handbook*. Ft. Worth, TX: Harcourt Brace.

VanOosting, J. (1985). *The business speech: Speaker, audience, and text*. Englewood Cliffs, NJ: Prentice-Hall.

CHAPTER 12

Wording Your Ideas

Objectives

After reading this chapter, you should be able to

1. explain the nature of language as a system of symbols;
2. explain the characteristics of language that often lead to miscommunication; and
3. apply principles of effective oral style to your own speaking.

Topical Outline

LANGUAGE AS A SYSTEM OF SYMBOLS

- Phonology
- Syntax
- Semantics
- Pragmatics

CHARACTERISTICS OF LANGUAGE

- Symbolism
- Denotation and connotation
- Abstraction
- Perception

QUALITIES OF EFFECTIVE LANGUAGE

- Appropriateness
  - Bias
  - Grammar and word choice
  - Oral style
- Clarity
  - Simplicity
  - Accuracy
- Vividness

Key Concepts

Accuracy
Appropriateness
Biased language
Bypassing
Catch-all words
Clarity
Clichés
Connotation
Denotation
Dialect
Figurative language
Grammar
Hyperbole
Imagery
Ladder of abstraction
Language
Metaphor
Metonymy
Oral style
Oxymoron
Personification
Phonology
Pragmatics
Referent
Scheme
Semantics
Simile
Simplicity
Stylistic devices
Symbol
Synecdoche
Syntax
Triangle of Meaning
Understatement
Vividness

Wording Ideas

PERSPECTIVE

I. Some of us have had English teachers who taught us to think seriously about our use of language. Indeed, not only is language use important in writing, but in speaking as well. When you prepare your outlines for your informative and persuasive speeches, please try to apply principles of effective language as you phrase your key ideas. As you deliver the presentations, you will adjust your language yet again.

A. Effective language is crucial to the success of a presentation and to the effectiveness of oral communication, in general.

1. If your language is too dry and lifeless, listeners may not want to pay attention to you.
2. If your language is too flowery and lacking in substance your listeners may consider you strange.
3. If your language is too abstract or too technical, listeners may not be able to understand you.
4. If your language displays grammar errors unacceptable to your listener, your credibility will suffer.
5. If your language is offensive to listeners, you will find it difficult to achieve your goals.

B. We often think of language too simplistically. We expect others to attach the same meanings to words we do. We fail to recognize the characteristics of language that frequently lead to ineffective communication. We fail to use techniques of language that will make it more understandable, acceptable, and interesting to our listeners.

II. ***Purpose statement***: Our goal in this chapter is to help you to improve the effectiveness of your language.

III. ***Preview***: First, we shall examine language as a system of symbols; second, characteristics of language that often lead to miscommunication; and, third, ways to make the use of language more effective.

Chapter Body

I. **Language as a system of symbols.** *Language* is a system of symbols that we, as human beings, use to share meanings. Like all systems, language has components, structure, and functions.

A. At the foundation of human language we find a set of *speech sounds* we combine to create *words*.

1. We refer to the speech sounds of the English language as consonant sounds and vowel sounds.

a. In English, we have nearly twice as many speech sounds as we have letters in our alphabet. Unlike many other languages (e.g.,

Spanish), we represent the same sounds with different letters (for example: "way" and "weigh"; "wait" and "weight").

b. *Phonology* is the description of the speech sounds of a language and the way these sounds change when combined with other sounds.
   (1) For example, most people born and raised in the United States pronounce the "p" sound in three different ways.
      (a) They pronounce the "p" in "pan" by releasing a noticeable puff of air.
      (b) They release less air when they produce the "p" sound in "span."
      (c) Finally, they release no air when they pronounce the "p" sound in the word "cap."
   (2) Individuals trying to learn U.S. American English as a second language often find it difficult to identify and learn the variety of ways we pronounce each speech sound.

2. We combine the sounds of our language to form words. Words are symbols we use to represent the way we view our reality.

B. The *syntax* of language refers to the rules that govern the way we combine words into phrases and sentences. Because it violates the rules of English syntax, the following sequence of words "makes no sense": "The shared girl sandwich boy and the." The same words make sense when sequenced according to our rules of syntax: "The boy and girl shared the sandwich."

C. *Semantics* refers to the meaning we attach to language.

D. *Pragmatics* is the study of the relationship between language and its users. For instance, pragmatics is concerned with the ways language restricts or promotes individuals' behaviors and the ways individuals' views of the world are related to the language they use.

II. **Characteristics of language.** Four interrelated characteristics of language help to account for the ease with which individuals can miscommunicate.

A. *Language is symbolic.*

1. A word is a symbol. The words of a language result from matching a set of sounds to each concept in the language. We have a concept we call "the street." Other languages use a different set of sounds for a similar concept resulting in different symbols [for example, "la rue" (French), "la calle" (Spanish), and "jalan" (Malay)].
   a. Even when individuals use the same word to refer to the same concept, the individuals' concepts always differ to a greater or lesser degree based on their own experiences and states of mind. For example, if you hear the sounds for the word "chair," you may think of a folding chair, an easy chair, a desk chair, your favorite chair, the chairperson of an organization, etc. You may even realize that you left a newly painted chair

outdoors and that it looks like rain. While you were worrying about your chair, you heard nothing else the speaker said. Communication can rarely be perfect if "perfection" is defined as sharing identical meaning.

b. When individuals don't know they are using the same word or symbol to refer to substantially different concepts, miscommunication is inevitable. One study (Strong, 1956, p. 28) revealed that the 500 most common words in English have over 14,000 different dictionary definitions. That's an average of about 28 concepts per word. A single word is ambiguous. Words don't contain meaning, people's minds do.

2. Ogden and Richards (1959) developed a model they labeled "The Triangle of Meaning" to remind communicators that a symbol is not the thing it symbolizes.

The Triangle of Meaning

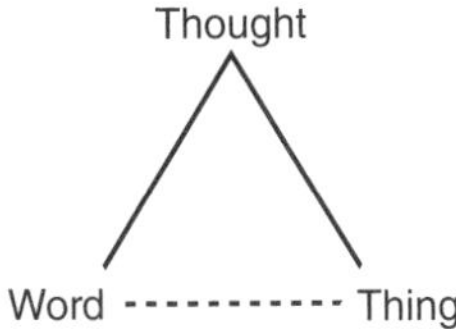

In the model, the line between the Word and the Thing (or Referent) is broken. The relationship between the word spoken and the thing symbolized exists in our mind. As communicators we must use techniques that increase the chances that our listeners will assign to our symbols (words) the meanings we intend.

B. Language allows us to create both denotative and connotative meanings. *The same word in a language can result in significantly different meanings for communicators.*

1. The words of a language evoke both denotative and connotative meaning in the minds of communicators.

a. Denotation

(1) The denotative meaning of a word is its dictionary definition.

(2) The denotative meaning refers to the specific, generally agreed upon definition of a word.

b. Connotation

(1) The connotative meaning of a word refers to all the feelings and attitudes associated with or implied by the word.

(2) Depending upon your experiences, a particular word may evoke positive, negative, or neutral thoughts and feelings you associate with the word.

2. The fact that *words evoke different meanings in different individuals*, suggests communicators must attempt to reduce the chances that their meanings are bypassing one another.
   a. Bypassing occurs when a receiver attaches a different meaning to a word than the sender intended.
   b. Because words have both denotative and connotative meaning, four types of bypassing are possible.
      (1) *Denotative–denotative bypassing* occurs when the sender intends one denotation for a word while the receiver attaches another. To illustrate, a speaker said to a friend, "I'm really keyed up. I need a couple of trips." The friend responded, "Oh, where are you planning to go?" "No silly. I need to take a couple of amitriptylines." Meanings bypassed because for the receiver "trip" denoted travel, while for the speaker the street slang "trip" denoted the drug amitriptyline, an antidepressant and muscle relaxant.
      (2) *Denotative–connotative* bypassing occurs when the sender intends one denotation while the receiver attaches an unintended connotative meaning. For instance, a speaker may use the word "postman" intending it to refer generically to men and women who work for the post office. A receiver may be thinking, "This person must not care about sexist language. The proper term is 'mail carrier.'"
      (3) *Connotative–denotative bypassing* occurs when the sender intends to convey feelings, usually in an indirect or figurative way, while the receiver attaches a literal meaning. For example, a student who joined a class during its second week asked the instructor if anything important had been covered so far. Intending to be sarcastic, the instructor said, "Of course not, I never cover anything important during the first few weeks of a term." The student responded, "Good. I was hoping so."
      (4) *Connotative–connotative bypassing* occurs when the sender implies one meaning while the receiver infers another. A supervisor once said to an employee, "Boy, you're hot today," meaning "You've done a lot of work today." The employee thought, "Another blatant case of sexual harassment."
   c. Bypassing can lead to confusion, waste, and even conflict.

C. Language contains words that differ in their *levels of abstraction*. Some words are quite abstract or far removed from the object or idea to which they refer. Other words are more concrete, that is they more precisely identify a specific object or idea. Take for example, the following series of words that refer to the same person:

The Ladder of Abstraction

thing
animate object
human being
adult human
woman
professor
Dr. Beth A. Messner

Whereas "Dr. Beth A. Messner" is a very concrete term that allows us to identify easily the person in question, "thing" is a highly abstract word. General semanticists, individuals who study the nature of meaning and its implications, refer to the progression of words from concrete to abstract as a ladder of abstraction. Hence, "to go higher on the ladder of abstraction" means to express a concept in more abstract language.

1. The more abstract a word is, the more likely that people will attach different meanings to the word. Hence, abstract words are more likely to lead to miscommunication than are concrete words.
2. As a receiver of messages, you should consider the abstraction level of a speaker. Sometimes speakers choose more abstract terms to mislead receivers. For instance, an individual could call an extreme case of physical abuse "physical contact." Another could call the murder of 50 children an "unfortunate event."

D. *Language affects perception.* Countless books and articles have been written about the relationships among language, perception, thought, feeling, and behavior. We shall focus only on some of the important relationships between a speaker's language and a receiver's perceptions.
   1. Whether you are engaged in public speaking or conversation, the language you use will influence the way others perceive you.
      a. Our language influences our credibility in the minds of our listeners.
         (1) From our use of language, listeners can draw countless inferences (to name but a few: our social class, educational level, competence, professionalism, stability, approachability, trustworthiness, friendliness, and enthusiasm).
         (2) If our listeners do not find us credible, they may reject valid points we are trying to make.
      b. Our language influences the ability of our listeners to understand the points we are trying to make. The words we choose will influence the clarity of our material.
      c. Our language influences the willingness of our listeners to give us their attention. Audiences are more willing to pay attention if our use of language is fresh and lively.

d. Our language influences our relationships with others. The language we use can attract or offend others.

2. The better you know your listeners, the better you will be able to use language that meets their expectations. If you do not know your audience well, you will probably make a better impression with too much formality in your language rather than too little. For instance, when referring to someone in the audience, use an appropriate form of address such as Mr., Mrs., or Ms. When you refer to the audience in general, "ladies and gentlemen" is a commonly used greeting.

III. **Effective language.** We recommend that you evaluate your language choices according to three standards of effectiveness: appropriateness, clarity, and vividness.

A. A speaker's language is *appropriate* when it suits or fits a particular purpose, listener, and occasion and helps meet the demands of oral communication. Hence, "appropriateness" is a relative term. For instance, language that is appropriate in a business training session may be inappropriate at an annual stockholders' meeting. As communicators, we need to avoid language that would offend our listeners or reduce our credibility. We need to adapt our language to the knowledge and expectations of our listeners. We need to recognize that the process of oral communication differs from delivering information in writing.

1. Effective communicators avoid biased language that would offend an individual they are trying to influence. In particular, you will reduce your chances of getting listeners to agree with you if you use offensive language that indicates bias against individuals on the basis of racial or ethnic group, age, disability, religion, sexual orientation, and so forth.

a. The *Publication Manual of the American Psychological Association* (1994) suggests two tests to identify bias in the use of language:

(1) Substitute the name of "your own group for the group or groups you are discussing or…[imagine] you are a member of the group you are discussing…. If you feel excluded or offended, your material needs further revision."

(2) "Ask people from that group…[to] give you candid feedback" (p. 46).

b. While we refer you to the *Publication Manual of the American Psychological Association* (1994, pp. 46–60) for an in-depth discussion of the issue, we would like to illustrate potential problems in language usage regarding gender and "other group" memberships.

(1) A sexist bias can result from language pertaining to the genders.
   (a) The use of "he" and "man" as a generic reference to both males and females can cause confusion and promote stereotypes.
      i. A sentence such as "The speaker needs to determine the best organizational arrangement for his speech" can be improved by saying "The speaker needs to determine the best organizational arrangement for his or her speech" or "A speaker should select the best organizational arrangement for the speech." To avoid overusing the phrase "she or he," try phrasing ideas in the plural, for example, "Speakers should organize their speeches well."
      ii. Using "man" or "mankind," when the speaker really means "people," can be both confusing and sexist.
      iii. Communicators should avoid occupational stereotyping (for instance, using "chairman" instead of "chairperson" or "chair") and sex-role stereotyping (for instance, using "mothering" when "parenting" or "nurturing" is more appropriate).
   (b) The words in constructions regarding the sexes should be parallel (for example, referring to adults as "girls and men," rather than "women and men," implies women lack maturity and stature).

(2) Biased language can result from the labels applied to groups of persons.
   (a) Referring to a group of people as "culturally deprived" is an example of biased language. "Culturally deprived" according to whose standards? Don't all groups have their own culture? Is different worse?
   (b) Because individuals may disagree about the most appropriate labels to describe their group(s), you should consider carefully the attitudes and traditions of your audience.

2. Effective communicators use grammar and words that are *appropriate* for their presentational settings. The grammar and words we choose will influence our credibility with a listener. Listeners who find a speaker's grammar too formal or too informal may not take the ideas in a presentation as seriously as they should.
   a. In most presentations, our language should be more formal than language we would use in a conversation with close

friends. Most college students can use appropriate grammar, but they may need to give grammar and word choice some conscious thought to ensure that their usage is acceptable to their instructors.

(1) For presentations in the college classroom, you probably should avoid major deviations from standard U.S. American English.

(a) Gregory (1987) provided a list of the type of grammar mistakes that may lead a listener (especially a college professor) to question your ability to use standard U.S. American grammar:

Nonstandard	Standard
He don't	He doesn't
You was	You were
I done it	I did it
Between you and I	Between you and me
I had went	I had gone
She's already went	She's already gone
I been thinking	I've been thinking
I've already took algebra	I've already taken algebra
Hisself	Himself
Theirself	Themselves
We seen it	We saw it
Her and me went	She and I went
Him and me went	He and I went
I come to see you yesterday	I came to see you yesterday
She ain't here	She isn't here
He don't love me no more	He doesn't love me anymore
He be late	He is late
I had wrote it	I had written it
Give me them apples	Give me those apples

(p. 257)

(b) We suggest that speakers avoid slang in a formal presentation unless its use would create a desired positive effect.

(2) Different regions of the country and various ethnic or racial groups sometimes develop the use of unique pronunciations, words, phrases, and grammatical forms. This unique dialect, or way of speaking, may differ

substantially from the dialect we call standard U.S. American English. Most dialects, however, include more formal usages and less formal usages.

(a) Using the appropriate form of a dialect may actually increase a speaker's credibility among listeners who speak the dialect.

(b) If the dialect includes pronunciations or usages that deviate significantly from standard U.S. American English, the user may have difficulty establishing appropriate credibility among those unfamiliar with the dialect. In extreme cases, nonusers of the dialect may have difficulty understanding parts of the presentation.

(c) We encourage you as a listener to avoid stereotyping or "tuning out" individuals who speak a dialect different from your own. However, we must recognize the fact that you cannot make your listeners grant you that same courtesy. Hence, we also encourage you to avoid becoming defensive if others point out significant deviations from standard U.S. American English in your speaking. Your ability to use the standard U.S. American dialect fluently can only increase your ability to function in a variety of careers where use of the dialect is an asset.

b. In most presentations, your grammar and word choice will be less formal than the traditional expectations of formal writing.

(1) Formal written style tends to be impersonal, using third person constructions such as "One can see..." "It appears..." and "The third issue under consideration..." Oral style is more personal, for example: "You can see...," "I think..." and "Let's consider a third issue..." Additionally, pronouns such as "we" and "our" can help a speaker establish a more personal bond with the audience.

(2) In formal writing, we seldom expect sentence fragments, contractions, or misplaced modifiers. In oral style, interpretation of the rules of grammar is more liberal, contractions are common, and usages are more colloquial (like those of everyday conversation).

(3) When engaged in reading, an individual can look up difficult words or reread difficult passages. When information is presented orally, the listener cannot "relisten" (unless the presentation is on audio or video tape). The speaker must help the listener follow the presentation and understand immediately.

(a) In oral style, effective presenters tend to use more simple sentences.

(b) In oral style, effective presenters tend to use more repetitions and restatements and internal summaries.

(c) In oral style, effective presenters tend to use more transitions to guide the listener through the presentation. Bormann and Bormann (1983) wrote, "Inexperienced speakers feel the need for transitions but have a tendency to use one or two words over and over again. Novice speakers say 'and another thing' and 'another point,' or overuse the word 'next' or 'also'" (p. 163). Study the following phrases to develop your ability to use a variety of transitions to help guide your listeners through your presentations:

"I will begin my argument by..."

"Because my purpose is..."

"Now that I have provided some background, I am going to..."

"First...Second...Third..."

"And now that we know that...are causing this problem, let's look at the possible ways to solve it."

"A third advantage is..."

"The way we're dealing with the problem of...just won't cut it anymore. Here's why..."

"If we look more closely at..., we'll find..."

"For example,..."

"Moreover, I hope..."

"Another way to look at this is..."

"Although most people believe..."

"Perhaps you're thinking this is an isolated example. I did. Until I found that..."

"Nevertheless, the scientists found that..."

"In answer to the first question..."

B. A speaker's language is *clear* when listeners attach to a message the same meanings and feeling the speaker intends. To achieve *clarity*, you must balance two, sometimes competing, needs: to be simple and to be accurate. You should avoid using simple words that could have many different meanings to your listener. Similarly, you should avoid the opposite extreme of using the "perfect" precise word that no one understands. In other words, select the simplest words and sentences that will convey the meaning you intend.

1. *Simplicity*. You can best achieve simplicity by using common, understandable words and minimizing long, involved sentences.
   a. Use simple words.
   b. Avoid polysyllabic words. The previous sentence violated the rule it expresses: Avoid long, unusual words when simpler ones will do. Additionally, using a big word you have difficulty pronouncing will harm rather than enhance your image.

c. Use words your listeners can understand.
   (1) Avoid technical language, or jargon, with listeners who are unfamiliar with the terms.
   (2) Avoid foreign expressions your audience may not understand.
d. Use the simplest sentence structure needed to convey your ideas. This does not mean you never should use compound, complex, or compound-complex sentences. You should vary your sentence structure to avoid boring the audience. You should, however, avoid the practice (of some novice speakers) of writing out long and involved sentences that require several breaths to deliver.

2. *Accuracy*. You can best achieve accuracy by using words that express the exact shade of meaning you intend.
   a. Avoid catch-all words. Catch-all words are highly abstract nouns and pronouns (for example, "thing," "stuff," "everything") that fail to create a definite idea.
      (1) If you feel you are about to use a catch-all word (for example, "Another thing to consider is..."), try to pick a more precise name for the catch-all word (for example, "My third reason for acting now is...").
      (2) One good rule of thumb is that a specific noun is usually better than a vague pronoun (such as "it").
      (3) When preparing for a presentation, use a dictionary or thesaurus to identify synonyms for ambiguous terms. A good word processing program will allow you to use its thesaurus with a touch or two of the keyboard. For example, take the word "growth." According to *Roget's College Thesaurus*, "growth" could be more specific by referring to: "development, evolution, increase, adulthood, maturity, harvest, crop, produce, yield, flora, vegetable, tumor, cancer, node, polyp, mole, tubercule, cyst, excrescence, swelling, protuberance, wen, expansion, prosperity, disease, convexity" (p. 214).
   b. Avoid vague adjectives and adverbs that fail to create a definite idea in the minds of the listener.
      (1) For example, the words "good," "pretty," "cute," and "just wonderful" fail to create a definite, similar idea in the minds of audience members.
      (2) Imagine, for example, that you are trying to describe a person. You say the person is "smart." According to *Roget's Thesaurus*, you might use a variety of other words: intelligent, quick, keen, acute, alive, awake, bright, sharp, canny, shrewd, astute, clear-headed, far-sighted, discerning, penetrating, piercing, clever, and brainy. In

actuality, you intend to mean the person is chic, stylish, jaunty, or dapper in appearance. On the other hand, you could have meant that the person is one who talks back, is a smart aleck, or obnoxious. The key is to use language with accuracy and precision—to give thought to using the most specific language that will evoke your intended idea.

C. The word "*vivid*" is a Latin adjective meaning lively. Synonyms for "vivid" include "bright," "brilliant," "fresh" and "intense." Hence, a speaker's language is vivid if it forms unique and striking mental images. Of course, you don't want to describe to the point of boring your audience, but you can increase your effectiveness by using vivid language that evokes desired images in the audience's minds. You can make your language more vivid by avoiding clichés, using imagery, and employing figurative language.
   1. Avoid clichés. Clichés are words or expressions that have been used so often they fail to create a meaningful image. When we hear classic clichés like the following, our thinking processes often "go into neutral": "pass the buck," "catch the brunt of it," "straddle the fence," "foot in your mouth," "cause hard feelings," "don't put the cart before the horse," "don't count your chickens before they're hatched," and "right as rain." More recently, phrases such as "You know?" "Ya know what I mean?" and "Ya hear me?" have developed into meaningless verbal filler.
   2. Use imagery. Words and phrases that appeal to our senses create imagery. Hence, there are as many types of imagery as we have ways to perceive reality. Good imagery allows the listener to experience the sensations associated with an experience.
      a. Imagery can appeal to our five basic senses.
         (1) Auditory imagery helps us hear an experience.
         (2) Gustatory imagery helps us taste an experience.
         (3) Olfactory imagery helps us smell an experience.
         (4) Tactile imagery helps us touch an experience.
         (5) Visual imagery helps us see an experience.
      b. Our sensations transcend our five basic senses.
         (1) Kinesthetic imagery helps us feel the tension, location, or movement of our muscles.
         (2) Systemic imagery helps us experience pain, nausea, dizziness, or positive internal feelings.
         (3) Thermal imagery helps us feel warmth or coldness.
   3. Use stylistic devices—with caution. The use of a word in an unusual manner or the arrangement of the words in a sentence in an unusual order can catch the attention of a listener in a way that causes enhanced thought, feeling, and appreciation. However, excessive use of stylistic devices can make a presentation appear

artificial or overdone. The absence of stylistic devices can make a presentation appear dull and dry. As a rule of thumb, the more formal the situation, the more appropriate the use of stylistic devices. However, many of the stylistic devices pertaining to words are used in everyday conversation. Additionally, if you study an episode of a television comedy known for its witty dialogue, you will probably be able to identify many of the figures of speech as the source of the program's humor and appeal. A danger in using figures of speech is that the audience may become confused by taking your words literally rather than figuratively. Students of rhetoric have studied figurative language since the times of the ancient Greeks. Hence, many of the techniques have retained the original names that the Greeks used to label them.

a. Use figurative language (sparingly). Eight common techniques of figurative language appear below.
   (1) Simile. A simile is a direct comparison usually using the words "like" or "as" (for example, "Like hornets from a dislodged nest, the students descended on the office of the department chairperson").
   (2) Metaphor. A metaphor is an implied comparison between unlike items that have something in common (for example, "The angry hornets descended on the office of the department chairperson").
   (3) Synecdoche. A synecdoche (pronounced si-NECK-da-key) uses a part of a concept to stand for the concept. Many popular slang words originated as a synecdoche (for example, "tube" or "TV" to stand for "television," "wheels" to stand for "automobile," and "hands" to stand for "workers").
   (4) Metonymy. A metonymy (ma-TAH-na-mi) uses a word associated with the concept to stand for the concept (for example, "badge" to stand for "police officer," "time" to stand for "prison term," and "light" to stand for "wisdom"). During the Vietnam period the motto "come home America" stood for "end the war." Additionally, a speaker used the phrase "greying of America" to stand for "the mean age of Americans is increasing." The speaker used the striking phrase to signal all the major transitions within the speech.
   (5) Personification. Personification gives human qualities to abstract ideas or inanimate objects (for example; "the crops beg for rain," "the engine talked back," and "Uncle Sam wants you").

(6) Hyperbole. A hyperbole is an exaggeration used for emphasis or effect (for example, "you're tearing out my heart," "America's favorite comic," and "the cat's death was the greatest tragedy of the century").
(7) Understatement. A deliberate understatement can create a desired effect such as humor (for example, "having lost my car, money, and credit cards, I felt a bit inconvenienced") or function to reduce the seriousness of an action (for example, having wrecked the family car, the adolescent says, "I had a little trouble tonight").
(8) Oxymoron. An oxymoron links two words that usually express contradictory sentiments (for example, "wise folly," "grateful hatred," and "lifeless passion").

b. The word "scheme" comes from the Greek word *schema* meaning shape or form. Hence schemes are differences in the normal order of words found in sentences. Look at the way you have phrased your key ideas in the speech. Ask yourself if you can improve the phrasing by adding words, by omitting words, by changing the order of the words, or by making coordinate ideas parallel in form.

Closing Remarks

Effective language use is essential to the success of a presentation. As you prepare to deliver your speech, use the suggestions in this chapter to enhance the overall quality of your presentation.

References and Suggestions for Further Readings

Bormann, E. G., & Bormann, N. C. (1986). *Speech communication: A basic approach*. 4th ed. NY: Harper & Row.

Casagrande, J. (ed.) (1983). *The linguistic connection*. Lanham, MD: The University Press of America.

Cherwitz, R. A., & Hikins, J. W. (1986). *Communication and knowledge: An investigation in rhetorical epistemology*. Columbia, SC: University of South Carolina.

DeVito, J. A. (1986). *The communication handbook: A dictionary*. NY: Harper & Row.

Ebersole, F. B. (1979). *Language and perception: Essays in the philosophy of language*. Washington, DC: University Press of America.

Gregory, H. (1990). *Public speaking for college and career*. NY: McGraw-Hill.

Morehead, P. D. (1978). *Roget's college thesaurus*. NY: New American Library.

Nickerson, S. (1995). *Breaking the language barrier*. Training & Development, *49*, 45–46.

Ogden, C.K., & Richards, I. A. (1959). *The meaning of meaning: A study of the influence of language upon thought and of the science of symbolism*. NY: Harcourt Brace Jovanovich.

Publication manual of the American Psychological Association. (1994). Washington, DC: American Psychological Association.

Silk, S. (1994). Making your speech memorable. *Association Management, 46*, 59–62.

Stewart, J., & D'Angelo, G. (1980). *Together: Communicating interpersonally*. NY: Addison Wesley.

Stewart, L. P., Cooper, P. J., & Friedley, S. A. (1986). *Communication between the sexes*. Scottsdale, AZ: Gorsuch Scarisbrick.

Strauss-Noll, M. (1984). An illustration of sex bias in English. *Women's Studies Quarterly, 12*, 36–37.

Strong, L. (1956). Do you know how to listen? In Dooher and Marquis (Eds.), *Effective communication on the Job*. NY: American Management Association.

Weylman, C. R. (1992). Mastering the use of 'power' words. *National Underwriter Life & Health*, 22, 21.

Zimmerman, G. I. (1986). *Speech communication*. St. Paul, MN: West.

CHAPTER 13

Your Persuasive Presentations

Objectives

After reading this chapter, you should be able to

1. apply principles and strategies of persuasion in your attempts to change the attitudes and/or behavior of others; and
2. construct effective persuasive presentations.

Topical Outline

- THE NATURE AND ROLE OF PERSUASION
- FUNDAMENTALS OF PERSUASION
  - The source
    - Competence
    - Trustworthiness
    - Attractiveness
  - The receiver
    - Types of audiences
      - Friendly
      - Hostile
      - Neutral
      - Apathetic
      - Mixed
      - Audience Dynamics
        - Selective exposure
        - Magnitude of change
        - Inoculation effect
        - Participation
        - Motivation
    - The message
      - Emotional appeals
      - Reasoning
      - Organization
    - The channel
- PREPARING THE PERSUASIVE PRESENTATION

Key Concepts

Attractiveness
Audience participation
Audience segmentation
Balance theory
Boomerang effect
Claim of fact
Claim of policy
Claim of value
Common ground
Competence
Counterarguments
Credibility
Dynamism
Emotional appeals
Ethics
Ethos
Friendly audience
Hierarchy of needs
Hostile audience
Inductive approach
Inoculation effect
Logos
Motivated sequence
Motives
Neutral audience
Pathos
Persuasive strategies
Problem–solution
Reasonable magnitude of change
Reasoning
Selective exposure
Trustworthiness
Values
Visualization

Persuasive Presentations

PERSPECTIVE

I. Some students consider persuasive speeches to be empty exercises. After listening to a few, however, they find that the speeches of their classmates influence their own attitudes and behaviors. In your career and social life, whether you try to "sell" an idea, product, service, or image of yourself, you will be engaging in persuasion. Researchers have studied extensively the difficult and complicated process known as persuasion. Scholars have written entire texts on persuasion. Hence, we cannot cover all of the related research in a short chapter. We encourage you to study the topic further in our course COMM 320, Persuasion. In this chapter, we present key concepts and principles of persuasion that apply not only to persuasive presentations, but also to one-on-one persuasion in interpersonal settings.

II. ***Purpose statement***: In this chapter, we seek to acquaint you with major principles of persuasion and to provide you with persuasive strategies appropriate for different types of target audiences.

III. ***Preview***: After discussing the nature of persuasion, we focus on four elements of the communication process: the speaker, the message, the channel and the receiver. We conclude the chapter by illustrating ways you can apply the principles to your own persuasive communication events.

Chapter Body

I. **The nature and role of persuasion.**
   A. Persuasive communication uses "arguments" to create conviction or change in a receiver or group of receivers. We define the word "argument" broadly to include logical reasons, emotional reasons, and reasons that stem from the receivers' reliance on others whom they feel are dependable sources of advice. We distinguish persuasive speaking, which encourages listeners to make choices consistent with the speaker's goals, from coercion, or attempts to eliminate choice on the part of the receiver.
   B. Everyday we persuade people on an informal, if not formal, basis. The possible examples are endless: the woman who persuades her date to go to the theater, the politician whose speech results in new supporters, the child who convinces his mother to buy him a new toy, the boss who motivates her secretary to learn a new computer program, the class who convinces the instructor to postpone the due date of their paper.
   C. In the course of the day we frequently engage in persuasion either as a source or a receiver.
      1. Not only do many situations involve persuasion, but there are many types of persuasion.

a. You may motivate your audience to do something it has never desired to do before.
b. You may motivate your audience to do something it has wanted to do but never has.
c. You may create in your audience one or more new beliefs and/or attitudes.
d. You may reinforce, or strengthen, beliefs and attitudes that already exist in your audience.

2. Some theorists view persuasive goals on a continuum. The form of persuasion on the left is far easier to achieve than the form on the right of the following continuum:

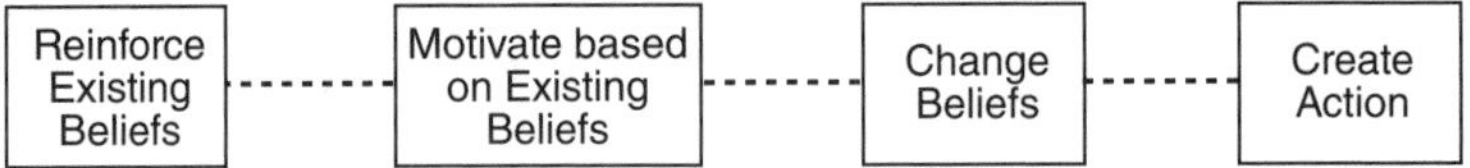

3. In addition, we can examine the audience's attitudes toward that which the speaker is advocating. In this case the audiences toward the left of the continuum below are harder to persuade than audiences toward the right side.

Opposed - Mildly Opposed - Neither Opposed Nor in Favor - Mildly in Favor - In Favor

II. **Fundamentals of persuasion.** Persuasion is one of the most complicated forms of communication. While there is no one single way to persuade another person, the use of persuasive techniques can increase your likelihood of persuading another person. Each persuasive event calls for a somewhat different way to approach the situation. To help you understand the process of persuasion, we return to the elements of Berlo's process model of communication—the source, message, channel, and receiver—to identify basic fundamentals of persuasion. Because characteristics of the message make little sense without considering first both the source and receiver, our analysis will begin with these two elements of the communication process.

A. *The source: Credibility.* Credibility is the image of a source held in the mind of each receiver. For a listener, a speaker with high credibility is more believable than one with low credibility. Hence, speakers who have high credibility, which Aristotle termed *ethos*, are more persuasive.

1. Notice that the Greek word *ethos* resembles closely the English word "ethics." The ability to persuade is a valuable skill that can be necessary for success, if not survival. Whether that skill is used for good or evil depends primarily on the ethics of the speaker.
   a. First, a lack of ethics may be demonstrated if the speaker is speaking for selfish interests, is dishonest, or negatively manipulates reasoning and support.

b. If the speaker is interested in the good of the audience (an audience that could range in size from an individual to a society or a group of societies), is honest in motives, and uses reasoning and support fairly, then the speaker is demonstrating good speaking ethics.
c. The ethical speaker cares about using and promoting positive values.
d. A wise speaker knows that unethical behavior may result in personal gain in the short run, but seldom results in gain in the long run. Eventually, the truth about an individual's unethical behavior "leaks out."

2. Credibility is important to persuasion because if a receiver perceives the source as knowledgeable, honest, and attractive (that is, charismatic), the source can more easily persuade the receiver in the desired direction. On the other hand, if the receiver does not like the message of a source, a source's credibility may suffer.
   a. Heider's balance theory helps to explain the importance of credibility in persuasion. Consider two different definitions: a *hostile audience* holds attitudes the speaker opposes (that is, desires to change); a *friendly audience* holds attitudes supportive of the goal of the speaker. The theory suggests that a condition of imbalance exists if listeners hold different attitudes than those of a speaker whom they like (that is, a speaker who has positive credibility but is facing a hostile audience). Similarly, a state of imbalance exists if listeners hold attitudes similar to those of a person whom they dislike (that is, a speaker who has negative credibility but is facing a friendly audience).
      (1) Balance theory states that if a condition of imbalance exists, an individual (in our case an audience member) will be motivated to change her or his attitudes in a direction that restores balance.
      (2) Hence, if you are presenting ideas the audience doesn't want to hear, the audience can restore balance by liking you less. In other words, by believing you are not credible.
         (a) To avoid such an occurrence, it's vital that you use techniques to maintain a high level of credibility.
         (b) If your credibility remains high, the audience will feel a pressure to restore balance by changing its attitudes to the ones you endorse.
      (3) On the other hand, if you present a non-credible image to a friendly audience, the audience will feel a pressure to be less favorable toward your position (or perceive you to be more credible than you deserve to be seen).
   b. From our discussion of Heider's balance theory, it should be clear that a speaker's credibility is neither static nor uniform.

It is a constantly changing image of the speaker in the mind of each audience member. In most cases, you will want those images to improve, not deteriorate.

(1) As a speaker, you will have initial credibility, a reputation you might say, when you begin to speak.

(2) Throughout the presentation, your image will alter—sometimes subtly, sometimes greatly—based on what you say and do.

(3) Hence, at the end of your presentation, you may have terminal credibility that is quite similar to or quite different from your initial credibility.

3. Dimensions of credibility. You can enhance your credibility by displaying your competence, trustworthiness, and attractiveness.

   a. *Competence*. To rely on you as a valid source of information, the audience must believe that you know the truth.

      (1) You can show competence by displaying your knowledge of and expertise on the subject, documenting your ideas with support and sources, and showing your personal involvement.

      (2) You should avoid errors in grammar and any other behaviors (verbal or nonverbal) that the audience could interpret as a lack of competence (for instance, making such statements as, "I'm really not sure I understand this argument myself, but it sort of goes this way…"; displaying nonfluencies such as "uh, uh"; mispronouncing words or repeatedly correcting your "slips of tongue"; and fumbling with visual aids or notes).

   b. *Trustworthiness*. To rely on you as a valid source of information, the audience also must believe you are telling the truth.

      (1) To enhance your image of trustworthiness, you can stress that which you have in common with the audience.

         (a) For example, your common ground with the audience might include referring to similar goals, similar experiences, and similar fears.

         (b) You also can enhance your image of trustworthiness by expressing your concern for the topic and the listeners and by approaching the topic objectively.

      (2) Avoid reducing your trustworthiness by unfairly attacking individuals or the opposing views or displaying any behavior that would make you appear dishonest, inconsistent, insincere, unreliable, excessive, or unsociable.

   c. *Attractiveness*. The third element of a speaker's credibility is attractiveness. Some individuals find this element of credibility shallow or difficult to accept, but research indicates that *an attractive physical appearance and/or personality tends to make a person more persuasive.* While the concept of physical attractiveness is easy to understand, the concept of an attractive personality may be less apparent. Think for a moment about a person who is physically unattractive yet attractive in nonphysical ways. Perhaps that person is helpful, interesting, or possesses skills you admire. One characteristic that most individuals find attractive in others is dynamism or energy.

(1) *Physical attractiveness.* A wise communicator will attempt to make himself or herself as attractive physically as possible. This principle of attractiveness has immediate and obvious implications for the persuasive speaker.

(a) You should give careful attention to your appearance, that is, the way you are dressed and groomed. One of our students tested this assertion. She dressed and used makeup in a manner she considered unattractive. She went to a local grocery store and asked several employees to help her locate specific items. She described their reactions as "disinterested" and "unhelpful." Two evenings later she returned to the same store, at the same time, but dressed and made-up in a manner she deemed attractive. On her second visit, each employee she approached helped her to the point of taking her to the item she asked for. The student learned in a firsthand way the value of attractiveness.

(b) Attractiveness may not compensate for faulty reasoning or bad ideas, but it does gain the audience's initial attention and favor.

(2) *Dynamism.* You also can make yourself more appealing or charismatic by displaying the qualities of dynamism: activity, energy, forcefulness, power, vibrancy, and vitality. Clearly, dynamism is associated with delivery.

(a) By making your delivery dynamic, you can demonstrate confidence and a desire to communicate with the audience. A smile and a "twinkle in the eye" can go a long way to persuade others.

(b) Just as too little dynamism can reduce your credibility, so can too much. Excessive dynamism (for example, being overly dramatic or expressive) may make you appear insincere, unreliable, or emotionally unstable. Hence, seek a balance between too little and too much dynamism.

B. *The receiver.* Although audience analysis and adaptation are important to any effective message, they are crucial in persuasive speaking.

Specific persuasive strategies that work with certain types of audiences often backfire with other types. In an attempt to clarify this phenomenon, we shall first consider five types of audiences then consider five general dynamics at work in most audiences.

1. *Audience analysis: Types of audiences.* In Chapter 3, we described five basic types of audiences: the friendly audience, the hostile audience, the neutral audience, the apathetic audience, and the mixed audience. For the purpose of planning a persuasive message, you must compare the beliefs, attitudes, and values of the audience to your persuasive goal. The outcome of your comparison will be your identification of your type of audience.
   a. *Types of audiences.* Audiences may be characterized as friendly, hostile, neutral, apathetic, or mixed.
      (1) A friendly audience is one that is positively disposed toward your persuasive purpose. In other words, the friendly audience holds beliefs, attitudes, and values that are consistent with your persuasive goal. For instance, an intended receiver may believe that the Children's Museum of your city is rundown and has too little space; he may feel that the city needs a new Children's Museum; and he may value civic responsibility. However, he has not made a contribution to the fund for a new building—your persuasive goal.
      (2) A hostile audience is one that is negatively disposed toward your persuasive goal. To illustrate, assume that your intended receiver believes that homosexual behavior is a threat to "family values"; she is opposed to any type of legislation that would guarantee specific rights to homosexuals; and she values protecting "family values." If your persuasive goal were to seek support to overturn legislation preventing the recognition of homosexual marriages, your hypothetical intended receiver would constitute a hostile audience member.
      (3) A neutral audience is neither for nor against your persuasive goal. The neutral audience is undecided.
      (4) An apathetic audience is one that has no knowledge or interest in your persuasive goal. In other words, the audience is unaware of the significance or importance of your persuasive goal. For instance, before the "war on terrorism," few Americans had any knowledge of or interest in the problems that the Afghan people faced as a result of the clash between the Taliban and other political groups.
      (5) A mixed audience contains listeners who fall into two or more of the four previously described types of audiences.

b. Throughout this chapter, we shall link the appropriateness of persuasive strategies to the friendly, hostile, or neutral/apathetic audiences.
   (1) We will not distinguish between the neutral and apathetic audiences in that the same strategies are generally applicable to both types of receivers. A strategy may, however, differ in intensity or purpose between the two groups. For instance, a persuader may stress the importance of the topic with the neutral audience to show the receivers the importance of making a decision on the issue. On the other hand, a persuader may stress the importance of the topic to motivate the apathetic receivers to learn more about the subject and become more involved. We trust you to recognize such subtle difference on your own.
   (2) We have not distinguished between the mixed and other audiences because, as was noted in Chapter 3, we recommend that you target your message to either the friendly, hostile, or neutral members of the mixed audience.
      (a) Most effective persuaders engage in audience segmentation. By that, we mean the persuader will target the message to the segment of the audience (those individuals) who can best help the persuader accomplish the goal of the presentation.
         i. For example, you may focus on the friendly members if you are seeking volunteers (or another immediate behavioral response).
         ii. On another occasion, you may choose to focus on the hostile members aiming to help them become more open-minded on the issue or trying to increase your credibility for future attempts to persuade.
      (b) Because the strategies appropriate for hostile audience members tend to be the most conservative strategies (hence, the "safest"), they seldom will offend the friendly or neutral members of the audience.
         i. On the other hand, using strategies for a hostile audience may be ineffective if you are seeking an immediate and overt behavioral reaction from your audience.
         ii. Similarly the strategies for neutral audiences tend to be "safer" than those for a friendly audience, but should not be your main focus if you are trying to reach hostile or friendly audience members.

c. Members of an audience may change their orientation toward your subject during your presentation. For example, hostile members may become neutral; neutral members may become friendly. Hence, you may need to change your strategies as the orientation of your receivers shifts.

d. We wish to stress that the chances of motivating an entire classroom audience to do something are rather slim. Persuasive appeals carefully adapted to the audience, however, can increase significantly your chances of successfully persuading a listener.

2. *Audience analysis: Audience dynamics.* In addition to considering the type of audience you are trying to persuade, you can enhance your effectiveness by considering and adapting to five general dynamics that operate within receivers: selective exposure, magnitude of change, the inoculation effect, audience participation, and motivation.

   a. Selective exposure. Humans tend to expose themselves selectively to messages and other experiences. Think for a moment about some experiences to which you might expose yourself: a carry-in dinner that follows evening prayers at a Muslim *masjid* (mosque); a concert by Bob Dylan; a lecture by a female journalist from India; a presentation sponsored by Spectrum—Ball State's Gay, Lesbian, Bisexual, Transgender, and Allied Student Association—during "Coming-Out" week; a home basketball game. Few individuals will regularly attend events that do not mesh with their personal interests. Even members of a specific audience tend to choose to use only the specific information that meets their own purposes and expectations. *Listeners tend to pay attention to the content of a message that supports their existing attitudes and avoid the content with which they disagree.* The process of selective exposure has important implications for a persuasive speaker.

      (1) First, you must be thoroughly knowledgeable about the attitudes of your audience if you are to succeed in adapting your message in ways that will be interesting and acceptable to your audience.

      (2) Second, even if you have been successful in weakening the confidence of the listeners in their initial beliefs and attitudes on an issue, you should expect them to seek out other sources of information to restore their confidence. In many instances they will seek out the very information that will contradict the position that you have been persuading them to accept. Thus, at the end of your presentation, it may appear that you have been successful. However, you may find that the information the listeners seek after the speech convinces them to hold more strongly the

position they held before you began speaking. Therefore, with an initially hostile audience, reinforce your point of view repeatedly, use techniques to bolster your credibility, and try to make the audience feel comfortable with their new attitudes and beliefs.

b. Magnitude of change. Because persuasion is difficult, a speaker seldom causes major changes in an audience. *Persuasive speakers must set reasonable goals.* A persuader only can set reasonable goals if the persuader knows the current position of the intended receiver(s). Although there are some cases of instant conversion, generally persuasion occurs slowly, by small degrees, over time. Therefore, in a single speaking event, the speaker needs to recognize the difficulty of the process and choose to accomplish a reasonable magnitude of change through the presentation. Pushing for a major change can result in a "boomerang effect" (the audience becomes more opposed to the position of the speaker).
   (1) When you address a hostile audience, persuasion will be very difficult. You may need to limit your goal to making the audience more open-minded on the issue. In some cases your primary goal may be to build up your credibility on the topic. Enhancing the audience's attitude toward you as a valid source of information should put you in a stronger position to change the audience's attitudes and/or behavior in the future.
   (2) When you speak to a friendly audience, usually your task will be to strengthen the convictions of the audience or move it to action.
   (3) When you speak to a neutral or apathetic audience, usually you will need to convince the listeners that the topic is important and relevant to their lives. If you accomplish this goal, you will probably see an initially favorable movement of the audience toward your goal.

c. Inoculation effect. Listeners will vary in the degree of resistance they have toward accepting beliefs and attitudes different than their own. An inoculation effect in communication is similar to the results of an inoculation in medicine. Medical inoculations are based on the principle that if the body gets a weak dose of an infectious disease, the body will build up its immunities.
   (1) Just as we have better resistance to disease after we have been inoculated, so do *we have more resistance to change when we have had a chance to build up counter-arguments against change. If, however, we have little exposure to an idea, we are persuaded more easily.*

(2) In preparing for persuasion, you should ask yourself, "What have my receivers seen or heard, believe, or feel, that contradicts my message?" You must be prepared to weaken the counterarguments of an audience that has been inoculated against your persuasive arguments.

(3) If, however, you encounter an audience that has not heard arguments against your position, then your task will be easier. Nevertheless, it's wise to present (at least a weak version of) the opposing position and refute it. In general, refutation of opposing ideas is more effective if presented after you support your own position. Providing refutation of opposing positions will help the listeners, after they leave you, to counter the opposition. Creating an inoculation effect is particularly effective if you are trying to motivate a friendly audience but want to immunize your listeners against opposing positions.

d. Audience participation. *Greater persuasion usually occurs if the audience participates in the persuasive event.* An audience may participate psychologically through mental and emotional involvement, and/or an audience may participate physically by following the instructions of the persuader.

e. Audience motivation. Human beings seldom change their beliefs, attitudes, or behavior unless they feel a motivation to do so. Hence, persuasive messages must stimulate motivation within receivers to believe, feel, or act differently.

(1) Ineffective persuaders tend to focus on their own reasons for bringing about a change; effective persuaders focus on the beliefs, attitudes, and values of the receiver(s) to uncover motives that are already existing in the receiver.

(2) We shall continue our discussion of audience motivation in our next element of the communication process, the message.

C. *The message: Emotional appeals, reasoning, and organization.* In addition to projecting a positive image that results in a speaker's credibility, an effective persuader uses and organizes information in a way that appeals to the listeners' emotions (motivational appeals) and reasoning (logical appeals). Aristotle termed these two aspects of persuasion *pathos* (appealing to the emotions) and *logos* (appealing to logic or reasoning).

1. *Emotional appeals*. You will be more effective in your persuasive efforts when you link the message directly to the motives of your listeners. Remember, however, that emotional appeals tend to influence humans in the short term. As time passes, emotional arousal decreases as other motives become more important to receivers. Especially when you are seeking an immediate action, however, you must reach the emotions and motives of your listeners.

a. A. H. Maslow's Hierarchy of Needs provides a useful way to look at the motivation of your audience members. Maslow asserted that once an individual meets a need, the individual no longer will be motivated by the need. A higher need will become the potential source of motivation.

Maslow's Hierarchy of Needs includes:

(HIGHEST LEVEL)

Self Actualization:	the need to contribute or fulfill one's full potential
Esteem:	the need for recognition, respect, or admiration from others
Social:	the need to be accepted by others or to receive love
Safety:	the need to preserve one's health, property, and security
Survival:	the need to meet basic requirements of life: food, water, shelter, and procreation

(MOST BASIC LEVEL) (pp. 153–174)

(1) Listeners are unlikely to be persuaded to act on higher needs if their lower needs are not met. For instance, you are unlikely to persuade people to give to a charity because it will make them feel better if they do not have enough money to eat.

(2) However, showing an audience the ways your ideas will help them meet their needs can be an effective means to persuasion.

b. A persuasive speaker should assume that human behavior is goal-directed and that humans can be set into action by appealing to various needs. There are numerous ways to classify *motives* in addition to Maslow's system. Consider the importance of the following motives on the behavior of your listeners:

(1) acquisition of material things
(2) adventure or achievement
(3) companionship
(4) competition or conflict
(5) creativity
(6) curiosity or discovery
(7) fear
(8) guilt
(9) imitation
(10) independence or freedom

(11)love
(12)loyalty
(13)peer acceptance
(14)pleasure
(15)power
(16)pride
(17)religious conviction
(18)revulsion or avoidance
(19)self preservation
(20)sex
(21)social responsibility
(22)status
(23)sympathy

c. You can motivate listeners by helping them see that they are not meeting their goals.
   (1) First, describe or allude to the goal(s) the listeners hold.
   (2) Second, show or allude to the fact that the audience's goals aren't being met.
   (3) Finally, show the listeners how your plan will help them accomplish their goal(s).

d. You can create motivational appeals by creating an emotional response in the audience and then showing that your plan is an appropriate way to deal with the situation. This approach is more psychological than logical. In fact, some speakers try to shortcut logical thinking in order to manipulate an audience to act. When the speaker moves an audience to take harmful actions, the technique is clearly unethical. Because any technique that shortcuts the logical process of providing sound reasons is subject to abuse, you should use this form of emotional appeal with care.
   (1) You will need to use stories or other forms of compelling evidence to create an emotional reaction in the audience. (For example, Jonathan Edwards, a famous colonial preacher, described hell so vividly that his listeners literally shook in fear.)
   (2) Next, you will need to link your plan to the emotion. (For example, Edwards told his listeners that, if there were not a hell, they would not be so moved, and that their only hope was to follow God.)

2. Reasoning and Support. While messages that appeal to the emotions of listeners tend to be short lived, messages that appeal to the reasoning of listeners tend to be longer lasting.
   a. For persuasion to have a long-term impact, the speaker must provide sound reasoning and evidence. (Please review

Chapter 9 where we discussed ways to reason using examples, statistics, testimonies, and analogies.)

b. You should assume that if you fail to provide sound reasoning and support, the audience eventually will be persuaded by a speaker who does. In the long run, the best reasons will prevail. You should expect that any fallacies in your reasoning will be exposed.

c. You should prepare for counterarguments in the audience's minds and ones that may be raised orally.

d. Repetition and reinforcement are crucial to the understanding and retention of your points.

3. Organization of the message. The organization of both main ideas and support becomes an important consideration for the persuader.

   a. Certain organizational techniques lend themselves well to persuasive messages.

      (1) Persuasive speakers often use the problem–solution pattern for organizing their ideas. The technique is straightforward. The speaker should identify and explain the problem, then offer an effective solution.

         (a) Many ineffective speakers violate this rule by telling the audience what to do (solution) then providing the reason they should do it (problem). By reversing the problem–solution order, speakers raise up the defenses of the listener before they get to their motivating material.

         (b) Many experienced speakers will develop their problem point with a causal pattern of organization.

            i. The speaker may analyze the problem by identifying effects (symptoms) of the problem and then the causes of the problem. Such an analysis will allow the speaker to identify a solution that eliminates or minimizes the causes previously identified in the problem point.

            ii. Similarly, the speaker may identify causes that are likely to result in predictable negative (i.e., problematic) effects in the future. Then, during the solution point, the speaker will identify actions to take to prevent the occurrence of the probable future problem.

      (2) A particularly effective way to organize persuasive messages is the Motivated Sequence developed by Alan H. Monroe.

         (a) Monroe, who stressed the importance of audience psychology, argued that "problems" and "solutions" are too abstract for most listeners.

i. A problem is not a problem to a listener unless it pertains to the listener's needs. (For example, antismoking advertisements prepared for young people once stressed the danger of an early death. Most young people, however, are not worried about death. They're worried about "looking cool." A more effective approach was to focus on the problems of having bad breath and offending one's friends. These "problems" became "needs" for the listener because of the motive to "be cool." *Pointing* was the label Monroe attached to the process of showing the listeners the way a problem affects them.)

ii. Similarly, a solution is not a solution unless it satisfies an individual's needs.

iii. Nor is a plan of action likely to appeal to a listener unless the listener can see the future effects of accepting or rejecting the solution.

iv. Finally, Monroe stressed that no communication occurs unless a speaker has the attention of the listener and that humans are most likely to act if they know exactly what to do.

(b) To use the Motivated Sequence, present your material in five steps:

i. Gain the **attention** of the audience. (By now you are quite familiar with this fundamental goal of a speech introduction.)

ii. Show that a **need** (a problem that points to a need of the individual) exists.

iii. Provide **satisfaction** of the need through a solution.

iv. Give positive and/or negative **visualization** regarding the implementation of the solution. In other words, paint a verbal picture that shows the audience what will happen if the solution is and/or is not put into place.

v. Call for **action**.

(3) A third common way to organize persuasive messages is to provide a list of reasons to believe or act in a particular manner.

(a) Because audiences tend to remember best the first (primacy effect) and last (recency effect) items in a list, effective speakers often place their most important ideas in the beginning and/or ending positions of their list, rather than in the middle.

(b) If you use a list of reasons, they should demonstrate at least a comparative (relative) advantage, if not an absolute advantage, for believing or behaving differently.

(4) Some speakers will organize persuasive messages as a single, emotionally stimulating story that illustrates a problem that clearly needs to be eliminated. After presenting the story, the persuader will commonly identify what the audience can do to help.

(5) If you are attempting to persuade an audience that holds attitudes very different from your own (a hostile audience), organize your material using an *inductive approach*.

(a) You can begin your presentation with information that the audience already believes (or at least does not find objectionable).

(b) You can delay revealing your main purpose until the listeners have accepted some of your evidence and argument thereby becoming more favorably disposed to your main goal.

b. A persuasive speech may include claims of fact, value, and/or policy. The nature of the claim(s) you present will normally shift specific responsibilities to you as the persuader. These responsibilities can best be met by using appropriate organization of your ideas.

(1) A *claim of fact* is a controversial statement that asserts or denies that something exists (is happening), existed (has happened), or will exist (will happen). The task of the persuader is to create an organized case to prove that the claim of fact is probably true.

(a) Clarify the meaning of any ambiguous or misleading terms in the claim.

(b) Identify the facts the audience already accepts that support your claim.

(c) Provide additional reasons and evidence (examples, statistics, analogies, and testimony) for believing that the claim is true.

(2) A *claim of value* is a controversial statement that answers the question "Of what worth or morality is something?" The task of the persuader is to justify the claim of value.

(a) Clarify the meaning of any ambiguous or misleading terms in the claim.

(b) Identify and rank in importance the values (criteria or standards) that should apply in cases similar to this one.

(c) Identify and develop the claims of fact that pertain to the situation.

(d) Illustrate or explain the ways the facts justify the claim of value in light of the proposed criteria.

(3) A *claim of policy* answers the question, "What should be done?" To develop a claim of policy, a persuader usually has to develop several claims of fact and/or value.

(a) Illustrate the existence of a problem that needs to be solved.

i. You may find it useful to identify the causes as well as the symptoms of the problem.

ii. Sometimes, you may need to argue that the problem can indeed be solved.

(b) Identify your specific plan for eliminating the problem.

(c) Illustrate that your plan is the best plan for solving the problem.

i. Show how your plan will address the problem.

ii. Show that your plan will not create new problems.

iii. Demonstrate that the benefits of your plan outweigh the costs of your plan.

D. *Channels of communication.* A speaker who uses a message that involves more senses than hearing often will be more persuasive than a speaker who does not.

1. Persuaders have long known the value of appealing to as many senses as possible. For example, marketers often try to provide potential customers with a multisensory experience with their product.
    a. A free sample of Lever 2000 Body Wash allows potential customers to "feel" and "smell" the product and its result.
    b. Grocery stores often provide in-store samples to promote the purchase of certain foods.
    c. Realtors and automobile salespersons let potential customers "experience" their products in ways that appeal to many different senses.
2. Persuaders have used the ambiance of special surroundings (such as a pleasant restaurant) to create a receptive mood. Speakers have used background music or the display of symbols such as the flag or pictures to create a receptive mood.
3. Ours is an image-oriented society; hence, you will probably be more successful if you use verbal imagery to paint mental pictures or to stimulate other senses of your audience.
4. Similarly, the use of visual aids capitalizes on the idea that "a picture is worth a thousand words."
    a. Computer graphics allow speakers to illustrate and reinforce ideas in a variety of striking ways.
    b. In some situations, you may even appear outdated or uninformed if you don't use computer technology. In other

situations, such as when speaking to individuals who are intimidated by or unfamiliar with computer technology, the use of visual aids not requiring a computer may be an asset.

5. Your challenge as a persuasive speaker is to discover effective appeals that go beyond the words you speak.

III. **Preparing the persuasive presentation.** Now that you have considered major fundamentals of persuasion as they relate to the source, message, channel, and receiver in the process of persuasion, you should be able to understand better, hence remember better, the suggestions we provide regarding specific persuasive strategies and general principles of communication.

A. *Persuasive Appeals.* Persuasive strategies vary in effectiveness depending upon whether the audience is friendly, neutral (or apathetic), or hostile. In other words, the appropriateness of a strategy depends upon whether the listeners' attitudes and behaviors coincide with those you are advocating.

1. The following techniques tend to be particularly effective with a *friendly audience.*
   a. Use strong, overt emotional appeals.
   b. Provide an underpinning of reasonable arguments to increase the chances that your presentation will have long-term effects.
   c. Stress your trustworthiness.
   d. If you have adequately strengthened the audience's convictions, make direct, concrete appeals for action.
2. The following techniques tend to be particularly effective with *neutral (or apathetic)* listeners (and if you can't sleep one night, watch "infomercials" on television to discover more).
   a. Illustrate the importance of the topic to the audience. Show them the ways the topic affects (or probably in the future will affect) their lives and/or the lives of those they love.
   b. Use a large variety of factors of attention (see Chapter 9).
   c. Use moderate, but not extreme, emotional appeals.
   d. While competence, trustworthiness, and attractiveness are all important with a neutral audience, be sure to pay attention to your dynamism. You will find it's nearly impossible to get people involved if you aren't involved and enthusiastic.
   e. As with the friendly audience, provide an underpinning of reasonable arguments to increase the chances that your presentation will have long-term effects.
3. You must prepare with extreme care and thoroughness when facing a *hostile* audience. In fact, if you and the audience strongly disagree in your attitudes before a speech, poor preparation will almost always result in greater disagreement by the end of your speech. Because of the audience's selective perception, they may

focus on those items of disagreement and any vulnerability you present in your credibility, emotional appeals, or reasoning.

a. Set reasonable goals for the presentation.
b. Pay careful attention to building all dimensions of credibility: competence, trustworthiness, and attractiveness. If the audience can reject you as a valid source of information, they can easily dismiss your ideas.
c. Be sure to stress your common ground with the audience. Downplay your differences.
d. Usually it's wise to organize your material taking the inductive approach. Start with the material that is most acceptable (or least objectionable) to the audience.
e. Don't forget the rule that applies to all audiences, but which is especially important when you have a hostile one: *never attack the values of the audience or make comments that could be interpreted as insulting or demeaning.*
f. Present well-documented evidence and arguments, preferably from sources the audience respects.
g. While it is certainly advisable to show the audience that your plan will meet their goals, avoid strong emotional appeals that might be perceived as manipulative.
h. It may be wise to deny or conceal your intent to persuade. We are not encouraging you to lie. We are encouraging you to think about the way you phrase the goal of your presentation. For example, when Senator Ted Kennedy once had to defend his involvement with the death of a secretary, he stated that he was not there to defend himself but to tell the events that led up to the unfortunate death. He did explain the details, but in a way that minimized his responsibility.

4. A *mixed* audience is a particular challenge to the persuasive speaker. To review what we presented earlier:
   a. One approach is to use the "safer" strategies associated with a hostile or neutral audience.
   b. A more effective approach, however, is to do what marketers do—target a segment of the audience. Identify the part of the audience that will best help you accomplish your goal and adapt the presentation to that audience segment, be it friendly, neutral, or hostile.

B. Schaefer (1984) provided some specific suggestions regarding how to give advice that apply almost equally well to most public speaking situations.
   1. Use a "soft-sell" approach.
   2. Don't get angry if your advice is not followed.
   3. Know what you're talking about.

4. Be trustworthy.
5. Give [advice] sparingly.
6. Be brief.
7. Be clear.
8. Respect views.
9. Display sincere caring.
10. [Schaefer goes on to advocate:] Don't preach, make windy orations, ramble, over-talk, complicate the simple, talk down, intellectualize, make convoluted interpretations, indulge in jargon, monopolize, keep attempting to convince, give a prolonged lecture, confuse through the multiplication of examples, use sarcasm, mumble, constantly re-explain, make fun of your own utterances or demean their import, hint at but never specify, endlessly contradict yourself or give double messages, never really mean or take responsibility for what you say, hesitate or tremble the words out, think aloud instead of beforehand, fall in love with and repeatedly promote your own causes and favorite themes, insist on the validity of your own interpretations, or communicate one line while living another. (pp. xii–xiv)

Closing Remarks

Persuasion is a complicated process. The ethical speaker needs to be aware of the needs and motivations of the audience. The degree to which listeners can be persuaded depends upon their initial agreement with the speaker and the speaker's credibility, reasoning, and motivational appeals.

References and Suggestions for Further Readings

Boster, F. J., & Mongeau, P. (1984). Fear-arousing persuasive messages. In R. Bostrom (Ed.) *Communication Yearbook 8*. Beverly Hills, CA: Sage, 330–377.

O'Brian, J. (1995). The gentle art of persuasion. *Supervisory Management, 40*, 14.

DeVito, J. A. (1986). *The communication handbook*. NY: Harper & Row.

Ehninger, D., Gronbeck, B., McKerrow, R. E., & Monroe, A. H. (1986). *Principles and types of speech communication*. Glenview, IL: Scott, Foresman.

Hale, J. L., Mongeau, P. A., & Rhomas, R. M. (1991). Cognitive processing of one- and two-sided persuasive messages. *Western Journal of Speech Communication, 55*, 380–389.

Heider, F. *The psychology of interpersonal relations*. New York: Wiley.

Hunt, Gary, (1987). *Public speaking*. Englewood Cliffs, NJ: Prentice-Hall. p. 159.

Maslow, A. H. (1954). *Motivation and personality*. NY: Harper and Row, pp. 153–174.

McGuire, W. J. (1964). Inducing resistance to persuasion: Some contemporary approaches. In *Advances in experimental social psychology*, L. Berkowitz, ed. NY: Academic Press, pp. 191–229.

O'Keefe, D. J. (1990). *Persuasion: Theory and research*. Newbury Park, CA: Sage.

Schaefer, C. E. (1984). *How to talk to children about really important things*. NY: Harper & Row. pp. xii–xiv.

Shelby, A.N. (1986). The theoretical bases of persuasion: A critical introduction. *Journal of Business Communication, 23*, 5–29.

Smith, M. J. (1982). *Persuasion and human action: A review and critique of social influence theories*. Belmont, CA: Wadsworth.

Synder, E. (1990). *Persuasive business speaking*. NY: AMACOM.

Wondriska, R. (1989). The persuasive edge: The executive's guide to speaking and presenting. *Library Journal, 114*, 75–76.

CHAPTER 14

Speaking on Your Special Occasions

Objectives

After reading this chapter, you should be able to

1. explain the basic principles that apply when speeches are delivered on special occasions;
2. prepare effective speeches for special occasions;
3. provide an effective rebuttal to the remarks of another speaker;
4. deal effectively with interruptions and heckling;
5. read written material effectively; and
6. speak before a camera.

Topical Outline

BASIC PRINCIPLES

- Expectations
- Values
- Accuracy
- Significance
- Role
- Sincerity
- Brevity

SPEECHES FOR SPECIAL OCCASIONS

- The Introduction
- The Presentation and the Acceptance
- The Commemorative
    - The Toast and the Recognition
    - The Welcome and the Farewell
    - The Commencement Address
    - The Dedication
    - The Eulogy

- The Devotional
- The Nomination
- The Speech to Entertain
- The After-dinner Speech
- The Roast

SPECIAL SPEAKING SITUATIONS

- The Rebuttal
- The Interruption
- The Oral Reading
- Speaking Before a Camera
    - Photographers
    - On Television

Key Concepts

Acceptance speech
After-dinner speech
Audience expectations
Commemorative speech
Commencement address
Dedication speech
Devotional
Eulogy
Farewell
Floor director
Heckling
Internal feedback
Interruption
Nomination speech
Oral reading
Rebuttal
Roast
Speaking before a photographer
Speaking for special occasions
Speaking on television
Speech of introduction
Speech of recognition
Speech of welcome
Speech to entertain
Televised interview
Toast

Speaking for Special Occasions and Situations

PERSPECTIVE

I. Ceremonies to dedicate a new building, to honor an outstanding accomplishment, or to say good-bye to an individual who has died are but a few special occasions that rely primarily on public presentations. Certainly, these speeches may be informative or persuasive in nature, but they are unique because of the situation involved. For various social situations, especially those that focus around speaking of one sort or another, audiences have come to develop various expectations of speakers. A wise speaker will be familiar with these expectations.

II. ***Purpose statement***: One of the goals of this chapter is to acquaint you with typical audience expectations so that you can approach a variety of special occasions with understanding and confidence. Additionally, this chapter will explore strategies for common speaking situations that occur in a variety of settings.

III. ***Preview***: We begin by focusing on special occasion presentations. First, we shall present general principles that apply to most special occasions; second, we shall examine typical audience expectations for a selected group of specific occasions. We conclude the chapter by providing recommendations for refuting the ideas of others, dealing with interruptions, reading literary or technical material, and speaking before a camera.

Chapter Body

I. **General Principles of Speaking for Special Occasions.** Human societies and organizations have developed a variety of rituals and ceremonies. A graduation ceremony may be highly formal. Welcoming a new member or employee to a group may be relatively informal. Regardless of its formality, a ceremony or ritual helps to give a group's members a feeling of unity and belonging, a sense of identity. A set of general principles apply at most special occasions.
   A. *Meet audience expectations.* A ritual, by definition, is an event that involves patterned behavior. In other words, certain behaviors must occur, usually in a specific order. Audiences become comfortable with the familiar. When speakers violate expectations and traditions, audience members usually become disoriented or distracted and occasionally become hostile. A major challenge when speaking at special occasions will be to meet expectations creatively without using clichés that might bore the audience.
   B. *Stress common values.* Humans are held together in groups by common values. A special occasion is the time to celebrate the common values of the audience.

C. *Be accurate.* If you make errors, the listeners may conclude that you are an "outsider," not a "true member" of the group.
   1. Be knowledgeable about the person, occasion, or event being acknowledged.
   2. In particular, learn the correct pronunciation of the name of any members to which you refer.

D. *Highlight the significance of the event.* In many situations you will need to refer to the significance of the occasion early in your introduction.

E. *Remember your role.* The content you use and the image you create should be appropriate. At most special occasions, you will be speaking for others as well as yourself. Reflect well upon the individuals or organization you will represent.
   1. <u>Demonstrate good taste</u>. Avoid statements or words the audience might find offensive.
   2. <u>Be sincere</u>. Allow your interest, love, concern, and/or enthusiasm to show through to the audience in your words and behaviors.
   3. <u>Avoid arrogance</u>. Humility is usually prized in speaking for special occasions.
   4. <u>Work for a smooth delivery</u>. A memorized or manuscript delivery may be particularly appropriate.
   5. <u>Exploit your ability to use language effectively</u>.
      a. The more formal the situation the more appropriate is the use of figures of speech (such as the metaphor and simile) and carefully crafted sentences. Language that would seem "flowery" in typical informative and persuasive presentations may add to the effectiveness of a speech in a formal special occasion.
      b. To avoid appearing "stuffy," personalize the content with humor and stories that create vivid images in the minds of the audience.

F. *Be brief.* Most audiences at special occasions appreciate short presentations.

II. **Speeches for Special Occasions**. You have probably already listened to or delivered a variety of speeches at special occasions. Throughout your professional and personal life, you will continue to expand your experiences. We encourage you to take advantage of these experiences. You will see what "worked" and what "crashed." If your experience is limited, perhaps you can learn about the expectations common when the following special occasions call for speeches.

A. *Speeches of Introduction.* A variety of situations requires that someone introduce a featured speaker to the audience. The general purpose of a speech of introduction is to create in the audience a desire to hear the speaker.
   1. The major goals of the speech of introduction are to create an appropriate mood, to arouse interest in the presentation, and to build the credibility of the speaker.

   a. <u>Mood</u>. The nature of the occasion and the speaker's presentation should guide your choices about your own levels of formality/informality and seriousness/humor. Depending upon the purpose of the key speaker, your speech of introduction should help the audience to feel like laughing at the entertaining speech, be ready to learn from the informative speech, and be open for change from the persuasive speaker.
   b. <u>Interest</u>. In the introductory speech, you will want to show the appropriateness and significance of the speaker's topic.
   c. <u>Credibility</u>. As the introducer, you have the responsibility to build the speaker's credibility in an appropriate manner.
      (1) The more familiar the audience is with the speaker's credentials and accomplishments the less time you should spend trying to build credibility. Perhaps you have heard the short introduction: "Ladies and gentlemen, the President of the United States of America."
      (2) Avoid citing a long, tedious list of accomplishments that would bore the audience or embarrass the speaker.
      (3) Avoid excessive praise of the presenter's abilities as a public speaker: let speakers demonstrate their skill. Stressing public speaking skill may not only place unfair pressure on the presenter, but also create unreasonable expectations among the audience.
2. We offer the following guidelines to help you prepare a speech of introduction.
   a. DO:
      (1) be as brief as possible;
      (2) learn and practice the proper pronunciation of the speaker's name;
      (3) make sure all of your "facts" about the speaker are accurate; and
      (4) focus on the occasion, the speaker, and the topic.
   b. DON'T:
      (1) draw attention to yourself;
      (2) summarize the speaker's presentation.
3. We offer the following guidelines for the actual delivery of the introduction.
   a. If possible, ask the speaker to review your remarks before delivering the introduction. If you have your remarks written out or outlined, the speaker can check them for accuracy and provide you with feedback.
   b. End your introduction with the speaker's full name. An embarrassing situation may result if the speaker rises to begin and then has to sit down because you have not finished your

introduction. A conventional, or traditional, practice that prevents such "false starts" is to avoid using the speaker's full name until the end of the introduction, where it functions as a signal to rise to begin.

c. After your introduction, pay close attention to the speaker.
   (1) If the listeners perceive that you are not attentive, they may question your sincerity and become distracted.
   (2) Speakers often refer to their introducers. If you do not react appropriately, you may look rather foolish.
   (3) Some situations require the introducer to thank the presenter at the end of the speech. The better your attention to the speech, the better you will be able to accomplish this function.
   (4) If your instructor requires that class members introduce speakers, he or she may also require that you critique the speech by identifying its strengths and areas needing improvement.

B. The Presentation and the Acceptance.
   1. *The Presentation Speech*. Speeches of presentation accompany the giving of an award or gift.
      a. The presentation should stress the importance, purpose, and/or history of the award and the reasons why the recipient is deserving of such recognition.
      b. In some formal situations, the speaker may need to explain the nature of the process used to identify the recipient.
   2. *The Acceptance Speech*. An acceptance speech acknowledges the support or recognition of others. One may accept an award, a political nomination, an office in an organization, or other forms of recognition and support.
      a. Although the speaker is expected to sound humble and gracious, the speaker should exhibit the characteristics that the group has chosen to honor.
      b. The speaker should show appreciation while striving to inspire confidence by showing he or she is made of the "right stuff."
      c. Although thanking individuals who helped you attain the award may be in order, avoid boring the audience with a long list of "thank you's." Perhaps you have seen an acceptance speech for the Academy Awards that exceeded the time limit given to recipients. For instance, Julia Robert's "long" acceptance speech in 2001 was ridiculed in the newspapers and late-night TV shows.

C. *The Commemorative Speech*. Commemorative speeches recognize events and/or individuals. Usually, a commemorative speech attempts to create an atmosphere of goodwill by downplaying evidence and argument while stressing common values and experiences. The effect of a commemorative speech often comes from the use of effective language (especially vivid language and striking stylistic devices) and the use of real examples (in particular, moving stories). A celebration, a solemn or informal ceremony, or a memorial may commemorate a person or event.

1. The Toast and the Speech of Recognition. The toast and the speech of recognition are probably the most common forms of commemorative speaking.
   a. The <u>toast</u>, a brief form of recognition, frequently occurs at parties or other ceremonies associated with graduations, engagements, anniversaries, business deals, and so forth.
      (1) Although toasts are seldom longer than a few sentences, to avoid the danger of "going blank," write and memorize your remarks in advance.
      (2) Stress the positive. A toast is no time to be critical or humorous in a way that will hurt the recipient or make the audience uncomfortable.
   b. The <u>speech of recognition</u> also contains remarks to acknowledge some form of achievement (for example: a promotion, a birthday, or an anniversary; getting an important new client or setting a record).
      (1) If you must recognize someone who is not a close friend or relative, you should talk to various people to learn more about the individual. Being knowledgeable and having a variety of perspectives will be helpful.
      (2) When talking about the individual, you may want to tell a story that will entertain your audience, while providing new information and insights into her or his character.
      (3) Avoid excesses. It's not your responsibility to portray the person as perfect.
2. The Welcome and the Farewell.
   a. A <u>speech of welcome</u> is designed to make someone feel a part of a group. Although persons joining a group are often excited and pleased about the new circumstances, they may also feel considerable apprehension.
      (1) The speech of welcome aims to help the new person and the members of the group feel comfortable together.
      (2) As a welcoming speaker, you should provide a little background information about the individual, say how fortunate the group is to have the new member, and invite some professional or social interaction that will enhance the forming of relationships.
   b. <u>Farewells</u> are designed to say good-bye in a way that shows appreciation and encouragement.

(1) The speaker may be the one who is leaving, or the speaker may talk about the person who is leaving.

(2) The farewell is usually a bittersweet event. The departing individual may be sad to leave but happy to face new challenges. Friends who remain may be feeling a keen sense of loss. The task of the speaker is to help everyone feel good about that which is ending by focusing on the past contributions and future opportunities of the departing member of the group.

3. The Commencement Address. A commencement speaker's primary goal is to praise, congratulate, and encourage a graduating class.
   a. Additionally, commencement speakers often refer to the contributions of friends and relatives (and perhaps the university itself) to the success of the graduates.
   b. To avoid the sedating effect of clichés and abstractions, effective commencement speakers often use vivid language and tell concrete stories about their own experiences or those of others to encourage the new graduates to make significant contributions in their future careers and personal lives.
   c. As with most forms of commemorative speaking, you should consider brevity a virtue.
4. The Dedication Speech. Dedication speeches are given to devote physical facilities (such as a new hospital wing), financial resources (such as scholarships or charitable trusts), organizations, or individuals to a particular purpose or cause.
   a. As a dedicatory speaker, you should stress the goals and potential benefits of the dedicated resources be they physical, financial, and/or human.
   b. You should acknowledge those individuals who made possible the object of the dedication.
   c. The dedication should be a rallying point for future activities as well as praise for a job well done.
5. The Eulogy. The eulogy is a tribute to an individual or individuals who have died. At funerals and memorial services, eulogies attempt to ease the pain of those who remain by praising the deceased and focusing on the future.
   a. Eulogies usually begin by acknowledging the grief of relatives and friends.
   b. The speaker often uses memorable stories to show that the person who died acted in ways that provide a praiseworthy and comforting model for those who are left.
   c. Family, friends, and associates will be touched in different ways by the loss. Make sure that you talk to significant individuals by name (especially the spouse or partner, children,

and parents of the deceased). Each person in the audience should perceive that you have spoken to her or him.

D. *The Devotional.* A devotional presentation seeks to inspire or reinforce faith.
   1. A devotional presentation often focuses on a scripture, inspirational text, or specific happening.
   2. Explain the relevance of the text or event to the process of spiritual development.
   3. Show the ways that spiritual development creates a sense of hope or confidence in the future.

E. *The Nomination.* Nominations are speeches that place an individual in the running for election to an office.
   1. You should talk in advance to the individual you plan to nominate.
      a. Make sure he or she wants to run for the office.
      b. Try to discover specific qualifications (about which you may not know) that make the individual appropriate for the position.
   2. Out of courtesy, you should show your manuscript for the speech to your nominee in advance and alter it according to his or her wishes.

F. *The Speech to Entertain.* The speech to entertain is designed to be a pleasant experience for the audience. Occasionally, organizations will schedule a speech to entertain at a special social event to rally its members. More frequently, organizations will schedule a speech to entertain in order to create a pleasant, positive atmosphere for its members attending a breakfast, lunch, dinner, or banquet.
   1. Speeches to entertain may make a serious point or provide new information to the listener; however, their primary purpose is to provide amusement for the audience. Hence, your approach should remain light. Avoid highly technical information and complicated argumentation.
   2. Humor often plays a major role in speaking to entertain. However, do not equate the speech to entertain with a stand-up comedy routine that presents a rambling string of jokes and one-liners. Like any effective presentation, a speech to entertain should develop a central idea and have an introduction, body, and conclusion.
   3. You should try to hold the audience's attention through the creative use of interesting and relevant forms of support that contain a variety of factors of attention (described in Chapter 9).
   4. You should try to increase the audience's interest with an engaging manner of delivery and a striking or amusing use of language.
   5. Many inexperienced speakers, unless they already have developed a captivating wit or keen sense of humor, find speaking to entertain a major challenge. If you experiment to integrate humor with the fundamentals of speech preparation, construction, and delivery, you should discover that your speaking to entertain can become a most enjoyable and rewarding experience.

G. *The After-dinner Speech.* Many organizations schedule presentations to follow a meal. Presentations following a breakfast, lunch, dinner, or banquet are called after-dinner speeches. Depending on the custom of the organization or the nature of the event, the after-dinner speech may be designed to inform, persuade, or entertain. Usually, however, even presentations to inform or persuade will remain light and pleasant.
   1. Although the speaker may tackle serious problems or important subjects, most audiences do not anticipate difficult work or controversial or shocking content right after they eat.
   2. Often the speaker will have to contend with considerable noise as people finish eating and the staff clears the tables. Such noise and movement may be distracting. Good-natured references to the distractions and improvised remarks to individual members of the audience may help you hold the audience's attention until the distractions subside.

H. *The Roast.* The roast is a speech designed to poke fun at an individual or group. Frequently, the roast substitutes for the after-dinner speech at a banquet. In some roasts, members of a group take turns "roasting" one person, while in others one person "roasts" several individuals in the group.
   1. An effective roast entertains the audience with good-natured fun that does not hurt feelings of the individual(s) being "roasted." A good rule of thumb is to avoid roasting the target(s) loved ones.
   2. The key to the roast is controlled playfulness. To minimize the chances that you might go too far, test your plans with someone who knows well the target of the roast.
   3. If you are roasting a group of people, make sure you take a pot shot at everyone. Normally, people do not publicly tease people they dislike. Thus, a person who is not included when everyone else is roasted may feel slighted.

III. **Special Speaking Situations.** From time to time, you may have to provide a rebuttal to the evidence or arguments of others, deal with abusive members of the audience, read material in public, and appear before a camera. We offer you suggestions for dealing with such special speaking situations.

A. The *Rebuttal.* A rebuttal is a chance to respond to assertions, arguments, or evidence with which you disagree.
   1. The key to an effective rebuttal is to listen carefully to the other person so that you can respond succinctly to the issues. Avoid becoming distracted or emotionally involved by statements with which you disagree. You may miss important information that the speaker says later.
   2. State the point with which you are disagreeing and provide a counterargument about the idea or challenge the speaker's evidence.

3. Avoid poking fun at the attitudes or attacking the personal characteristics of the speaker, because you probably will lose credibility with audience members who may justifiably perceive your behavior as unfair or unprofessional.

B. *The Interruption.* In response to disruptive behavior such as heckling, avoid panic or becoming defensive. By showing your good nature and ability to maintain control of the situation, you will earn respect from the audience.
   1. If you suspect serious disruption is likely to occur, you should make prearrangements with security personnel of the facilities and/or plan your verbal and nonverbal responses.
   2. You may be able to ignore one interruption, but you should probably respond to any more.
   3. The use of humor and assertiveness are probably the best ways to handle disruptive behavior.
      a. A demonstration of anger will probably please the hecklers because they will know that you are losing self-control.
      b. By asking for the support of the audience, you may be able to keep them on your side.

C. *The Oral Reading.* Especially on formal and important occasions, you may need to read material orally to your listeners. The reading of a literary or technical text shares much in common with the delivery of a speech from manuscript. An effective reading depends on your ability to express the thought and feeling of the text through effective delivery. You will have an advantage if you can read the passage in advance and practice saying it aloud before the speaking situation.
   1. Study the text. As you read the material, consider carefully both the ideas and the feeling that the author has tried to express.
      a. Be sure you understand the meaning of all terms and references.
      b. Be sure you know the expected pronunciations of unusual terms and all proper names.
   2. When possible, prepare your text as you would the script for a speech from manuscript.
      a. Select a font size, line-spacing, and margins that will allow you to read the text easily.
      b. Select an unobtrusive binder that will help you handle your text in a professional manner.
      c. Use highlighting or underlining to provide yourself cues about the way you will emphasize words.
      d. Include notes about the way you wish to deliver the ideas. For example, identify the exact locations where you want to change your rate, volume, or tone of voice. Identify the spots where you need to pause for emphasis.
   3. Appropriate delivery is the key to effective oral reading.

a. Eye contact is important in all speaking situations, even reading. You may want to follow the words unobtrusively with your finger or keep a card on the current line so that you can find your place easily after looking up at the audience.
b. As you read the ideas, attempt to express the meaning and feeling of the text with vocal variety.
c. Be alert to problems common among oral readers.
    (1) Some people have a tendency to end most sentences that they read on a high pitch. Try to avoid such a tendency.
    (2) Other common mistakes in oral reading are reading too fast or talking too quietly.
    (3) Before you begin, yawn unobtrusively to relax your throat and remember to breathe fully. A well-supported voice will provide a good basis for varying your rate, tone, volume, and pitch according to the meaning of the passage.

D. *Speaking Before a Camera.* Occasionally, you may find a photographer with a still or video camera recording the speaking event. On other occasions, you may need to deliver your ideas completely by means of a televised broadcast or a videotaped presentation.
1. Try to be sensitive to photographers with still and video cameras when you speak in public. The experienced speaker will notice when a photographer moves into position and holds up the camera. At that point, the experienced speaker often looks directly at the camera while speaking. Of course, you should not look only at the camera. Look at the audience in the general direction of the camera until the photographer finishes shooting.
2. Speaking before a television camera has become quite common. Although a variety of situations are possible, you should understand the special demands of the televised medium and ways to handle yourself both in presentations and interviews.
    a. Television is an intimate medium that generally requires that you deliver ideas quickly and concisely within strict time limits. You will appear in several close-up shots that will magnify or emphasize your facial expression, gestures, and general appearance.
        (1) On television, you will face the challenge of appearing and sounding enthusiastic and sincere without becoming overly dramatic.
            (a) We recommend that you practice using a video recorder to assess and modify your style of delivery. You will see if your style is appropriate and pleasing to a viewer. With a little practice, you will rapidly develop a sense of internal feedback that will allow you to know the type of image you are projecting.

(b) For television, you should give special consideration to your appearance.
   i. You may need to use more makeup than usual and should probably at least powder your face so that the strong lights do not glare off your skin.
   ii. Pastel and medium colored clothing tends to look better than very dark or very light clothes. White, stripes, plaids, and wild prints can cause problems.
   iii. Jewelry may cause distractions by reflecting light or making noises.

(2) For television, you should probably memorize your key ideas and the evidence that will support these ideas.
   (a) If you are making a presentation, you will want to be able to look directly at the camera. If you have seen a televised lecture, you know how difficult it is to pay attention to a speaker who reads notes or pages of manuscript.
   (b) For televised interviews, you should phrase ahead of time the points you wish to communicate to the viewers. You also should have evidence ready to prove that your points are reasonable and important.
      i. When the interviewer asks you a question directly related to a point you have prepared, you will be ready to answer with confidence and clarity.
      ii. When the interviewer asks you a question you do not want to answer, you will be able to explain the reasons why you would rather address another issue that you can justify as more important.

(3) You can maximize the impact of your presentations if you capitalize on the fact that television is a visual medium. Few events are more tedious than watching a television speaker who uses no visual aids.
   (a) In most occupational settings, you will have a support staff to prepare visual aids. However, your responsibility will be to tell the staff the nature of the aids you need.
   (b) If you must supply or create visual aids yourself, remember the shape of the television screen. Be sure to leave large margins on your visual aid so that the rectangular nature of the screen does not cut off important elements of the visual aid.

b. In the preparation of televised presentations, a floor director will stand next to the first camera to be used and point a finger at you when you are to start.
   (1) Do not look at the floor director.

(2) Look directly into the lens of the camera before you start, while watching the floor director in your peripheral vision.

c. Occasionally, you may need to move your position for shots from differently positioned cameras.
   (1) The floor director will help you make such changes.
   (2) After you have finished speaking, continue looking directly into the camera lens until you are sure that you are no longer being photographed.

d. Being interviewed on television, especially if you are representing a group or organization in controversial circumstances can pose difficult challenges. Entire books and even workshops are available to prepare executives and representatives of organizations to deal with such circumstances. We would like to mention just a few of the considerations you should always keep in mind about the two-person televised interview.
   (1) For studio interviews, the production staff will use at least three cameras. The camera positioned behind the interviewer will capture the interviewee from the interviewer's perspective. A second camera will be behind the interviewee, and a third will take shots that include both the interviewer and interviewee.
      (a) Most of the time, as an interviewee, you should ignore the camera and maintain eye contact with the interviewer. The production staff will select the camera that is most appropriate at any given time.
      (b) If you want to emphasize your sincerity when making an important point, look directly into the lens of the camera behind the interviewer. Hopefully, the production staff will select this camera.
   (2) Maintaining a steady gaze is particularly important when listening to an accusatory question or making a serious point. If your eyes dart back and forth or look down, you may appear "shifty" or guilty.
   (3) Avoid the common habit of nodding your head up and down when you are listening to questions. In conversation, we often nod to signal that we are listening. If you nod your head when an interviewer presents negative information or accusatory questions, you may give the viewer the impression that you are agreeing with the damaging information or admitting to guilt.

Closing Remarks

We believe that growth and success come from a willingness and resolve to learn constantly about an ever-changing world. We have offered you the knowledge of speaking in some of the special occasions and situations we have experienced. We hope this knowledge contributes to your success. However, the world and the expectations of audiences are changing constantly. We encourage you to evaluate and take advantage of the suggestions we have provided and challenge you to discover the newly developing expectations of the audiences you will face in your own lives and times. Best wishes.

References and Suggested Readings

Andrew, P. H., & Baird, J. E. (1995). *Communication for business and the professions.* Madison, WI: Brown & Benchmark.

Brislin, R. (1994). *Intercultural communication training.* Thousand Oaks, CA: Sage.

Evans, T. (1992). *Well-done roasts: Witty insults, quips & wisecracks perfect for every imaginable occasion.* NY: St. Martin's.

Gamble, T., & Gamble, M. (1994). *Public speaking in the age of diversity.* Boston: Allyn and Bacon.

Grice, G. L., & Skinner, J. F. (1995). *Mastering public speaking.* Needham Heights, MA: Allyn & Bacon.

Hanna, M. S., & Gibson, J. W. (1995). *Public speaking for personal success.* Dubuque, IA: Wm. C. Brown.

Iapoce, M. (1988). *A funny thing happened on the way to the boardroom: Using humor in business speaking.* NY: Wiley.

Lucas, S. E. (1995). *The art of public speaking.* NY: McGraw Hill.

MacArthur, B. (1994). *The Penguin book of twentieth-century speeches.* New York: Penguin.

Powers, J. (1994). *Public speaking: The lively art.* NY: Harper Collins.

Shea, G. F. (1984). *Managing a difficult or hostile audience.* Englewood Cliffs, NJ: Prentice-Hall.

Sprague, J., & Stuart, D. (1992). *The speaker's handbook.* Ft. Worth, TX: Harcourt Brace.

Synder, E. (1990). *Persuasive business speaking.* NY: AMACOM.

CHAPTER 15

Your Communication in Other Settings

Objectives

After reading this chapter, you should be able to

1. prepare effectively for an employment interview;
2. participate effectively in team presentations;
3. contribute to the effectiveness of small, task-oriented groups.

Topical Outline

EMPLOYMENT INTERVIEWS

- Forms and purposes of interviews
- Preparation for the employment interview
- Practicing for the interview

GROUP PRESENTATIONS

- The panel discussion
- The symposium
- The forum
- The team presentation

COMMUNICATING IN SMALL GROUPS

PURPOSE AND CHARACTERISTICS OF GROUPS

GROUP MEETINGS

GROUP DYNAMICS

- Norms
- Roles
- Cohesiveness
- Physical environment
- Conflict management
- Decision making
    - Problem-solving agenda
    - Brainstorming
    - Nominal group technique
    - Consensus

Key Concepts

Agenda (for a meeting)
Brainstorming
Central negative
Cohesiveness
Conflict management
Consensus
Description
Empathy
Employment interview
Equality
Forum
"Groupness"
Group dynamics
Group meeting
Group presentation
Image management
Information provider
Interview (preparation)
Interview (types of)
Leader (of a meeting)
Nominal group technique
Norm
Panel discussion
Physical setting
Problem orientation
Problem-solving agenda
Provisionalism
Résumé
Role (of group members)
Self-centered roles
Social level (of group communication)
Social roles
Socio-emotional leader
Spontaneity
Supportive climate
Symposium
Task leader
Task level (of group communication)
Task-oriented group
Task roles
Team presentations
Tension releaser

Speaking in Professional Contexts: Employment Interviews, Team Presentations, and Group Meetings

PERSPECTIVE

I. The fundamental principles of speech construction and delivery that you have already studied will serve you well in a variety of oral communication settings. We conclude this text with a discussion of three important types of oral communication you are likely to encounter in your professional careers: the employment interview, the group presentation, and the group meeting. Being able to perform well in each of these contexts will contribute to your personal success in your career. We alert you that we present a limited number of concepts and principles pertaining to each context. Each of these contexts for communication is the topic of a course offered by the Department of Communication Studies.

II. ***Purpose statement:*** We believe you can increase your ability to succeed in business and other professions if you can prepare effectively for employment interviews, work well with others in team presentations, and function effectively in group meetings. The purpose of this chapter is to acquaint you with fundamental concepts and principles of these three forms of business and professional communication.

III. ***Preview:*** First, we shall focus on ways to prepare yourself for effective employment interviews; second, for effective team presentations; and finally, for productive performance in groups and teams. The discussion should give you valuable suggestions you can apply in your everyday life.

Chapter Body

I. **Employment Interviews.** One formal type of speaking situation is interviewing. An interview has many characteristics of both public speaking and interpersonal conversation. Most effective interviews need research, planning, and organization—skills that are especially important in public speaking. The interaction, however, may contain many elements of spontaneous conversation.

   A. Interviews can take a variety of forms and have a variety of purposes.

      1. The typical interview involves only two individuals. In some circumstances, however, an interviewer may interview several individuals together or several interviewers may question a single interviewee.

      2. Interviews may center around information gathering, persuasion, or social pleasure. In your career you will probably find yourself selling an idea, if not a product or service, to another individual. Additionally, you will evaluate and be evaluated by others in interviews. You also may find yourself in two-person situations involving counseling, grievances, and other business and professional circumstances. Before you can pursue your career, however, you will need to use interviewing skills to obtain the professional position you desire.

B. *Preparing for the Employment Interview.* In an employment interview, you as the interviewee should have specific objectives. You will want to present a favorable image, find out more about the company and the position, and sell yourself so that you get the job (if indeed it is one that appeals to you). You can never be prepared for every possible question, but you can be prepared for the interview. Your preparation should include researching the organization and position, preparing résumés and applications, planning ways to project an appropriate image, and practicing for the interview.

1. Before the interview, you will need to learn as much as possible about the organization. The reference librarian can help you locate information about most organizations. You may learn helpful information from someone who works for, or has dealings with, the organization. You should learn as much as possible about the prospective employer.
   a. How long has the company been in existence?
   b. What are the main functions of the company?
   c. Who are some key officials in the organization?
   d. What kind of economic success has the organization had?
   e. What might they look for in a particular employee?
   f. What do they expect in the job under consideration?
   g. What is the typical salary range for the type of position for which you will be interviewing?
2. Your preparation for the job interview should also include the creation of a résumé.
   a. Typically, college students and recent graduates will prepare a résumé in one or two pages.
   b. You may want to prepare several résumés, each emphasizing different skills or interests, depending upon different positions that interest you.
   c. You should copy or laser print your résumé on high quality (containing cotton) white or ivory paper. Today, many professional copy shops will prepare a computer file for you and print your résumé on a high quality printer, an approach with several advantages.
   d. Your goal in the preparation of a résumé should be to communicate your abilities and special skills in a document that looks professional.
      (1) Most résumés contain the applicant's name, address, telephone number, educational background, employment experiences, and special skills.
      (2) Often a list of references with their positions, addresses, and telephone numbers are provided on a separate piece of paper with the applicant's name, address, and telephone number at the top.

e. Sending a résumé to an employer by mail seldom gets a job, but it can help open the door for an interview. If possible, stop by the company and talk to the interviewer in person. Just seeing the potential employer for a minute—to say you are applying and want to know if he or she needs any additional materials—will make you a "known quantity" and give you an edge in the application process.

3. Often, you will need to complete an application for the position.
   a. Like the résumé, the application should be neat. Because applications are often copied for files, you should use black ink or type your application.
   b. It's a good idea to keep a copy of a completed application (or a list of your vital statistics) with you during your job hunt so that you will know dates, addresses, phone numbers, and other information. Thus, you will be able to complete job applications more easily and accurately.
   c. Because of federal laws and sanctions against discrimination, employers normally prefer that applicants not attach a photograph to résumés or applications.
4. Image management. The image you project will come primarily from your appearance and nonverbal behaviors. Based on initial impressions, interviewers may decide in a matter of seconds whether they will consider you a viable candidate for the position.
   a. Of course your appearance should be neat and appropriate both when you interview and when you pick up or deliver an application. A general rule of thumb is that you should dress slightly more formally than the people in the position currently dress. Clothes that are simple but business-like are a good idea. Remember that physical attractiveness increases a person's persuasiveness; you can use your appearance to enhance your chances of success.
   b. Through your physical behavior you should attempt to project personal characteristics appropriate for the position.
5. You can prepare for the interview by anticipating likely questions, phrasing answers, planning your own questions, and attending to your image. You should anticipate the expected and the unexpected.
   a. You should prepare concise answers to frequently asked questions. The following are some of the frequently asked questions.
      (1) What do you want to be doing with your life in five years? Ten years? Twenty years?
      (2) What do you know about our company?
      (3) Why do you want this job?
      (4) Why should I hire you?
      (5) What are your greatest strengths? Weaknesses?

(6) What do you have to offer over the other applicants?
(7) How do you think you will fit into this company?
(8) Aren't you rather young (old, inexperienced, over-qualified, or whatever) for this position?

b. Many interviewers are not trained in effective interviewing techniques. Hence, be prepared for the unexpected.
   (1) Although certain questions are not allowed in interviews because of possible discrimination, many interviewers ask them out of ignorance or insensitivity.
   (2) Some interviewers are shy and expect the interviewee to carry the ball.
   (3) Some interviewers are too talkative and dominate the interview so that the interviewee has difficulty getting a word in edgewise.
   (4) In case you need to take the initiative, be prepared to work into the conversation concise statements that illustrate your strengths. Additionally, prepare appropriate questions that you can ask the interviewer.

c. Use your sensitivity to guide the interview with your own nonverbal behaviors, questioning, and comments. The more practice you undertake and the more interviewing experience you gain, the greater will be your confidence and potential for success.
   (1) The wise job applicant will *practice aloud* answers to a list of potential questions.
      (a) We recommend you try recording yourself role playing an interview with a friend. Seeing and/or hearing yourself will allow you to evaluate and adjust your image. If recording equipment is not readily available, at least practice before a mirror.
      (b) Many universities have mock interview programs associated with their placement centers or academic departments. Consider taking advantage of these valuable services.
      (c) Before you schedule an interview for the position you want most, you may want to schedule interviews for positions you find less desirable. You may find not only that you like the "less desirable" position but also that you can gain interviewing experience.
   (2) Any form of practice will help you to feel more confident and enable you to prepare answers that say what you want to say.

II. **Team Presentations.** Frequently in business and professional settings, speakers must work together to provide a program or presentation. While the basic skills of speech construction and delivery apply, these settings have features worth considering. Effective team presentations demonstrate a sense of unity and teamwork. To project these characteristics, *speakers must coordinate their efforts*. In this section, we strive to acquaint you with four common presentational methods—the panel discussion, the symposium, the forum, and the group presentation—to enhance your chances of success in such situations.

A. In a *panel discussion*, a small group of individuals (frequently with different experiences and perspectives on a topic) holds a discussion of ideas in front of an audience. The panelists come prepared to discuss their ideas and make points they feel are important. In that the chair or moderator guides the discussion, a panel often resembles an interview with one interviewer and several interviewees. However, spontaneous, free-flowing, conversational discussion among the participants usually dominates an effective panel presentation.

B. In a *symposium*, several individuals deliver related speeches in front of the audience. A chair or moderator may introduce each speaker, provide transitions, and handle audience questions. Sometimes a respondent or critic is included to raise issues with the various speakers. As a member of a symposium, you should adhere strictly to the time you are allotted. Stealing time from other speakers may make you look unprofessional.

C. In a *forum*, audience members ask questions of speakers who respond with brief impromptu speeches. Usually, a forum follows a panel discussion or a symposium.

D. In a *group presentation* or report, an individual or a team of speakers presents the findings of a task group's deliberations.
   1. In most business or professional settings, the group leader or another individual member of the group will deliver the presentation. The speaker should approach the situation just as a speaker would approach any informative or persuasive presentation. The speaker, however, should take care to speak for the group, representing accurately the group's deliberations and conclusions.
   2. Often in classroom presentations and occasionally in business presentations, several members of a group will contribute to a presentation. Members of the speaking team will need to work together to make sure the overall presentation has an introduction, transitions, and a conclusion. The group members should avoid any behaviors that would suggest a lack of unity and teamwork.
      a. Each speaker for the group should be familiar with the material that other members plan to present.
         (1) If speakers unintentionally repeat or contradict material already covered, the audience probably will infer that your group did not work well together.

(2) If speakers do not pay close attention to the presentations that precede them, they will not be able to adjust to deviations from the original plan.

b. All members of the team should consider themselves "*on stage*" during the entire presentation. Members of the team should fix their attention on the individual currently speaking. Team members should avoid engaging in any behavior that would draw attention away from their speakers.

(1) If team members appear bored or disinterested, the audience is likely to feel the same way.

(2) If team members speak to one another during the presentation, they are likely to distract listeners.

(3) If team members stand or move during the presentation, they are likely to draw attention away from the speaker.

c. Team members should decide in advance who will assist with visual aids and who will provide transitions to "cover" should anything go wrong.

III. **Communicating in Groups.** *The ability to work cooperatively is a fundamental skill valued in the U.S. workplace.* Experts predicted that by the turn of the century, especially in high-tech firms, team performance will contribute more strongly to an employee's assessment than will individual performance (Benson, 1992). The predictions have become reality. There are a variety of types of groups depending upon their purposes and functions. Communication in groups always operates on two levels, the task level and the social level. Effective communication on the task level advances the work to be done. Task communication involves such behaviors as offering information and opinions, suggesting ways the group should attack its problem(s), and summarizing the ideas and plans of the group. Effective communication on the social level helps maintain the group and meet the interpersonal needs of its members. Social communication involves such behaviors as praising ideas or actions, harmonizing relationships, and releasing tensions. In some groups, task concerns dominate the interaction. In other groups, social concerns dominate. This section focuses on task-oriented groups but recognizes that social concerns are important in all groups.

A. *Purpose and Characteristics of Groups*

1. We define a "group" as individuals who communicate together over time for a common purpose. By this definition, several people waiting in line for concert tickets are not a group, but a collection of individuals. To be a "group" or team, an association of individuals must demonstrate the following characteristics of "*groupness*":

a. meeting (usually in a face-to-face situation) over time for a period of several hours, days, weeks, months, or even years;

b. relying on one another to accomplish at least one common objective or goal;

c. developing specialized roles and rules of behavior (norms) for its members; and
d. having a small number of people (approximately 3 to 25 people).

2. Advantages and Disadvantages of Groups.
   a. When people work in a small group, they generally expect certain positive results. Through a division of labor, tasks impossible or difficult for an individual become feasible. Normally there is increased accuracy in the work involved and enhanced commitment to the decisions made.
      (1) The saying "two heads are better than one" reflects the notion that additional people tend to increase the quality of decisions by contributing additional knowledge, perspectives, and insights. (In some cases, however, groups instead demonstrate "pooled ignorance.")
      (2) When a group of individuals comes up with its own solution to a problem, the members are more likely to feel committed to their solution than if a policy or plan is imposed on them. They will probably work harder to implement the plan of action they have selected themselves.
   b. Although group problem solving has advantages, the major disadvantage is that the process is less efficient than individual problem solving.
      (1) Because of the interaction among the group's members, group work takes time.
      (2) If you are facing a routine matter or are in the midst of a crisis that requires immediate action, you should probably make the decision yourself (or allow a decision to be imposed by your leader).
3. The task-oriented group. A task-oriented group focuses on a common interest. Whether the interest is a hobby, a social concern, or a work problem, an issue or interest brings the members together. For example, a learning group may meet to study an issue or concept or to prepare for an exam or classroom presentation. A problem-solving group may meet to identify the causes of and the solutions to a problem. A quality improvement team may meet to find ways to make an organization more efficient and effective.

B. *Group meetings*. Group meetings may vary in their levels of formality. Some group meetings are highly formal using an agreed upon set of rules such as parliamentary procedure. Other group meetings may be short and spontaneous, resembling an informal, conversational discussion. We shall focus on the typical planned business or professional meeting that emphasizes open discussion of issues and possible plans of action. Meeting will be more productive if both the leader and participants prepare for the meeting and understand basic principles of group dynamics.

1. The leader of a meeting can facilitate effective group deliberations by preparing the members for a meeting and providing guidance during the meeting.
   a. The leader should prepare and distribute an *agenda*, or plan for the meeting. With prior notice, members will know the issues to be discussed and be able to prepare appropriately.
      (1) In particular, the leader should notify individuals who need to give reports or supply information needed by the group. If needed information is not available, the meeting may not only waste time but also frustrate and demoralize members.
      (2) Distributing a written report or information prior to the meeting may save valuable meeting time.
   b. The meeting leader should move the group through the discussion in an orderly and efficient manner by providing the following functions:
      (1) initiating topics and providing needed background information;
      (2) recommending procedures;
      (3) seeking opinions and information;
      (4) regulating participation (encouraging the quiet to speak and interrupting tactfully the overly talkative);
      (5) encouraging members to test ideas and opinions; and
      (6) keeping the group on track (summarizing when appropriate).
   c. A follow-up after the meeting is often appropriate to remind members of the decisions and commitments they have made and to maintain the group's momentum for the next meeting.
      (1) If someone is taking minutes (a formal record of the decisions and actions taken by the group), he or she should type up the minutes as soon after the meeting as possible and have them checked by the chair or another group member before distribution.
      (2) Additionally, the leader should check with members between meetings to make sure they are gathering information or taking actions necessary for the next meeting.
2. Members must assume personal responsibility for the success of the group. Thoughtful participation is key to an effective group. Members need to contribute information and opinions, ask questions, and test ideas to maximize the group's performance.

C. *Group dynamics.* Too often, members blame "poor leadership" for a group's lack of productivity. Any member of a group or team can help to provide guidance and help to solve problems that the leader has failed to address. Group members (including the leader) will be more effective if they understand basic concepts and apply basic principles of group dynamics.

1. Norms. Norms are the habits, expectations, or "rules for proper behavior" that develop in a group. A group's members come to expect that they will follow certain procedures and participate in particular ways. A group will develop expectations about the way it will use time, handle disagreements, and treat members who violate group norms. Group norms prescribe the standards for appropriate attire and physical appearance; group norms govern whether refreshments are served (and if so, which kind are appropriate).
   a. Group members should attempt to develop norms that help the group to accomplish its task.
   b. Group members should attempt to suppress or eliminate happenings that would reduce effectiveness were they to become habitual.
      (1) Many leaders will begin meetings exactly at the appointed time to prevent the development of the norm that the group will wait until all members arrive.
      (2) Many groups will develop formal or informal sanctions to "punish" members who come unprepared or let the group down. Such sanctions make it clear that the group values responsibility and commitment.
      (3) Many groups will avoid adjourning a meeting because members are not prepared or eager to work. Instead, the effective group will attempt to find another significant goal it can accomplish during the meeting. Such action prevents the development of a *"no-work" norm* that may ultimately destroy group effectiveness.
2. Roles. Over time, members of the group will come to expect individual members to behave in specific ways, that is to assume certain roles. Because these behaviors become expected, roles are a form of group norms. An effective group will encourage its members to assume or share productive roles suited to their knowledge, skills, and personalities. An effective group will discourage behaviors (roles) that reduce group effectiveness.
   a. Beneficial roles may be classified as *task roles* (for instance, initiator of procedures or opinion seeker) that advance the work of the group or social roles (for instance, encourager or harmonizer) that facilitate interpersonal relationships in a group and strengthen the group as a team. Both task and *social roles* are important to the effectiveness and stability of a group as a social unit. While communication scholars have identified twenty or more beneficial roles in small groups, we wish to focus on the five which Cragan and Wright (1980) argue are essential to having a good discussion. If members of your groups are not demonstrating one or more

of these roles, we encourage you to provide the functions of the missing role(s).

(1) *Task leader.* The task leader will help to set goals and create agendas. The task leader will seek ideas and seek members' evaluation of ideas. Additionally, the task leader will summarize when necessary and regulate participation.

(2) *Socio-emotional leader*. The socio-emotional leader will promote a productive interpersonal climate in the group. The socio-emotional leader will praise accomplishments and appropriate behavior and attempt to resolve conflict that has become personal. Additionally, the social-emotional leader will encourage the group to analyze and deal with its problems in working together.

(3) *Information provider*. The information provider will contribute ideas.

(4) *Central negative* (or devil's advocate). The central negative will instigate conflict by evaluating ideas and assessing opinions.

(5) *Tension releaser*. The tension releaser will help members feel comfortable with one another. The tension releaser will use appropriate humor to break tensions.

b. Effective groups will not encourage members to display nonproductive roles. Members should understand that problematic behavior continues because the group is rewarding the "offender" by meeting his or her personal needs.

(1) *Self-centered roles* stem from the "offender" trying to meet his or her personal needs at the expense of the group's needs. Typical self-centered roles include acting overly aggressive, blocking group progress, seeking recognition (through boasting or clownish behavior), and acting helpless.

(2) Initially, members should deal with inappropriate behavior in the least threatening manner that will allow the "offender" to "save face." If serious disruption continues, the group should address the problem directly.

(a) Usually, an appropriate initial reaction is to ignore the inappropriate behavior. Laughing at inappropriate clowning, for example, will encourage more disruptive behavior.

(b) If problems continue, the leader or a member should discuss in private how he or she feels when the "offender" engages in the nonproductive behavior.

(c) If the "offender" continues to engage in highly damaging behaviors, the group should discuss the problem with the "offender" to try to establish appropriate expectations.

3. Cohesiveness. Cohesiveness refers to the commitment of group members to the goals of the group and to the group itself.
   a. As cohesiveness increases, members tend to feel more free to disagree on important issues and group productivity will increase. If cohesiveness becomes excessive, through members allowing maintenance of the social climate to become their primary goal, disagreements may disappear and the group may become nonproductive.
   b. A group can increase its cohesiveness by focusing on its identity and successes.
      (1) By developing traditions and rituals a group can help members feel they are a part of a cohesive group. Similarly, by referring to past experiences and "inside jokes," members can foster a sense of belonging to a unique and important group.
      (2) By setting and accomplishing realistic short-term goals, a group enhances a feeling of success and pride. A sense of progress or accomplishment contributes to a group's attractiveness to its members.
      (3) By praising group and individual accomplishments, group members can enhance cohesiveness.
      (4) Occasionally, the most effective way to develop group cohesiveness is to identify a common enemy or outside threat.
4. Physical setting. The physical setting in which a group meets can influence interaction significantly.
   a. Seating arrangements can influence significantly the interaction of group members. Leaders sometimes seat members by using name cards to facilitate or discourage particular types of interaction.
      (1) A circular arrangement allows each person to see and respond nonverbally to the others in the group.
      (2) By seating a quiet group member directly across the table, a leader can more easily increase the quiet member's contributions.
      (3) By sitting at the side of a rectangular table rather than at the head, a leader can create a greater feeling of equality among the members. By sitting at the head of the table, the leader can increase her or his dominance.
      (4) Individuals are more likely to talk directly to others seated across the table. Hence, a leader may choose to seat two members with a history of personal conflict on opposite ends of the same side of a rectangular table.

b. Members are more likely to work cooperatively in a pleasant, comfortable environment.
   (1) Appropriate refreshments tend to contribute to a spirit of cooperation and cohesiveness.
   (2) Hot or cramped quarters tend to increase the aggressiveness of members.
   (3) Distracting noises tend to increase the level of frustration among members.

5. Conflict Management. Effective conflict management is important to the success of a group. A group without conflict is often a group that is too tense to test ideas. Conflict shows that people feel free to express themselves and to disagree. Without conflict, a group cannot risk, change, grow, and develop. But while conflict over ideas and methods often helps a group reach its goal, other personal conflict can destroy a group. Hence, a group needs to develop ways to manage its conflict.
   a. One important characteristic of effective conflict is to keep disagreements on the idea level and not allow them to become personal.
   b. Another fruitful way to handle conflict is to encourage those who are disagreeing to focus on their common interests or goals rather than on the positions they are holding or the demands they are making.
   c. In effective groups, at least one member of the group will function in the role of conflict manager or tension releaser. When conflict over ideas starts to become personal, the conflict manager will help to mediate the dispute and/or the tension releaser will use humor to stop further escalation of the dispute.
   d. An important skill in interpersonal communication is the ability to use language in a way that promotes a *supportive climate.*
      (1) If people feel supportive rather than defensive, they are better able to avoid and/or manage conflict.
      (2) To promote supportiveness, Gibb (1961) suggests using description, problem orientation, spontaneity, empathy, equality, and provisionalism.
         (a) *Description* gives information and details rather than passes judgment.
         (b) A *problem orientation* focuses on identifying and solving a problem together rather than on trying to impose a personal solution. The emphasis is on "we" rather than "I."
         (c) *Spontaneity* occurs when we remain free and open to ideas rather than plotting to manipulate others.

(d) *Empathy* involves trying to think and feel about issues and events from the perspective of the other person. Acting in a cool, uncaring, overly objective manner, can add substantially to the frustration and defensiveness of others.

(e) *Equality* occurs when we act as though we respect the worth and talent of other individuals, rather than as though we are superior or arrogant.

(f) *Provisionalism* (tentativeness) can reduce defensiveness in others by showing we are open-minded and willing to consider change. When we insist on having our own way, others often become defensive.

6. Decision making. A tendency among humans is to be solution oriented rather than problem oriented. Many groups try to identify solutions before they understand the problem at hand. Too frequently, group members will "go along" with the suggestions of an important, powerful, or outgoing individual and fail to provide the knowledge and perspectives they possess. You can minimize the potential for such problems by using a problem-solving agenda, brainstorming, nominal group technique, and consensus decision making.

   a. *Problem-solving agenda*. Often the purpose for forming a group or team is to solve a problem. By following a methodical and comprehensive problem-solving agenda, a group can reduce its chances of "solving" problems that really don't exist. Below are the steps commonly used in problem solving.

      (1) Define the problem. Describe the symptoms, history, and scope of the problem.

      (2) Determine the criteria that need to be met for a solution to be judged appropriate. Is it important to eliminate the causes of the problem? How do such considerations as money, time, location, and participation, limit our possible solutions?

      (3) Identify possible alternative solutions. Come up with as many ideas as possible.

      (4) Apply the criteria. How do the solutions measure up according to the criteria for judgment?

      (5) Select the best solution.

      (6) Plan a step-by-step method for implementing the solution.

      (7) Evaluate the effectiveness of the implementation and determine what changes are necessary.

   b. *Brainstorming*. One effective way of generating creative ideas is brainstorming. The group leader should remind members to follow faithfully the rules of brainstorming: Members are to generate ideas as quickly as possible without responding verbally or nonverbally to any idea; a member of the group should record ideas for later clarification and evaluation by the group.

(1) The objective is to generate ideas. Even an "off-the-wall" idea may help a group member to think of a valuable idea.

(2) By putting off evaluation until an entire list of ideas is formulated, the results are apt to be comprehensive and creative.

c. *Nominal group technique*. Nominal group technique is but one of the many techniques now widely used by teams in business and the professions to promote continuous quality improvement (see for example, Scholtes, 1988; & Cornesky, 1995). Nominal group technique is a formalized process of brain-storming that helps reduce the inhibiting influence of group members who have high status. For nominal group technique to be effective, the leader (or facilitator) should make certain the group follows each of the specified steps of the technique.

(1) The leader should explain the steps of the process to the group. This step should normally require 5 minutes.

(2) The leader should pose a question or problem to the group. The leader should ask members to list their answers or ideas silently on paper within a specified amount of time (15 minutes should be adequate for a complex issue; 5 minutes may be adequate for a simple one). The leader may repeat the question while members are working silently or place it in writing before the group.

(3) Using a flip chart or other suitable medium, the leader will prepare a master list of ideas from the group. The leader will call upon each member in turn to read one item remaining on his or her individual list. The leader will instruct members to cross off of their personal lists any idea already on the master list. Once all members have presented one idea, the leader will continue again around the group, taking one idea at a time, until no items remain on the lists of the individual members. If at the end of 20 minutes, members still have items remaining on their lists, the leader will (for the last time) ask the members to give the most important idea that they have not yet struck from their individual lists.

(4) The leader will display the master list of items for all to see. The leader will repeat each item asking if members understand the idea. If an item is not clear, the leader will ask its proposer to clarify the issue. The leader will

not allow members to debate issues at this time, only to clarify. This stage should take no more than 15 minutes.

(5) Based on the number and complexity of items, the leader will ask each member to consider the importance of each item on the master list to the issue at question. The leader will then ask the members to rank (silently and individually) a specified number of items from most important to less important. For a complex issue, the specified number may be 5 or 6—for a simple issue, 3. The results are tallied to identify initial group priorities (If members are asked to rank the 5 most important items on the master list, an individual's most important item will receive 5 points, the second most important item will receive 4 points, and so on. The leader will tally the points to identify the items receiving the highest number of points from the rankings by individual members). This stage should take fewer than 15 minutes.

(6) The leader will ask participants to discuss the results of the ranking. The leader will encourage members to develop, defend, or dispute the rankings. Members may even discuss items receiving a low ranking. The leader will encourage members to participate but discourage members from dominating. The leader will encourage members to group similar items into a single category. This phase should take fewer than 30 minutes.

(7) Following the potentially stressful nature of the debate, the leader may want to give the group members a short break.

(8) After the discussion of items, the leader again will ask each member to rank privately a specified number of items in their order of importance. The items again will be tallied (as in step 5) in order to prepare a master list of group priorities. These priorities will provide a focus for future group discussion.

d. *Consensus*. Consensus occurs when all members agree with a decision. We encourage you to promote decision making based on consensus when working in groups or with teams, especially if they are small. Consensus avoids compromise or voting by attaining a true agreement among all members. Although it may seem difficult to reach, consensus can be facilitated by following a logical problem-solving method and focusing on the common interests and goals of the group members.

(1) Majority rule occurs when the group votes and the wishes of the larger portion of the group prevail.

(a) This approach is often used in elections, and although the process may work well in a variety of settings, majority rule often causes problems in a small group.

(b) The problem with this approach is that you may have a significant and unhappy minority. In a group of five people, a vote of three to two may have a crippling effect on the continued success of the group.

(2) Minority rule happens when a strong, vocal, or powerful minority imposes its will on the group through intimidation or threat.

(3) Compromise occurs when both sides give in to accept some middle-of-the-road position. Granted both sides receive some of what they want, but again, probably neither side is happy with the final decision. Additionally, decisions reached through compromise often are weak ones.

Closing Remarks

In this chapter we have explored a limited number of concepts and principles that should help you in employment interviews, in team presentations, and in group meetings. Should you desire to study these topics in greater depth to refine your personal skills, the Department of Communication Studies offers courses each semester dealing with each of these three broad areas: COMM 325, Interviewing; COMM 330, Group Decision Making; and COMM 375, Presentational Speaking. When you are considering general electives for your academic program, please consider the potential personal value you can obtain from these courses.

References and Suggested Readings

Benson, T. E. (1992, April 6). Quality and teamwork. *Industry Week*, 66–68.

Brilhart, J. K., & Galanes, G. J. (1986). *Effective group discussion, 6th ed.* Dubuque, IA: Wm. C. Brown.

Cline, R. J. W. (1990). Detecting groupthink: Methods for observing the illusion of unanimity. *Communication Quarterly, 38(2)*, 112–126.

Cornesky, R. A. (1995). *Turning continuous quality improvement into institutional practice: The tools and techniques*. Port Orange, FL: Cornesky & Associates.

Cragan, J. F., & Wright, D. W. (1980). *Communication in small group discussions: A case study approach*. St. Paul, MN: West Publishing.

DeVito, J. A. (1986). *The communication handbook: A dictionary*. New York: Harper & Row.

Gibb, J. (1961). Defensive communication. *Journal of Communication, 11*, 141–148.

Messmer, M. (1995). The art and science of conducting a job interview. *Business Credit, 97*, 35–36.

Napier, R. W., & Gershenfeld, M. K. (1993). *Groups: Theory and experience*. Boston: Houghton Mifflin.

Pavitt, C., & Curtis, E. (1994). *Small group discussion: A theoretical approach*. Scottsdale, AZ: Gorsuch Scarisbrick.

Scholtes, P. R. (1988). *The team handbook: How to use teams to improve quality*. Madison, WI: Joiner Associates.

Stewart, C. J., & Cash, W. B. (1994). *Interviewing: Principles and practices*. Madison, WI: Brown & Benchmark.

Tubbs, S. L. (1995). *A systems approach to small group interaction*. NY: McGraw-Hill.

APPENDICES A–D

Appendix Introduction

Objectives

After reading this appendix, you should be able to

1. select an appropriate topic for a speech;
2. recognize and evaluate your own level of public speaking anxiety;
3. consider possible sources of receiver stress;
4. name and use several methods of reducing communication apprehension;
5. identify the elements of an argument; and
6. construct and refute arguments.

Key Ideas

- You should select speech topics about which you have knowledge or interest, that you can adapt appropriately to the audience and the occasion.
- Once you select the speech topic, you will need to narrow it, and determine your specific purpose.
- There are many potential causes of stage fright and communication apprehension.
- Misconceptions sometimes cause people to give poor advice for controlling communication apprehension.
- You can reduce your public speaking anxiety by using a technique that works for you:
  Systematic desensitization
  Visualization and relaxation techniques
  Cognitive restructuring
  Skill development
  Movement
  Practice
  Developing confidence

Key Ideas (continued):

- Communication stress can be a problem for listeners.
- Toulmin has provided a model of argumentation comprised of 6 elements.
- The warrant of an argument determines the type of argument.
- Each type of argument can be strengthened or rebutted in unique ways.

Key Concepts

Argument
- Causal reasoning
- Deductive reasoning
- Inductive reasoning
- Reasoning by analogy
- Reasoning from authority
- Reasoning from sign

Assigned topics
Attitudes, speaker
Audience knowledge
Backing (Toulmin)
Brainstorming
Claim (Toulmin)
Classroom setting
Cognitive restructuring
Communication apprehension (CA)
Communication apprehension, causes
Communication apprehension, misconceptions
Communication apprehension, reducing
Communication stress
Data (Toulmin)
Deep breathing and CA
Developing confidence
Impromptu speeches
Movement and CA
Occasion
Practice and CA
Rebuttal (Toulmin)
Real world settings
Relaxation techniques and CA
Skill development and CA
Sources of topics
State versus trait anxiety
Stress
Systematic desensitization
Title for the speech
Qualifier (Toulmin)
Warrant (Toulmin)

APPENDIX A

Selecting a Topic

Perspective

Many students struggle over selecting a topic for a speech. They want to chose a topic in which both they and their class have interest. Certainly the audience must be considered, but we recommend that you choose something you care about, in which you feel genuine interest and enthusiasm.

A professor remembers a student, Michael, who gave a speech more than 20 years ago about "hogs." Now "hogs" is not one of her favorite topics. In fact, she didn't remember having any interesting conversations about hogs, unless you wanted to include discussions about the Arkansas Razorbacks. At the time of this student's speech, Joan didn't know much about hogs nor did she want to know much about hogs. This student and his family were hog farmers, however, and not only did he know about hogs, he thought hogs were great.

Joan confessed that she had never heard a more enthusiastic speaker. Michael talked about why he liked hogs, how they were used, what they were like to raise, and the whole time his non-verbal behaviors reflected a genuine knowledge and enthusiasm that the class could not ignore. His audience listened responsively, and when Michael finished his speech, they applauded with the same kind of enthusiasm he had used while he spoke.

If Michael had asked in advance, "Do you think 'hogs' would be a good speech topic?" all of us would have incorrectly said "no!" His expertise and interest were contagious, however, and his speech turned out to be one Joan has remembered throughout the years, after having forgotten hundreds of other speeches.

We think the most important way to chose a topic is to select something you really care about. Many students of public speaking procrastinate when it comes to selecting a topic about which to speak. They periodically think about the assignment, roll a few topics around in their minds, but put off making a decision. We recommend that you give serious thought to topic selection early, making sure the subject is one in which you have genuine interest, then begin to prepare your speech.

The purpose of this appendix is to review ways to choose a topic and gear it to your audience and situation. The second part will discuss speech anxiety and how you can control it.

Speech Topics

There are several sources of topics for public speaking situations. First, the topic may be assigned. Some instructors assign general topics to expose their students to topics that will increase their knowledge or views—for instance, a country, medical advances, ways to help others, and so forth. You may find yourself in a business situation, for example, where the boss says: "In our staff meeting next Monday, I'd like for you to talk 5 to 10 minutes about how your department can improve customer satisfaction." Or perhaps in another course your professor says: "Each student will give an oral report on a topic I will assign from the following list." Perhaps a friend is moving away, and another friend who is having a party says: "For fun, each of us is going to tell a story about Pat, so be prepared."

In a way, you have an advantage when the topic is preselected. The topic is probably preselected for one of a few reasons: (a) you know about the topic and are asked to speak about it because of your knowledge; (b) the topic is something you are expected to learn, so you will be an "expert" by the time you give the message; or (c) the audience or occasion calls for a specific topic. You may be given a general area to discuss, a specific topic, or even a specific purpose or title for your speech. In these cases you will still need to refine your topic for the occasion and audience, but then you are ready to get to work on preparing the speech.

Although you may be given a general type of topic or a general purpose (to persuade, to inform, or to entertain), in many situations you will select your own topic. The general rule of thumb is: *select a topic you know something about or want to learn something about.* You, as speaker, have several potential sources: hobbies, personal experiences, personal beliefs, travel, events, and ideas or concepts.

Brainstorming: Topics for a Speech to Introduce Oneself

Hobbies

The way I spend my time

Television

Favorite film

Favorite film directors

Managing my time

My major

Why I selected my major

Languages I speak

Part-time jobs

My values

My most central value

My three greatest assets

A famous person I like

A famous person I dislike

The woman I most admire

My favorite course in college

My favorite professor

An organization I belong to

My favorite television program

Why I decided to attend this college

The biggest advantage in being me

Something that really bugs me

If I could change the world, I would...

Why I decided to attend college

How my family is different

The biggest problem I faced while growing up

Ways I have earned extra money for college

Ideas for managing money while in school

Who I would like to be if I were not me

What I want to do ten years from now

What I want to accomplish before I die

The most important thing I learned in high school

A prejudice I have observed that needs changing

When I leave the world, I will have made it different because

The country I would most like to visit outside the U.S.

The difference between film and television techniques

The advantages/disadvantages of going away to school versus staying near home

Choosing a Topic

Self criticism and self-doubt will inhibit your creativity. If you find yourself procrastinating in picking a topic, try brainstorming. In brainstorming, you start by giving yourself a goal (for example, "I'll come up with 40 topics in 5 minutes"). Repeat to yourself, "I won't criticize myself. I'll write down any idea that comes into my head—no matter how wild or crazy." Start writing down topics as quickly as possible without evaluating any idea. Even a silly idea may help you think of a good idea. On the previous page is a list of topics brain stormed for an assignment: To introduce oneself.

When you have reached your time limit, review your list. See if the topics you wrote make you think of any other topic. If so, add them to the list. Now is the time to evaluate the list. Place a star by all topics that are interesting to you. Place a check mark by all the topics that you think would be of interest to your audience. Review the items with both a star and a check to pick the best topic.

Issues to Consider in Topic Selection

There are three basic factors to consider in topic selection: the speaker, the occasion, and the audience.

The speaker. Any speaker should have interest, knowledge, commitment, and appropriate attitudes regarding the topic. For example, one student decided to give a speech in class on wearing seat belts. Is she interested in this topic? Yes, her father worked in safety at Chevrolet, and he instilled a genuine interest in safety. Does she have knowledge? Yes, her father frequently discussed tests conducted at Chevrolet, so she has more knowledge than the average person. Does she have commitment? Yes, her husband was in a serious car accident and is alive only because he was wearing seat belts. Does she have appropriate attitudes regarding the topic? Yes, she never moves a car unless she and her passengers are wearing seat belts. Thus, the topic of seat belts appears appropriate from the standpoint of the speaker.

The occasion and setting. The occasion is another important issue to consider. Certain topics may be more appropriate in some situations than others. Think of a variety of speech settings: a funeral home, a classroom speech, a synagogue, a sorority, an auditorium, a business meeting room. As you think of each setting, you probably see a different type of room, differences in the way people dress, differences in the age of people in attendance, and more. The setting affects the nature of the speaking situation.

A student wants to give a speech on birth control. Is this topic appropriate for a classroom situation? Probably. Will the requirements of time limitations be adequate? Perhaps not for a thorough discussion. Can and how might visual aids be used? The student will need to talk to the course instructor. Some topics may be inappropriate in a college classroom. Some that would be appropriate in a college classroom would be offensive for an after-dinner speech. Often the occasion will dictate the type of topic and purpose that are (and are not) appropriate. You will also need to consider the physical context of your speech. Is your classroom too small to comfortably seat the students? Is the temperature uncomfortable? Will there be distracting noise from a busy street outside the room? These are some environmental factors the speaker needs to consider. Is the occasion special or unusual? Are you the only speaker or one of a series of speakers? Have you been invited to speak? Will the time and place of the speech matter for your given topic? If you are the last presenter on Friday afternoon, your boss and colleagues may lose interest quickly. If you are the invited speaker to a group's centennial celebration, you'll need to make reference to that. You may not be able to change the occasion, but you'll need to adapt to it. And the occasion may not make any difference in your topic selection in the long run, but having considered the possibilities of this influence, you'll be better prepared.

The audience. Finally, you should consider the audience. A student wants to talk about nuclear disarmament. What are the knowledge, interest, and attitudes of the people who are listening to the speech? Do classmates feel the same urgency about the problem? Will the audience agree or disagree with the principle? Do they have the same values as the speaker? How knowledgeable about the topic are the students? Especially regarding sensitive topics, you should know your audience's knowledge, interest, and attitudes.

Imagine that your professor made the assignment that you "give an informative or persuasive speech on a topic of particular interest to college students." Obviously, you would consider the special nature of college students, their interests, the way they like to spend time, issues on your particular campus, and so on. If you brainstormed for a minute about topics for class, you might come up with a list like the following:

Sample Topics of Interest

AIDS
Apathy
Attendance (punctuality) in classes
Bargains in...
Best... (restaurant, theater, apartment complex, fraternity, campus organization, course on campus, etc.)
Birth control
Books
Campus museum
Challenges
Clubs
Competition
Dressing more fashionably
Driving and drinking
Eating out
Entertainment
Exercise
Faculty office hours
Films
Health
History
Homesickness
Honesty (Problems with plagiarism, computer sabotage, etc.)
Improving your GPA
International students
Intramural sports
Job placement services
Local culture
Meeting new friends
Maintaining long distance relationships
Nutrition
Parking problem on campus
Physical fitness
Planning
Pool
Religious/spiritual support
Research
Safe sex
Safety
Scientific contributions by alumni
Shopping
Speakers on campus
Sports
Sororities and fraternities
Student advising
Student performances (choir, orchestra, theater, art, etc.)
Student politics
Student union
Study abroad
Study habits
Study groups
Time management
Town-gown relations
Winter activities

You may find some of these topics completely inappropriate for you as a speaker. Others may be ones you would rather not listen to. Most topics, however, can be adapted to the particular speaker, audience, and occasion. Some of these topics would be of interest to more than just college students, but you would need to adapt them differently depending on the audience. For example, an elementary or high school student might be as interested in the topic of "study habits" as a college student. You would not, however, give the same speech about "study habits" to elementary students, high school students, college students, and parents. The most effective public speech would adapt to the knowledge, interests, and attitudes of the particular audience.

Generally in the classroom setting you will have a youthful and educated audience—probably open-minded about many issues—that is interested in learning. What will your classmates know about your topic? How can you arouse interest in the topic?

You will need to select a topic that is appropriate for assignments, so that you fulfill the instructor's requirement. For example, if your instructor assigns an informative speech, you should choose a topic about which you have knowledge or will do research so that you have knowledge before you speak. A speech that only entertains the class may be popular among classmates but would be inappropriate for the informative assignments.

In this course you will be evaluated and probably graded based on your communicative success. In the "real world" your public speaking success may influence such factors as people's opinion about you, your potential for advancement in a company, respect for you by community members, and more. Real world settings can be complicated when you try to select a topic appropriate for the audience. As with your classmates, you will often know your real world audience. They may be people who belong to your club, other parents at your child's school, or coworkers, for example. In other cases, you may know very little about the audience. The more you know, however, the better chance of adapting appropriately for an effective message. It is helpful to know audience characteristics, including the audience's knowledge, composition, beliefs, and requirements of the occasion.

Topics to Avoid

Some professors of public speaking recommend that students avoid certain topics. The suggestion may be made because of university regulations, ethical considerations, past experiences of the professor, the exceedingly controversial nature of a particular topic, sensitive or offensive material, or simply because the professor has already heard so many speeches on a certain topic. Some instructors have a list of "forbidden topics," which may include topics such as abortion or capital punishment. Instructors may prohibit speeches that advocate illegal actions or adherence to a particular religion. Some instructors have rules prohibiting the use of animals, weapons, illegal materials, drugs, alcohol, illegal, or shocking materials in the classroom. These decisions may have been made because of the teacher's understanding of audience expectations.

Be sure that you know your teacher's policies on appropriate topic selection, as well as the specific requirements of your course instructor. But more importantly, use mature judgment whenever you talk to any group of people. You should consider carefully the potential reaction of your classmates and instructor before you speak and show them the sensitivity and respect they deserve. Terry, for example, gave an informative speech about cancers caused by chewing tobacco. He brought some photographs that many people would consider sickening. Terry showed good judgment, however, when he warned the class in advance that he had shocking photographs and they need not look at the pictures if they didn't want to. Only about two thirds of the class actually looked at the pictures that he displayed at the back of the room. Thus, Terry found a good compromise approach for a sensitive presentation.

Problems with Topics

There probably are more problems with speakers than there are with subjects. Some problems with subjects may include dull subjects, difficult subjects, controversial subjects, preselected topics, and impromptu speeches.

It is difficult to decide if a "dull topic" is dull because the material is inherently dull or the speaker's approach to the material is dull. The problem is more likely to be the latter. A teacher will find certain subjects easier to teach because they are more interesting. The difference is actually the teacher's perception of what is interesting rather than the class's perception. One teacher developed an instructional board game for class that students always seem to enjoy. She takes what she considers a dull topic and makes it interesting by converting it to the game format. Thus, one key to making the speech interesting is to use a creative approach in finding support.

Although you may generally consider the subject of water and water bills to be dull, two friends discussed their water bills because of a copy of *Water News* (Vol. 7 No 1, Summer, 1988) which contained a series of statistics about water: "An individual person uses 168 gallons of water daily…It is possible to drink water that was part of the Dinosaur era...95% of a tomato is water…It takes 11 gallons of water to process 1 chicken…It takes 1,500 gallons of water to process one barrel of beer," and so on. The pamphlet proved to be quite interesting to the two women because of the variety of unusual information it contained.

Thus, anyone can be successful with a "dull" subject depending on the approach. If the speaker finds unusual, humorous, or important support and gives an enthusiastic delivery, the audience will probably perceive any topic as interesting.

Special Considerations

Sometimes a topic is preselected for the speaker. Perhaps you will find yourself assigned to give a speech on a study area in a class, or a specific talk to a community group, or a pep talk at work. Whatever the situation, you will have less freedom with a preselected topic. You will need to search for a variety of support—remember that beginning with early research is helpful—and develop an interest and enthusiasm about the topic.

An impromptu speech is one that comes up at the spur of the moment. In a speech class, the instructor may simply give you a topic and you must immediately begin a message. Perhaps you are in a meeting and decide to give an impromptu speech about an important issue. Concentration on one or two key ideas will help. You should think of support while you talk and examine your audience's reactions so that you can best adapt to them.

There are some topics that prove difficult, usually because they are about something the audience considers private or emotionally charged. One teacher had a guest speaker come to a communication fundamentals class to talk about Acquired Immune Deficiency Syndrome Disease (AIDS). Societal attitudes, prejudices, fears, and misinformation made AIDS a difficult topic for the speaker to discuss and for the students to listen to open-mindedly. To prepare for the speech, the teacher gave students a brief quiz about their knowledge and attitudes and how the topic should be approached in the classroom. In order to give a background, clarify information, and instruct, the guest speaker had to use explicit language. The result was that while some students were uncomfortable about the topic and chose not to attend class that day, in contrast, other students evaluated the speech as the most worthwhile part of the entire course. Some listeners had tears in their eyes, perhaps thinking about someone they knew, as did the speaker as she talked about men, women, and children she has watched die from AIDS. Both the teacher and the guest speaker approached this controversial topic with great care.

There are many things you can do to enhance your effectiveness with problem topics. Speaking sensitively, recognizing audience attitudes, warning your audience, and telling them that it is okay to show emotion are a few techniques that can help with difficult topics.

Title for the Speech

Many speakers never actually title their speech. For example, a business executive may give a message to the company staff without ever formally titling the speech. In other cases, the title may be important in encouraging people to listen to you. You have probably seen, for example, the catchy title of a sermon on a sign outside a church. If the speech title arouses interest and thought, the title may actually induce some members to attend. An effective title may arouse curiosity or encourage pre-thinking about the idea of the speaker. The title may give the listener a handle to help him or her remember the speech.

Generally, the effective speech title will portray the speech essence and arouse interest in the speech. Too often, students begin a speech with something like: "Today, I'm going to talk to you about wearing seat belts." The problem with this approach is that some students who don't wear seat belts automatically turn off the speaker because they don't want to hear something that conflicts with their behavior. Those students who do wear seat belts may mentally turn off because they already wear seat belts and don't think they need to listen. Beginning a speech by announcing a controversial topic is usually a mistake.

Imagine that a fellow student planned a speech on how we communicate through the use of our eyes. A speech entitled "Eyes" would arouse less interest than one entitled "The Eyes Have It" or "You and Eye." If your speech will be introduced by someone who will announce the topic or if the topic is used for publicity, the title should be one that will arouse attention.

Closing Remarks

Choosing a topic for your speech is critical to your communication success, but considering yourself, the audience, and the occasion and setting can increase the chances of your being an effective speaker.

APPENDIX B

Coping with Stress in Communication

Perspective

One day before class Don, a student in his late twenties, came to his professor's office to talk about his speech. He said he was nervous about giving his speech and he started to cry. The professor thought he was trying to be funny. Don had spoken in class discussions many times and the professor didn't expect him to be especially concerned about his first speech. As they talked, the professor realized he was extremely upset. Don was so nervous about his speech he had lost control.

One time a professor had a student who had missed several classes, including ones in which he was supposed to give a speech. John brought in a doctor's excuse. The excuse just happened to be from the professor's own doctor, so she knew it was real. But when she read the excuse, it only listed the days and times of her public speaking class. That seemed rather fishy, so the professor asked the student about it. "Why does the doctor just excuse the days and times of my class?" she asked. The student responded: "Because I start vomiting about a half an hour before I'm supposed to come to your class."

Another student said the first day of class that she had dropped (had withdrawn) from the required public speaking class four times. She was a graduating senior and needed to pass this time. By using relaxation and positive visualization, her professor helped her. The student not only survived the course, but received a high grade.

Although these examples are extreme, they make the point that public speaking is a severe problem for some people. If you are "typical," the idea of giving a speech makes you nervous. This section explains the concept of stress or communication apprehension and gives you methods for handling the nervousness you may feel in public speaking situations.

Speech Anxiety

Usually during the first class of a public communication course, someone will ask "how many speeches do we have to give?" Any response seems to prompt a few groans, as students complain about the idea of "getting up in front of a group." Anyone learning public speaking should give attention to the concept "communication apprehension" (or CA). For some individuals CA is a personality trait that leads them to avoid all situations involving oral communications. For such individuals, the stress of communicating far outweighs the benefits they expect from communicating. Other individuals have little difficulty communicating with others except in public-speaking situations. For these individuals, the stress of succeeding when the outcome is unknown leads to a strong case of *stage fright*. Nervousness during public speaking is a topic of serious concern to many students.

In one classic study, when asked to list their fears, the individuals who responded listed public speaking more often than the fear of death! Other studies have supported research that fear of public speaking is, indeed, a common apprehension (Grice and Skinner, 1993; Lucas, 1986). A number of specific things can be done, however, to manage communication apprehension and stage fright. There are all kinds of reactions to giving a speech: vomiting, shaking muscles, tears, forgetfulness, procrastination, and more. Most people, however, can learn ways of coping with nervousness during speaking.

No matter whether you call the concept "stage fright," "fear of speaking," "shyness," "anxiety," "communication apprehension," "public speaking anxiety," or some other term, virtually everyone has experienced "it." Research indicates that a normal or typical reaction to new or stressful situations is some nervousness or fear, that is, a feeling of stage fright. When we talk to other people, we are risking ourselves, opening up, and making ourselves more vulnerable. This process does, and should, create some tension. In fact, the person who feels no tension is as unusual and atypical as the person with debilitating anxieties (Richmond & McCroskey, 1985). The good news is that public speaking experience reduces or eliminates excessive stage fright for most individuals. If you do not experience a reduction in stage fright during this course, you probably possess CA.

Most of the time, we cope with nervousness because the communication is desirable for other reasons. We want to meet new people, so we engage in small talk and think of something to say. We want to get the new job, so we endure the dreaded job interview. We want to land the account, so we give a persuasive presentation to the prospective client. We want to pass the course, so we give the oral report that goes with a written term paper. Usually the advantages of the communication outweigh the risk of the communication.

Causes of Communication Apprehension

There are different theories about what causes communication apprehension. Some theorists believe that genetic reasons partially explain the apprehension. Perhaps you know someone who is rather shy and you have noticed that one of your friend's parents is the same way. There is some evidence that there could be a physiological basis for this behavior.

Others believe that the causes are environmental. If your parents are outgoing, you observed their behaviors, and you probably learned how to be outgoing also. If your father, for example, enjoyed giving speeches at work, and you watched him practice with confidence at home the night before, you may have acquired more skills and confidence than other people who did not have the advantage of a positive role model. Often, individuals who are shy have one shy parent and one dominating parent.

Some theorists believe that the causes of reluctance to communicate are sociological in nature. Some people simply may not have learned effective communication skills due to sociological or cultural factors. Socioeconomic factors influence the things to which we are exposed. While some students may not have been exposed to, or learned, needed communication skills, others may simply not care to interact in traditional ways. Another sociological aspect is that we feel more comfortable with people who are similar to us. A student who differs from the majority of college students around him or her—because of age or race or ethic background, for example—may feel more uncomfortable and thus more apprehensive than other students. Some students may be "different" or perceive themselves as different from others, accept their difference, and have no desire to change. In this case, their behavior is their choice, so being required to act in other ways causes apprehension.

Misconceptions. Most students have certain misconceptions about communication apprehension. First, students typically believe they are unique because they are apprehensive. In actuality, apprehension is an extremely common attribute. Most students believe that everyone around them can tell how nervous they are when they give a speech. In actuality, audiences—even public speaking instructors—generally fail to accurately perceive the level of nervousness the speaker is experiencing. Another misconception is that overgeneralized advice can help others control their communication apprehension. We typically hear advice such as "just imagine the audience with their clothes off." Actually, that could be an even more frightening or distracting thought. Some people say "relax and take a few deep breaths." A student who tries to follow this advice, however, may hyperventilate and feel dizzy and disorientated. The suggestion "Look over the audience's heads at a spot in the back of the room!" results in a lack of concentration on the audience, poor audience adaptation, and failure to maintain eye contact. Such advice can cause a serious problem because most listeners consider good eye contact one of the most important delivery aspects of an effective public speaker.

There is an ongoing debate in the research on communication anxieties regarding whether the anxiety speakers experience is a state or a trait. Is it something caused by a given situation or is it just one manifestation of a more generalized anxiety? The intention here is not to get into the psychological nature of communication anxiety, although you may find individualized psychological counseling to be effective if you have problems you need to work through. The intention is, however, to give you some specific coping devices that can help you in this course and later in life.

Systematic Desensitization. Systematic desensitization works like allergy shots. If you are allergic to pollen for example, your physician may give you injections of pollen. The injections are very small amounts of the antigen that allow you to desensitize yourself against the pollen. Then when you next are exposed to the pollen, you can handle it more easily with a less severe allergic reaction.

The same technique works in communication apprehension. Either in your imagination or in reality you expose yourself to the public speaking situation in small doses. Perhaps one time you simply walk into the classroom in which you will give your speech. Then the next day you walk up to the front of the room. The next time you walk to the front while there are students in the classroom and you look out at the students. Another time you practice giving your speech while no one is in the room. One student with severe apprehension gave his first speech from the back of the room, another gave his first speech sitting down, another gave her first speech to the first three students who showed up for class while another student kept the rest of the class outside until she finished. Success in these small preliminary doses made it easier for these students to give their regular or next speech.

Many counseling centers will provide a more formal type of systematic desensitization for individuals who have debilitating fears (be they of public speaking or spiders). Basically the method involves teaching the subject to relax. Once the subject is relaxed, the counselor will ask the subject to visualize an extremely mild form of the situation or object that causes fear (for example, "Imagine that you might be telling two coworkers about a new policy"). The counselor will ask the subject to imagine a more threatening situation. As soon as the subject signals he or she is feeling tense, the counselor will ask the subject to repeat the prescribed relaxation exercises. Once the subject relaxes again, the counselor will start again with a less threatening scenario and begin working upward toward more threatening ones. The process continues until the subject can imagine an extremely threatening situation without feeling tense.

Visualization and Relaxation Techniques. Even without a counselor, you can apply a variety of visualization and relaxation techniques that will help you face your fears. You have probably heard of or known a woman who has experienced "natural childbirth." In this case, the woman learns to consciously relax her body so that she can give birth more easily with less discomfort. The same kind of conscious relaxation techniques can be used to calm oneself when experiencing communication apprehension. Basically, the student tenses her or his body muscles, then relaxes them. By learning the difference between tension and relaxation, the student can recognize tension and consciously relax more easily. By visualizing various public speaking situations, then checking for tension and consciously relaxing, the student can better control communication apprehension. This technique has proven successful as a means of reducing speech anxiety (Ayres & Hopf, 1985).

Most students who use relaxation and visualization techniques find success by listening to commercially prepared relaxation audio tapes. Another approach is to make an audio tape for yourself. You will probably do best if you speak slowly, calmly, and distinctly when you make your recording, with pauses that allows you to consciously relax while listening. Listening to such a tape throughout the semester—even during the few minutes before your class starts—may be helpful. A sample script for a self-made relaxation tape appears at the end of this section.

Cognitive Restructuring. Cognitive restructuring is a process by which individuals can change their thinking. Usually this approach is used during psychological counseling, but you may find it helpful to talk about your fears with a close friend, with another member of your communication class, with your instructor, or in an open class discussion. Perhaps you could discuss why you are nervous about the speech. You might talk about what has happened in previous public speaking situations. You may want to discuss what might be the worst thing that could possibly happen. Then you will need to focus on "restructuring" your thinking so that you can replace the negative experiences of the past or unrealistic expectations of failure with positive images of the future.

One approach to cognitive restructuring is to write out affirmations, record them on an audio tape recorder, then listen to the tape on a daily basis. Affirmations are positive thoughts, helpful concepts, and inspirational promises you make to yourself. These statements should be designed to restructure old patterns about public speaking so that your thinking processes will be the way you want them to be. You can make a tape for yourself. Even if it is only five or ten minutes long, you can listen to the tape in the car while driving to school, on your Walkman while exercising, or at night while you are relaxing in bed just before you fall asleep. Remember, a key to restructuring your thinking is that you should listen to the tape daily or at least regularly.

Skill Development. Most people can make major strides in controlling nervousness as they acquire new skills. In public speaking, when one learns specific skills related to how to conduct research, how to plan a speech, how to increase the effectiveness of reasoning and support, and how to provide effective delivery, the process of delivering a speech becomes easier. Learning the needed skills will help you keep your nervousness under control.

Movement. Tense muscles will shake. While you read this passage, take a moment to tense all your muscles. Make a fist, make your body stiff, tense every part of you as hard as you can. Tense yourself more and more until you start to shake. Then move your arm. Moving muscles are less able to shake. If you show your nervousness through trembling knees, for example, you will probably tremble less if you walk while speaking. By gesturing while you talk, walking (not pacing) rather than stand rigidly behind a lectern, or using a visual aid, the movement may reduce shaking as you help yourself concentrate on your message and your audience.

If you don't allow your muscles to be stretched tightly, but instead allow them to move, you may help calm yourself in other ways. For one thing, you won't have to worry about anyone noticing your shaking knees.

Practice. The way we plan things in our minds is not the same as they will come out of our mouths. But at least by planning, we can have some effective visualizations. In most cases, you should practice a speech at least once. You may find it interesting to talk to yourself in the mirror or give your speech to a friend. Some people find success giving their speeches to a dog or cat (who is usually a noncritical listener). Others practice saying their ideas aloud while driving. Still others record their speech on audio or videotape, then analyze the play back. Practice will help control nervousness while speaking.

Developing Confidence. Sometimes when we need encouragement, we should ask for encouragement. You probably have a friend, for example, who is willing to tell you what a fantastic communicator you are. Sometimes we feel that if we ask for compliments then they aren't any good. Nonsense! If we need compliments to help build our self-confidence, then we should ask for compliments, and bask in their glory when we hear them. If you tell a close friend that you are really nervous about giving a speech...that you need their encouragement and support...that this course is difficult for you and you need to be taken seriously...then that friend will probably find a variety of ways to encourage you. If you practice the speech, ask for compliments (not criticism), and ask your friend to assess your communication ability in positive terms, those compliments may fortify you sufficiently to make giving the speech easier. Sometimes our confidence reserves get too low for our effective performance, in which case, a boost from a friend (or classmate or teacher or family member) can do wonders.

Sharing the Stage. Sometimes you can reduce your communication apprehension by sharing the stage with someone else. If you are introducing someone, for example, you can focus attention on the person being introduced. If your hand is shaking while you try to hold up a visual aid, ask someone in the audience to hold the visual aid for you. With a friendly helper on which the audience can focus some of their attention, you may feel more at ease.

Audience Stress

As a listener, you also may feel stress. Each audience member brings values, culture, experience, and perceptions to the communication situation. There are several areas in which the audience may feel stress.

Our *need to predict* and feel comfortable in a speaking situation may be a problem when an audience member is unfamiliar with the situation. Consider, for example, the situation of the family of four—Presbyterians of European decent—who decides to try the Unitarian church. The woman pastor introduces a Cherokee who is giving the message. The family is in a new environment, knows no one in the worship service, is unused to the religious rituals of the group, and is unfamiliar with the Cherokee speaker's style. For the family to listen openly to the situation requires adaptation to the unfamiliar.

Audience empathy may be a problem if the speaker shows considerable discomfort. If a business manager drops her speech notes and cannot find her place, for example, empathetic audience members will feel considerable stress in the situation.

Listening to ideas that *conflict* with your beliefs, force you to reconsider your values, or challenge your behaviors can also create stress. Some speakers confront us with issues that we would rather ignore. To be informed is to decide if and how we take responsibility to act on what we know. Consider the ideas presented in this speech introduction:

"Jenny was a fourteen-year-old girl when she attended a birthday party in the camper in the backyard of her friend's house. As the night went on, her friend's older sister brought several boys to the party. After getting the girls to drink beer, the older sister helped the boys drag Jenny out of the trailer. There in the backyard, with her friends cut off from helping, the boys gang-raped her for four hours. This story is not only true, but part of a growing trend. Today, of the reported rapes in this country, 25% are gang-rapes. There is a growing incidence of teen rapists who are often able to escape punishment because of legal age limits. The purpose of my speech is to inform you of this tragic trend in our society."

This type of information can create stress because the audience is uncomfortable with the topic. The speaker needs to be aware of the potential stress and treat the subject sensitively.

Closing Remarks

Stage fright and communication apprehension are common and controllable. In fact, the person who feels no stage fright is the unusual or "abnormal" person. Although it may have various causes, you can work on reducing apprehension through the techniques we presented.

References and Suggestions for Further Readings

Allen, M., Hunter, J. E., & Donohue, W. A. (1989). Meta-analysis of self-report data on the effectiveness of public speaking anxiety treatment techniques. *Communication Education, 38*, 54–76.

Ayres, J., & Hopf, T. S. (1985). Visualization: A means of reducing speech anxiety. *Communication Education, 34*, 318–323.

Ayers, J., & Hopf, T. S. (1987). Visualization, systematic desensitization, and rational emotive therapy: A comparative evaluation. *Communication Education, 36*, 236–240.

Beatty, M. J., & Andriate, G. S. (1985). Communication apprehension and general anxiety in the prediction of public speaking anxiety. *Communication Quarterly, 33*, 174–184.

Biggers, T., & Masterson, J. T. (1984). Communication apprehension as a personality trait: An emotional defense of a concept. *Communication Monographs, 51*, 381–390.

Grice, G. L., & Skinner, J. F. (1983). Mastering Public Speaking. Englewood Cliffs, NJ: Prentice Hall.

Hopf, T., & Ayres, J. (1992). Coping with public speaking anxiety: An examination of various combinations of systematic desensitization, Skills Training, and Visualization. *Journal of Applied Communication Research, 20*, 183–198.

Lucas, S. E. (1992). 4th ed. *The art of public speaking*. NY: McGraw Hill.

McCroskey, J.C. (1978). Validity of the PRCA as an index of oral communication apprehension. *Communication Monographs*, *45*, 192–203.

McCroskey, J. C., & Lashbrook, W. B. (1970). The effect of various methods of employing video-taped television playback in a course in public speaking. *The Speech Teacher*, *19*, 199–205.

Richmond, V. P., & McCroskey, J. C. (1985). *Communication: Apprehension, avoidance, and effectiveness*. Scottsdale, AZ: Gorsuch Scarisbrick, Publishers.

Vital Speeches of the Day. Southold, NY: City News Publishing. (This monthly publication has numerous speeches on current issues.)

Watson, A. K. (1987, November 5). *Helping communication apprehensive students as part of the developmental speech course*. Paper presented at the Annual Meeting of the speech Communication Association. (ERIC Document Reproduction Service ED 295 260)

Zakahi, W. R., & Duran, R. L. (1985). Loneliness, communicative competence, and communication apprehension: Extension and replication. *Communication Quarterly*, 33, 50–60.

APPENDIX C

Preparing a Personal Relaxation Script

As mentioned earlier in Appendix B, "Visualization and Relaxation Techniques," you may benefit from preparing your own relaxation tape. Once you have prepared your personal script, record the script using a calm, soothing vocal quality with pauses between major ideas. Prior to using such a tape you should practice tensing and relaxing parts of your body (including your throat and face) until you can recognize the "feel" of tension and relaxation. When using your self-prepared relaxation tape, you should stop the tape if you feel tension in order to relax the part of the body you feel is becoming tense. Once you relax the tensed muscles restart the tape (or, better still, rewind the tape a bit before you restart it). The point of using a self-made relaxation tape is to master a relaxed feeling while visualizing the situation in which you must perform.

An Example of a Personal Script for Dealing with Anxieties

(The words in regular type are the words of the script. The italicized words provide instructions or optional script.) Everyone should have a home base. Home base is someplace where I feel relaxed. *[Insert a description of your personal home base. Perhaps your home base is lying on a warm beach listening to the waves gently brush against the shore. Perhaps your home base is a place where you always felt safe as a child. Select the scene that works for you. The rest of this sample script will be based on a beach as home base.]* When I feel nervous, I can go to my home base no matter where I am. I can feel the warm sun and gentle breeze against me. I can feel calm, warm, and relaxed just by thinking of home base. As I think now, I can see a calm place for

me. I can hear the sounds. I can see myself there. I can feel the calm come over me. I can feel at peace. I can feel good about myself.

As I relax, I will check my body to relax any muscles that are tense. I will practice feeling the difference between tension and relaxation. *[If you decide to make a tape for this class, you probably have severe anxiety and tension about speaking. Hence, you will benefit from including instructions to yourself within the script to check for tension. For example, "Now I am checking my face for tension. I am making an ugly, all tensed up face. Now I am relaxing my face. I can feel the difference between tension and relaxation in my facial muscles, my jaw, and my throat....." As you become familiar with visualizing success in any situation in your life that causes you anxiety you may simply remember to check for tension throughout your body as you visualize yourself succeeding at the activity that concerns you. For instance, after checking for facial tension, you would go on to the other parts of your body. To illustrate: Now relax. Feel the difference between tension and relaxation. Now, take a deep breath, tense the chest, and relax. Tense the right arm, make a fist, tense, then relax. Tense the right arm, make a fist, tense the muscles, then relax. Check the right leg, curl the toes, feel the tension. Now relax. Check the left leg, curl the toes, feel the tension. Now relax. Now think about the entire body. Check for tension (if you feel any tension is in the body, it is time to release that tension by first inhaling, then tensing the muscle[s] fully, pausing, then concentrating on relaxing the muscles with a prolonged and complete exhalation of the breath. Many people benefit by imagining they are exhaling from or through the part of the body that they have tensed). Continue until you feel totally relaxed. As you play your tape, if you feel any tension, stop the tape and follow the four-part relaxation process we have just described.]*

Now I am thinking about attending my speech class. We are discussing the principles of public speaking. As I think about that, I will check to see if any tension creeps into my body, and if it does, I will relax and release the tension.

My instructor has assigned a speech to be given in class. The instructor gave the specifics of the assignment, and I am thinking about a possible topic. I consider the class as the audience, think about the classroom situation, and adjust my topic to the circumstances. I narrow the topic and decide on my specific purpose. Now I am checking my body. If any tension has entered my body, I will release the tension. I may go to my home base for a moment. It is some place where I feel warm, comfortable, calm, and relaxed. I feel deeply relaxed. Any tensions, worries, or anxieties, will float away...out of my body...up to the clouds and away with the breeze.

I have decided on my specific purpose, I begin planning the speech. I write down the main ideas of my speech. I go to the library and do the necessary research. I find a variety of support for my ideas. I take careful notes so that I can cite the sources of my research. Then I write an outline of my speech. I begin by writing the speech body. After my ideas are written down and supported, I decide on an introduction and a conclusion to the speech. I organize the message in a logical format and carefully prepare the outline. *[As you think these thoughts, continue to monitor your body. If you feel any tension has entered your body, stop the tape. Release the tension by returning mentally to your home base or go through the four steps of inhaling deeply, tensing fully the muscle(s) that are tense, pausing, then concentrating on exhaling away the tension from the tense muscle(s). After but a few hours of practice you will probably be able to relax simply by repeating the "home base" script: "I am in my home base. Here, I feel warm, comfortable, calm, and relaxed. I feel deeply relaxed. All tensions, worries, and anxieties are floating away…out of my body…up to the clouds and away with the breeze."]*

I am listening to a classmate give a presentation. My presentation is due next week. Now I am practicing my speech before I give it. Now a supportive friend is listening to me practice the presentation. I make some adjustments, and I am ready to give my speech. It's now the day that I am going to give the speech. I get up in the morning, get ready, and go through the day up to the point of my public speaking class. I go to the class and see the various people in my class. I feel calm and in control. I know that I am ready to give the speech. The instructor calls on the first student. I carefully listen to that speech, concentrating on what the student has to say. I can see the people in the class. Now I am checking my body. If any tension has entered my body, I will release the tension. I may go to my home base for a moment. Here I feel warm, comfortable, calm, and relaxed. I feel deeply relaxed. Any tensions, worries, or anxieties, are floating away...out of my body…up to the clouds and away with the breeze.

Now it's my turn to speak. I get up with confidence and go to the front of the class. I look around at the class members. Several people are looking at me. Each of these individuals is a human being, just like me. If I treat them like a friend they will treat me like one. If we help one another, each of us will grow. The material in my presentation will help these people. Because I am helping these people, they will respect me. I look back with confidence and collect my thoughts. I start with the introduction. Then I begin the speech body. I discuss my first key idea and support the idea. I look at the audience members and try to read their responses. I adapt to their feedback. I proceed through each of my key ideas. I occasionally look at my notes. Although I have planned the message, the actual words come as I speak, because I am concentrating on helping this audience, not thinking about myself. I am my natural self. I feel free to gesture, use vocal variety, handle a visual aid, and move appropriately. My delivery affirms what I am saying. I can see some of the people in the class. As I read their reactions, most look attentive. One person seems busy writing. Someone else looks confused. Another person smiles and nods. I see the instructor. I concentrate on the members of the class and their reactions, because the instructor is grading me on how well I relate to the entire audience. As I talk, I watch my time. I adjust my message to the audience. I even think of a new example to explain one of my ideas.

[As you listen to the script and visualize your performance, monitor your body. At any point you feel you are tensing up, relax. Yes, you know the routine by now, but we are repeating it so that you over-learn and don't forget it: either return to home base (I'm checking my body, I feel tension. I can release the tension by returning to my home base for a moment. Here I feel warm, comfortable, calm, and relaxed. I feel deeply relaxed. Tensions, worries, and anxieties, are floating away...out of my body...up to the clouds and away with the breeze,). If your imagination refuses to return to your home base, you can always take control of your tensions physically with the four-part relaxation technique (inhale, tighten to the max the tense area, pause, exhale away the tension through the area that's tense).]

I finish the speech with confidence. I have discussed all the key ideas and provided a variety of support. My conclusion helps to make my speech memorable. After I finish, someone in the group raises a hand. I listen to her question and answer it carefully. Another student raises a hand and makes a comment. I disagree with the comment; so I restate his point then explain my reasons for disagreeing with it. I remain calm and make my responses brief and to-the-point. After I finish, I maintain my composure. I walk back to my seat, continuing to realize that class members are watching me and thinking about what I have said. I sit down. I feel good about my speech. My speech didn't go exactly the way I expected, but my speech was effective. I feel good about what I have done. I can listen to criticism with confidence because I have a desire to improve. The instructor calls on the next speaker. I now concentrate on listening to that speaker. As I listen, I realize that I really am enjoying the class. The students are getting to know each other. Our presentations are getting better and better. We're growing in competence. The instructor seems to be a caring person who wants all of us to improve—I think; or hope, no, I know; or will make it so—I'm in control! I'm glad I'm in my public speaking class. Who am I kidding? Most people fear public speaking more than death! But, as I think about it, the fear of public speaking is something I can conquer. Wow! What else can I conquer? Whatever's out there! I'm never going to let fear cramp my life!

OK, get a grasp. I'm on Earth not Jupiter. OK, I have to keep checking my body. If any tension has entered my body, I will release the tension. I may go to my home base or breathe effectively. No, I like my home base where I feel warm, comfortable, calm, and relaxed. I feel deeply relaxed. Any tensions, worries, or anxieties, will float away…out of my body…up to the clouds and away with the breeze.

[If this script is getting a bit weird for you, don't panic. The point is as humans we can write our own scripts. The best ones help us grow, be competent, help others, and be happy.]

APPENDIX D

Reasoning with the Toulmin Model

Twenty-five-hundred years ago, Aristotle identified in his *Rhetoric* what he called three forms of artistic proof: ethos, pathos, and logos. Today we call these forms of persuasion, credibility, emotional appeals, and reasoning, respectively. Chapter 13 of this text goes into some detail regarding ethos and pathos. We deal with reasoning here in a self-contained unit. Hence, our instructors can assign this material whenever they choose. In Chapter 9, we provide additional material regarding the use of evidence and the nature of fallacies in reasoning. Our focus here, however, is on the process of reasoning. In particular, we shall look at ways to build, bolster, and refute arguments based on a model developed by Toulmin (1958), a British philosopher. The model shows us the relationships among the 6 elements of an argument. Understanding the 6 elements should help you not only to construct a sound argument, but also to analyze the arguments of others (and know ways to refute or attack them).

Toulmin has identified 6 parts of an argument:

Elements of the Model

CLAIM
DATA
WARRANT

(These top three are essential elements of an argument; the bottom three elements complete an argument.)

BACKING
RESERVATION
QUALIFIER

The **claim** is the *point an arguer tries to prove*. The **data** is *the evidence that the arguer uses to prove a point*. Examples of evidence include expert testimony, examples, parallel cases (analogies), statistics, and other factual data. The **warrant** is the part of the argument that *justifies leaping from the data to the claim*. Most individuals find the warrant the hardest part of the model to understand. Hence, pay your closest attention to the examples and explanations provided below. Soon we shall see that each form of argument has a different, that is to say "unique," warrant. However, before we examine types of arguments, let's examine the way Toulmin diagramed the 3 core elements of his model:

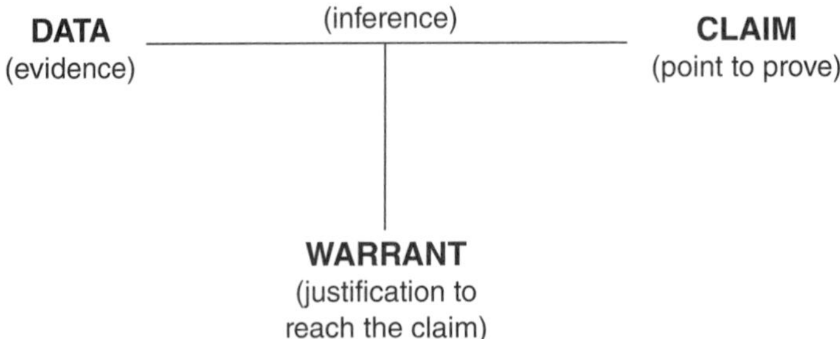

Below is the diagram of a simple argument by analogy, i.e., we argue that what happened in one situation can be expected to happen in another. The data is a known case of weight loss that will predict what could happen for someone else.

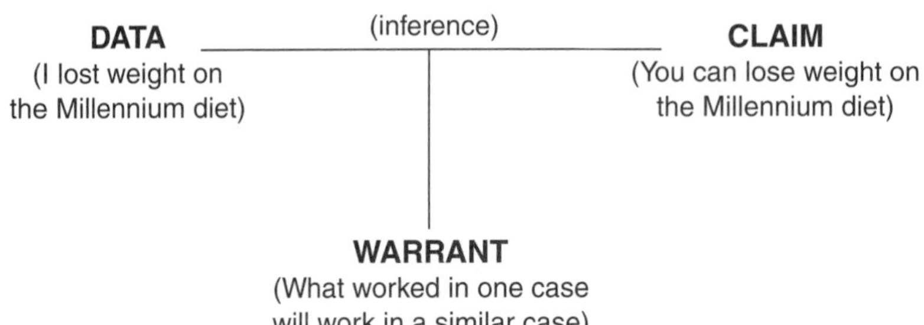

When we argue, we seldom state all 3 parts of the argument. For example, in the most recently presented argument, the speaker could say, "I lost 20 pounds on the Millennium diet [data]. You can too![claim]" or "I lost weight on the Millennium diet [data]. What worked in my case can work in yours [warrant]." Usually a speaker just omits saying what the audience already believes. If that warrant or evidence is false, the argument will be fallacious, even though the argument is valid. Early women astronauts report that even though they weighed less than the men (when payload weight was important) they were not allowed to fly in that those in charge argued that "the space program will be over if a woman dies in space." Do you buy the warrant that would support that claim? Did you know that women test pilots of the same era were forced to change into a skirt and high heels before they could climb down from the planes they had just landed? Do you buy the warrant that "women must be dressed 'appropriately' when they appear in public?"

As noted earlier, each type of argument has its own unique warrant. In the most recent diagram, the essence of the warrant (what worked in one case will work in a similar case) is always the justification for accepting the claim in an argument by analogy. Lets look at the warrants in 6 basic arguments:

1) *Inductive reasoning*—what's true of the examples is true of the group (or class) they represent. **Data:** In my 2 classes that meet on Friday, about 40% of the students have been absent each week. **Claim:** Many BSU students skip their Friday classes. (Implied) **warrant:** My students are typical Ball State students.
2) *Deductive reasoning*—what's true of a group (or class) is true of its members. Most of us have heard the most overworked example of deduction. **Data:** Socrates is a man. **Warrant:** all men are mortal. **Claim:** Socrates is mortal [or Socrates will die]. Can you pick out the elements of the following argument? "The ousting of Saddam means the people of Iraq will not suffer anymore from the atrocities of the former regime. That justifies the invasion and war conducted by the coalition of the willing." (Yes, the first sentence is the **data**; the second is the **claim**; and the implied **warrant** is, "Saving a people from a sadistic dictator justifies war against that dictator and his people.")
3) *Reasoning from parallel case (analogy)* (you should have this one down pat by now)—what happened in one situation will hold true in a similar situation. Let's look at an argument made before your time. "Miami of Ohio's DAPR system works extremely well there. Our students have the same advising needs as Miami's students. We should buy the DAPR software from Miami of Ohio."
4) *Reasoning from authority*—the authority is an expert whose opinions should be believed as accurate. "The war in Iraq is necessary (**claim**). The President says so (**data**)." Implied **warrant:** "The President is a man of integrity who has access to secret information."
5) *Sign reasoning*—X is a sign of Y. Smoke is a sign of fire. Ice is a sign of a temperature below 32 degrees. "Dr. B must have arrived early to her office on March 24 (**claim**). Her truck was in the first spot as you enter the south gate of the Emens structure (**data**)." Implied **warrant:** "Getting a good parking spot is a sign that someone arrived early."
6) *Causal reasoning*—the warrant presents a causal relationship between antecedent(s) and consequence(s), i.e., A, or As, cause E, or Es. The cause–effect relationship should have come from research, experience,

and/common sense. "Sarah demonstrates the symptoms of spousal abuse (**data**). Abuse in a relationship usually causes spousal abuse syndrome (**warrant**). Hence, Sarah may have been abused by her significant other (**claim**)." Up for another? "Jack has been coming to work every day with alcohol on his breath. He'll probably be fired soon."

Notice that words like "must," "probably," and "may" are showing up in the previous few examples. We can say with certainty that given oxygen, a fuel source, and its kindling temperature a block of wood will burst into flame. In human affairs, however, we seldom have situations that are absolute. Hence, we need to qualify our arguments. A qualifier is 1 of 3 remaining elements of the Toulmin model.

A **qualifier** is a word or phrase that reflects our *estimate of the degree to which we are confident of our claim*. Common qualifiers are "there's a chance," "possibly," "probably," "certainly," and so forth. **Backing** provides *additional support for the warrant*. The **reservation**, or **rebuttal**, identifies the *applicable weaknesses of, or ways to attack, a particular type of argument*. Adding our 3 additional elements to the basic diagram of an argument looks like this:

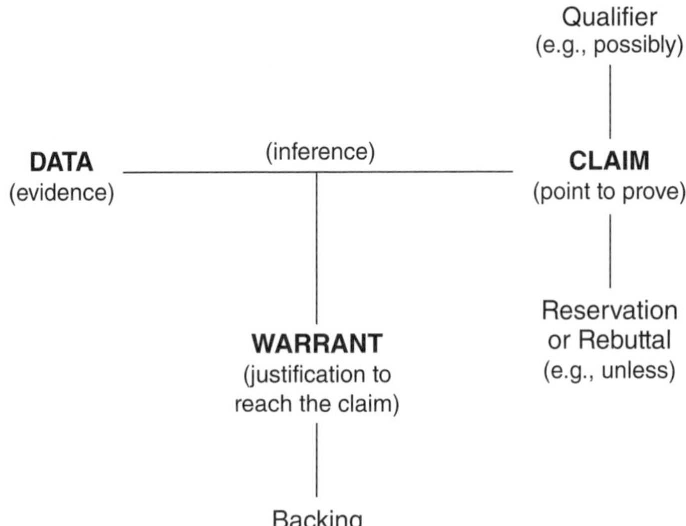

Let's flesh out our argument by sign to see the relationships among the 6 elements of a complete argument. In an argument by sign, we need to test the **reservation** that the sign may be fallible (that is, not a fast rule)—X could be the sign of some other Y. In our case, Dr. B could have taken the parking spot after someone else left. So her parking space could have been the result of luck rather than arriving early. We could provide additional backing for our warrant. We could note that she gave a special lecture to COMM 210 students at 8:00 a.m. and that she did not leave campus all day. Based on our backing, we can conclude that she definitely arrived at her office early on March 24. Or can we? Let's take a look at our argument by sign. Note a new reservation and qualifier:

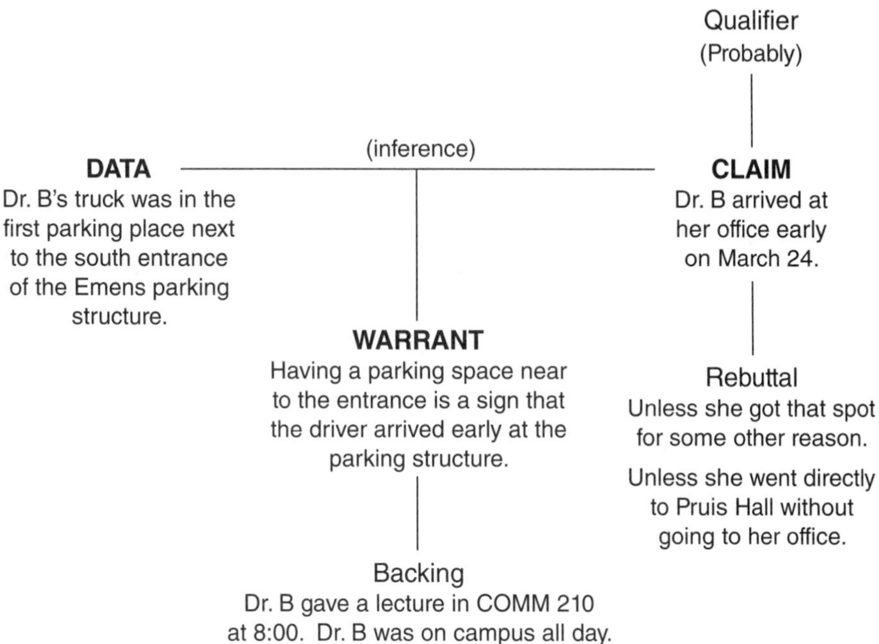

Let's look at a few ways to back the warrants of our arguments:

1) *Inductive reasoning*—what's true of the examples is true of their class. Show that the examples are typical and relevant. Cite authorities who support the typicality of your evidence. Use relevant statistics to show typicality of your evidence.
2) *Deductive reasoning*—what's true of a class is true of its members. Think of this as showing that a rule or conclusion applies in a particular case. Show that your principal or rule is well accepted, for example, it has been true in the past.
3) *Reasoning from parallel case*—what happened in one situation will hold true in a similar situations. Describe the similarities between the cases. Show that the similarities outweigh the differences.
4) *Reasoning from authority*—the authority is an expert, or possesses unique knowledge (e.g., an eyewitness). Try to find reasons that would show the authority is competent, reliable, and honest. We especially tend to believe the "reluctant witnesses" who testify in a way that goes against their own best interests. Cite the qualifications of the authority. Show that other sources or facts agree with the conclusions.
5) *Sign reasoning*—*X* is a sign of Y. Back up the accuracy of the sign relationship. Attack alternate explanations.

6) *Causal reasoning*—a causal relationship accounts for the issue at hand. Explain the causal relationship. Show that it is supported by research, experience, and/or common sense.

Now that we know how to back up our arguments, let's look at the ways these arguments can be attacked. Knowledge of the reservations will help you rebut the arguments of others. Additionally, this knowledge can help you anticipate ways others may attack your claims:

1) *Inductive reasoning*—show that the examples (data) are not typical and/or relevant.
2) *Deductive reasoning*—show that the rule or principle is wrong or does not apply in this case.
3) *Reasoning by analogy*—show that the differences outweigh the similarities.
4) *Reasoning from authority*—show that the alleged authority is not an expert (for example, has become outdated or unacquainted with current research or s/he could not have perceived the data s/he is reporting as an eyewitness) and/or is biased and/or dishonest. Show that the authority is benefitting personally from the testimony.
5) *Sign reasoning*—show that the sign is fallible.
6) *Causal reasoning*—show that the causal relationship does not apply or exist. Show that just because an event occurred in time before another, the first event is not necessarily the cause of the second. Suggest an alternative causal relationship.

Closing Remarks

We hope you will find that use of the Toulmin model will help you enhance your critical thinking.

Reference

Toulmin, S. (1958). *The uses of argument*. Cambridge, England: Cambridge University Press.

COMM **210**

Index

A

B

C

D

E

F

G

H

I

J

L

M

N

O

P

Q

R

S

T

U

V

W